Holy Ghost-like mind is a Good Mother-like character

A 365-Day Devotional

Mizraiim Lapa-Pethe

Holy Ghost-like mind is a Good Mother-like character
A 365-Day Devotional

First published in Australia by Mizraiim Lapa-Pethe 2020

Copyright © Mizraiim Lapa-Pathe 2020
All Rights Reserved

 A catalogue record for this book is available from the National Library of Australia

ISBN: 978-0-6485541-2-7 (pbk)
ISBN: 978-0-6485541-3-4 (ebk)

Typesetting and design by Publicious Book Publishing
Published in collaboration with Publicious Book Publishing
www.publicious.com.au

No part of this book may be reproduced in any form, by photocopying or by any electronic or mechanical means, including information storage or retrieval systems, without permission in writing from both the copyright owner and the publisher of this book.

DEDICATION

This book is dedicated to my gorgeous one-year-old baby boy, Blessed, to the glory of the Father, Son and the Holy Spirit. The gift of Blessed from above has brought me closer to the Holy Spirit as a mother. This book, *Holy Ghost-like Mind is a Good Mother-like character*, was inspired by the Holy Spirit because while I was writing I knew I needed God's grace to be that good mother and also his mercy to forgive me for having my own way most of the time. Thus I continue to repent as I am a work-in-progress and am trying my best to be on track with the guidance of the Holy Spirit.

At two months into my journey of pregnancy with Blessed, I didn't know the gender of the baby yet. While eating a Twisties, the Holy Spirit spoke clearly to me, asking from deep within my heart, 'What are you eating?'

I remember looking at the Twisties packet and saying, 'Twisties'. The Holy Spirit responded saying, 'Yes, you are eating Twisties, that is what the name says on the packet, and so, that is what the packet contains inside. You are going to give birth to a baby boy and you will name him Blessed. Blessings will flow out from him because that is what his name is. He is given to you to remind you of God's Son who removed your curses from disobedience to restore you to live a blessed life'.

I was numb and speechless for some time. Then many thoughts rushed through my mind that I can't give a name to as it is not commonly used; it was the enemy driving all negative thoughts through my mind. Walking daily with the Lord every day in His Word and prayer convinced me to name him as instructed. From birth, Blessed entered this world with smiles and joy; seeing a newborn baby smiling with his eyes still closed even gave me tears of joy. I also called him 'the living joy of the Holy Spirit from inside of me'.

Thank you Holy Spirit for inspiring, mentoring, teaching, correcting and strengthening me through this motherhood journey I have come through so far. I know You will continue as we journey towards eternity together.

Every day is mother's day. Every day is the Lord's day to be in the Spirit (Revelation 1:10) – Holy Ghost-like mind is a Good Mother-like character.

****

I would like to make a special mention of those godly mothers who partnered up with me in getting this book published. The encouragement and support you all gave is eternally invested in the kingdom of God. We are all doing it for our Father's glory. I am so grateful and I will continue to praise and thank God for all of you in my life for walking with me on this part of my journey through this book, *Holy Ghost-like mind is a Good Mother-like character*. With the help of the Holy Spirit, our helper, we will continue to grow every day into the good mother that God originally designed.

Hildeanne Wefin, Debra Alim, Emma Somare, Leah Nandie, Anna Ingip, Margaret Morre Rus, Maggie Kawa, Nou Gamu, Jean Koaea-Molo, Kathy Wangatau, Miriam Samol, Mary Egu, Sonia Koltop Thyme, Nancy Yari, Sarah Kiniafa, Mitchiel Kandiu, Jennifer

Gagau, Kimberly Kanimba, Boio Vegoa, Elizabeth Kuri and Marcella Lase Tingkum Birie. Thank you so much.

To my two dear young girl friends, I know without doubt that, when your day of happiness comes, you will both be great mothers. Thank you so much Lorina Liora Tina and Albertina Posa for being part of my journey through this book.

To my dear husband, Thomas Pethe, thank you so much for the support you have given. I would never have found the time to write this book if you had not given your time to me by looking after our beautiful children, Angelilly (5 years' old) and Blessed (1 year old). It is my prayer that God will reward you back with more time and strength to continue to play your role as a wonderful husband and good father.

CONTENTS

Why I wrote this book	i
You should read this book	iii
The revelation of the Holy Spirit	iv
How this book will help you	vi
About the author	vii
What should readers do?	viii
What readers said about my previous book	x
January	1
February	38
March	70
April	104
May	138
June	171
July	205
August	240
September	279
October	312
November	348
December	383

Why I wrote this book

In my previous book, *Christ-like mind is Child-like character*, a 365-day devotional book, I wrote about how the kingdom of God is like a child; a 365 daily read of how the character of a child is like the kingdom of God, all scripture linked. (This is a beautiful inspiring book to own if you don't already.)

This book is about how the Holy Spirit was teaching me about the kingdom of God through the character of my child, Angelilly, from when she was almost three to four years old. I dedicated this book to her and wrote about how her child-like character had taught me about the kingdom of God.

When I gave birth to Blessed, Angelilly said, 'Mum, you should write a book about Blessed, he is not going to be happy if he sees that you wrote a book about me'. Angelilly was four years' old when Blessed was born.

The close relationship I was developing with the Holy Spirit, along with the encounter I had with Him in naming Blessed, encouraged me to pick up my pen and start writing. The rest is history; I was available and the Holy Spirit just used me to note everything down in a journal. The title of the book and its contents filled me with joy making me hungry to grow closer to the Holy Spirit. I have to say that if in a day I didn't get to sit down to hear from the Holy Spirit and write something for the book, I felt so empty; it was a feeling of missing someone I love that I was supposed to meet but didn't.

I am obeying the voice of the Holy Spirit in writing this book to help all mothers so that we can now do our daily motherly roles with joy and worship unto God with His holy ones in His throne room. We are now part of God's team as all our daily roles are in worship to God.

You should read this book

Holy Ghost-like mind is a Good Mother-like character is a book that every girl and woman should have to read daily to help prepare for motherhood. God nurtures us through Mother Nature to meet our physical needs, and He supports us through the Holy Spirit who meets our inner needs as a mother. Mother Earth was made by the Holy Spirit breathing life into the spoken Word of God to bring it into existence (Genesis 1:2). This is why many times your spirit will feel so complete and connected to nature when you sit calmly and absorb its beauty.

The Holy Spirit is a friend, teacher, comforter, nurse and supporter of all the roles that a mother plays in her house.

Written in a calendar format for each day, just five minutes of reading will bring new insights and challenges.

The revelation of the Holy Spirit

It takes NINE MONTHS for a baby to fully develop in a mother's womb and to be born resembling its parents. It also takes nine months for us to be fully matured and developed in producing the NINE FRUIT of the Holy Spirit for us to give birth to the image of Christ in all seasons.

A mother goes through the pain of childbirth to give new life which is her very own flesh and blood. Her pain is soon forgotten after the birth as she experiences the joy of seeing her baby. Jesus told His disciples in John 16, 'You are sad now that I am going away but it is for your good that I must go, so He (Holy Spirit) will come.' You see, Jesus told His disciples that they will see Him again because the Holy Spirit will come. When we produce the fruit of the Holy Spirit, we are giving birth to the image of Christ, and the Holy Spirit reveals Christ to us. The joy from the revelation of Christ by the Holy Spirit that a person receives is indescribable. This is what Jesus meant when He said, 'You will see me again, and your hearts will rejoice, and no one can steal that joy'. The enemy comes to steal, kill and destroy but he can't steal your joy from the revelation of Jesus by the Holy Spirit.

> *When a woman is giving birth, she has sorrow because her hour has come, but when she has delivered the baby, she no longer remembers the anguish, for joy that a human being has been born into the world. So also you have sorrow now, but I will see you again, and your hearts will rejoice, and no one will take your joy from you. (John 16:21-22, ESV).*

Keep listening for and hearing the Word of God so that the Holy Spirit can breathe life into it to make the Word become flesh (John 1:14), and so you can give birth to the image of Christ and see the Holy Spirit revealing Him to you.

How this book will help you

This book will help you to want to develop a more intimate and closer relationship with the Holy Spirit. The greatest blessing of this book is that it will help and teach you to produce the fruit of the Holy Spirit in your everyday life to face the difficult people that come your way. The LOVE of God flowing out of the nine fruit of the Holy Spirit will cause you to have compassion towards difficult people. You will come to understand that, like Jesus, these people are blind and they do not know what they are doing.

Instead of comparing yourself to others, you will start comparing your OLD SELFISH life to what your NEW LIFE should be in the Holy Spirit. Your new character is the mindset of the Holy Spirit and you will start to renew your mind to have the mind of Christ (1 Corinthians 2:16).

About the author

Mizraiim Lapa-Pethe practised as a tax accountant before deciding to take a full-time role parenting her children. Her first book, a 365-daily devotion, *Christ-like mind is Child-like character* is a great, inspiring book to read. Children's characters – 365 in total – are closely linked with scriptures showing how the kingdom of God looks.

Her experience of motherhood in effectively applying the use of the blood of Jesus and remaining connected in Word and prayer every day will open your eyes to see how you can live a victoriously joyful life every day.

She is married to Thomas Pethe, and they live in Sydney, Australia with their two beautiful children, Angelilly, five years' old, and Blessed, one year old.

What should readers do?

Every reader must fill themselves with the Holy Spirit by being full of gratitude and giving thanks to God; making music and song in their hearts unto the Lord until the end of time.

> *Don't be drunk with wine, because that will ruin your life. Instead, be filled with the Holy Spirit, singing psalms and hymns and spiritual songs among yourselves, and making music to the Lord in your hearts. And give thanks for everything to God the Father in the name of our Lord Jesus Christ (Ephesians 5:18-20, NLT).*

This is how you will inherit the eternal joy and peace from the kingdom of God that flows out from God into His Spirit into us.

> *I pray that God, the source of hope, will fill you completely with joy and peace because you trust in him. Then you will overflow with confident hope through the power of the Holy Spirit (Romans 15:13, NLT).*

Every day is the Lord's day where we are to be in the Spirit. To be ready to go to heaven is to make every day the Lord's day by being in the Spirit.

> *I was in the Spirit on the Lord's day, and I heard behind me a loud voice like a trumpet (Revelation 1:10, ESV).*

When someone is so blessed or something so nice happens to them we say, 'today is your day'. When it's someone's birthday, we say 'today is your day'. The day is centred only around that person making them even more special. Everyone who knows about it makes that person feel even more special by saying all kinds of good things. It's as if they are praising and worshipping that person. They speak and act in goodness and kindness. There is so much love and joy. God also wants us to make every day His day; He made the day and gave it to us so we could make it His day. We make it His day when we rejoice and be glad in the day He has made. By doing that we are filling ourselves with the Spirit. To make it His day we are to be in the Spirit. We fill our spirit with His Spirit by being full of thanksgiving and joy through acts of hymns and praises to God.

> *This is the day that the Lord has made; let us rejoice and be glad in it (Psalm 118:24, ESV).*

At a birthday party there is so much joy and celebrations of music taking place for that person. Every day God gives birth to your new day, it's your birthday from God, celebrate with the angels around you and the Holy Spirit inside you.

What readers said about my previous book, the 365 daily devotional book: Christ-like mind is Child-like character:

I am speechless, thank you Holy Spirit, thank you Abba Father...Your book is amazing with powerful truths. Truths we need for our everyday lives. It was the Holy Spirit that gave you every word to write down. I am just crying reading your book. Most parts brought me back to when my kids were babies, and as a mother I was raising them in the Word and principles of the Kingdom.

~Emma Somare~
Mother of three children.

Congratulations on writing this book. It is truly anointed by God, I could literally feel it, as I held the book and read it. I had to buy another copy again for a dear friend.

~Lyn Laws~
Mother of two and grandmother
of three children.

In my every beginning of my new day as I mother two toddlers at the moment, I find refreshing contents and am overwhelmed by the outcome of the spiritual nourishment of this book. Serving me well with my times spent with my children. It's an honour and blessing to have it hand delivered to me here, in London, UK, by inspiring and true friend, Mizraiim and her beloved daughter, Angelilly.

~Maggie Kawa~
Mother of four children.

This wonderful Holy Spirit inspired book written by my friend Mizraiim is such a blessing. A daily encouragement for all. Written with such love and respect, first to the Lord and then showing us how precious our little ones are, to nurture, and guide them into adulthood in relationship with our wonderful saviour.

God Bless you, for taking up the challenge (the Sword), and using it in this battle (called life) that we are all experiencing and giving us such lovely guidelines to follow and encourage us on our journey.
Love in Jesus,

~Val Bergan~
Mother of six, grandmother to eleven,
and great-grandmother to seven children.

I am proud of your achievement and so happy for you. Your book gives me strength in thought every day, sometimes I am in a situation and I pray!,... then I open the book to read the daily message and it would be all about what I can do to overcome trials and hardship, and understanding situations. The Lord has truly used you as a vessel to share God's love through this book. Thank you again for this blessing.

~Michelle Ososo~
Mother of one child.

The Spirit of the Lord has surely inspired you to write this book. I even share it to my boss and others.

May God continue to use you as a vessel for his glory.
Well done.

~Leah Nandie~
Mother of three children.

I have been enjoying the devotional since the day I purchased online! Learning new things, looking at life, and the scriptures from a different perspective now, and I love it. Always looking forward to the daily readings. I had to buy two hard copies again for myself and a friend. All glory to God and blessings to you and your beautiful family.

~Kathy Wangatau~
Mother of three children.

JANUARY

~ Renewing your mind to live in Your new spirit and heart ~

4 May 2020. I remember on this day that the Lord spoke to me and said, 'Your children will only ever have one mother; the same from which they are birthed from your flesh'. They will have new relationships with others but they will always have only one father and mother of their flesh.

The kingdom of God is like this. You cannot see the kingdom of God unless you are born again in the Spirit. You receive a new heart and spirit in your new relationship with Christ when you are born again. You will still have the same mind from your flesh, even if you have a new relationship with Christ in the Holy Spirit, with a new heart and new spirit.

> *And I will give you a new heart, and a new spirit I will put within you. And I will remove the heart of stone from your flesh and give you a heart of flesh (Ezekiel 36:26, ESV).*

Your old mind knows your OLD SELF and will constantly tell you what to do. God wants us to renew our mind because we cannot allow old thoughts into a new heart and spirit. This is the reason the Word has become flesh. So our mind of the flesh from the fruit of the knowledge of good and evil can be renewed to what God says of us in the fruit from the Tree of Life, which is Jesus. We will still have the same mind of the flesh as along as we are living in our body. Just as we will still have the same mother and father of our flesh.

The new heart and spirit are the righteousness of Christ. We become self-righteous when we allow our old mind to pour its thoughts into our new heart and spirit. Self-righteous people praise themselves and tell others how good they are at doing something.

> *Let another man praise you, and not your own mouth; a stranger, and not on your lips (Proverbs 27:2, NKJV).*

Jesus explained this in a parable in Matthew 9:16-17 when John's disciples questioned him about how they and the Pharisees fast.

> *One day the disciples of John the Baptist came to Jesus and asked him, 'Why don't your disciples fast like we do and the Pharisees do?'*
>
> *Jesus replied, 'Do wedding guests mourn while celebrating with the groom? Of course not. But someday the groom will be taken away from them, and then they will fast.*
>
> *'Besides, who would patch old clothing with new cloth? For the new patch would shrink and rip away from the old cloth, leaving an even bigger tear than before.*
>
> *'And no one puts new wine into old wineskins. For the old skins would burst from the pressure, spilling the wine and ruining the skins. New wine is stored in new wineskins so that both are preserved.' (Matthew 9:14-17, NLT).*

Jesus said it right there, we cannot put together the old and the new version of anything or it will become and look terrible. We, as mothers, have to be that good mother and not think negative and ill thoughts towards other parents' children and how they are raised. When we allow such negative ill thoughts, our children can end up becoming bad and terrible in life. The kind of energy and vibes we create around us affect everything under our care and concern. We have to renew our mind to think good heavenly thoughts.

Finally, brothers and sisters, whatever is true, whatever is noble, whatever is right, whatever is pure, whatever is lovely, whatever is admirable – if anything is excellent or praiseworthy – think about such things (Philippians 4:8, NIV).

On each day of the month of January, and EVERY DAY renew your mind daily in the Word of God, so new fresh thoughts of LIFE can enter your new heart and spirit.

January 1

~ *A good woman and mother* ~

This is the day that the Lord has made; let us rejoice and be glad in it (Psalm 118:24, ESV).

I remember three years ago, (2017) God showed me in a vision how EACH DAY He made was good. He showed me the latest model of a classic four-wheel drive, blue in colour and brand new. The four-wheel drive was going on a bumpy road full of holes. It was going up and down. The ride was not smooth. I could see from time to time, little pebbles hitting the side of the car. The dust was getting onto it too and leaving some marks. The inside of the car was brand new as it was straight from the manufacturer with plastic covering still on it.

****

This is what the Lord said: 'You see, that new four-wheel drive is just like a new day I give you. Every day I give you is brand new. The problem is it enters an evil world. And so, for 24 hours, your good day that I have given you has to go through a rough ride with you. How you get in charge and control it through is up to you.' This is the reason you need to fuel up in the Word of God, so the

Holy Spirit can bring the Word alive in you for you to reproduce His fruit of righteousness in this sinful world. You can control what is in you and stay new like that four-wheel drive. Whatever the world throws at you can just remain where it should be, and you keep remaining new and clean in Christ.

> *Then God blessed them, and God said to them, 'Be fruitful and multiply; fill the earth and subdue it; have dominion over the fish of the sea, over the birds of the air, and over every living thing that moves on the earth. (Genesis 1:28, NKJV).*

So is a woman. Everything I made is good. The first woman I made was good until the day she took into her the fruit of the knowledge of good and evil and exposed herself to evil. This problem is now sorted from when the Holy Spirit entered the woman by the spoken WORD, through the virgin birth of Jesus. I created a good mother out of a woman that was deceived, shamed, naked and lost. I sent my Spirit into the womb of a woman who was going to be the mother of the Saviour of the world. Every mother must receive into them EVERY DAY the Word of God, just as I give a new day every day. The Word you receive into you will draw the Holy Spirit to produce His fruit of righteousness in you; to be fruitful and multiply in the same way as I told the first man and woman.

> *But the fruit of the Spirit is love, joy, peace, patience, kindness, goodness, faithfulness, gentleness, self-control; against such things there is no law (Galatians 5:22-23, ESV).*

****

Each day of your every NEW day take into you the Word of God and plant it in your house. Be fruitful, and multiply in reproducing the fruit of the Holy Spirit.

January 2

~ *Living and moving in Christ* ~

For in him we live and move and have our being (Acts 17:28, NIV).

A good mother is the strength that keeps her household alive and moving. She is like a wheel that easily moves her house and all that is in it. She only fuels herself with positive vibes to move. She pays careful watch to be moved only by what God says of her and not anyone else. She lets God's Word be her truth and all men a liar.

Let God be true, and every human being a liar (Romans 3:4, NIV).

The Holy Spirit is the strength and power of God within us to keep us alive and moving in Christ. We move and have our being in Him. He fuels us in His fruit of righteousness to energize and strengthen us to continue walking on the path of righteousness.

I pray that out of his glorious riches he may strengthen you with power through his Spirit in your inner being (Ephesians 3:16, NIV).

Every day make a move that shows Jesus is alive in you through His Spirit, and in Him you move and live.

January 3

~ *Clothe yourself with compassion* ~

Therefore, as God's chosen people, holy and dearly loved, clothe yourselves with compassion, kindness, humility, gentleness and patience (Colossians 3:12, NIV).

I remember people doing bad things to me and as I was thinking about it the Holy Spirit taught me this: A good mother always has compassion for those who mistreat or do bad things to her. She has the Spirit of understanding and understands that they do not have the Spirit of knowledge and so they do not know what they are doing.

My people are destroyed from lack of knowledge (Hosea 4:6, NIV).

The final words of Jesus at the cross are that He forgave those that crucify Him. He had compassion towards them knowing that they did not understand what they were doing.

The Holy Spirit inside us understands and knows us very well. He is the Spirit of God the very breath of God that breathes life into us. He is the Spirit of knowledge and understanding. He has compassion towards us, understanding and the knowledge that we live in a world of evil that attacks us everywhere all the time.

The Spirit of the Lord will rest on him – the Spirit of wisdom and of understanding, the Spirit of counsel and of might, the Spirit of the knowledge and fear of the Lord (Isaiah 11:2 NIV).

Each and every day spend time in Word and prayer to understand and know the Spirit of understanding and knowledge, so that you can understand and know why people are doing what they are doing to you and forgive them with compassion and love from the Holy Spirit.

January 4

~ Build up your life in wisdom ~

For the foolishness of God is wiser than human wisdom, and the weakness of God is stronger than human strength (1 Corinthians 2:25, NIV).

A good woman will always be a good mother even if she marries a foolish man. She knows and understands that God's foolishness is wiser than human wisdom. A foolish act from her husband will only make her wiser if she applies the wisdom of God's Word in responding. This is how a good woman builds her household in wisdom.

By wisdom a house is built, and through understanding it is established; (Proverbs 24:3, NIV).

The Holy Spirit is the Spirit of wisdom that we house, and in Him we live in the fear of the Lord. We are His house that He builds in wisdom and understanding, so we can become more stronger and wiser in Him.

The fear of the Lord is the beginning of wisdom; all those who practise it have a good understanding. His praise endures forever! (Psalm 111:10, ESV).

If God's foolishness can be wiser than your human wisdom, how amazing your life will turn out if you ask and seek God's wisdom in His Word every day.

January 5

~ *The peace and comfortableness of the Holy Spirit* ~

Therefore, since we have been made right in God's sight by faith, we have peace with God because of what Jesus Christ our Lord has done for us (Romans 5:1, NLT).

A good mother assures her children that she will always be with them. They feel safe and at peace knowing the presence of their mother is always around them. The peace and comfort she gains in the Word and from her prayers is released into her children. Even when she transits out of earth to her heavenly home, her children know that her spirit has gone back to God and become a good spirit to care for them and keep bad spirits from destroying them. She is their angel that heaven has gained.

Therefore, angels are only servants – spirits sent to care for people who will inherit salvation (Hebrews 1:14, NLT).

[...]and the dust returns to the ground it came from, and the spirit returns to God who gave it (Ecclesiastes 12:7, NIV).

We feel comfortable and at peace knowing the living Spirit of God lives in us. Jesus finished His work on the cross and offered His Spirit to the Father. His Spirit is the good Spirit that resurrected Him from death and made Him victorious over devil and death. The same Spirit that resurrected Jesus from death and gave Him life is inside us. He produces goodness for us to overcome evil.

And if the spirit of him who raised Jesus from the dead is living in you, he who raised Christ from the dead will also give life to your mortal bodies because of his Spirit who lives in you (Romans 8:11, NIV).

The angels are all around us and the Holy Spirit within us, no evil can destroy us.

January 6

~ *The only way is Jesus* ~

> *However, as it is written: 'What no eye has seen, what no ear has heard, and what no human mind has conceived' – the things God has prepared for those who love him (1 Corinthians 2:9, NIV).*

A good mother changes the way she prays. She prays and asks God to prepare her to receive what He has made ready for her. What God has prepared no eyes have seen, no ears have heard and no mind has perceived. The life she is living is all about how God wants her to live. She is living her life in the LIVING LIFE. This is the only way she wants her house to live because Jesus is the only way to every way and path that leads to the way of life, prosperity and abundance.

The Holy Spirit within us is the Spirit of the Father, and Jesus Christ is the only way to the Father.

> *Jesus answered, 'I am the way and the truth and the life. No one comes to the Father except through me (John 14:6, NIV).*

Jesus is the only way for us to go to the Father, and the only way for the Holy Spirit to come live in us.

January 7

~ *Think heavenly* ~

Finally, brothers and sisters, whatever is true, whatever is noble, whatever is right, whatever is pure, whatever is lovely, whatever is admirable—if anything is excellent or praiseworthy—think about such things (Philippians 4:8, NIV).

A good mother doesn't think about all the bad things her children do to use it against them. She thinks of things that are of good nature and heavenly. She points out what those wrong acts are and directs them to do the right thing. She speaks 1 John 3:7 into herself and her children's life.

Whoever practises righteousness is righteous, as he is righteous (1 John 3:7, ESV).

The Holy Spirit doesn't condemn us; He convicts us of our wrong deeds to do the right thing. He is always available to help us renew our mind in the Word of God so we can have the mind of Christ (1 Corinthians 2:16)

Do not conform to the pattern of this world, but be transformed by the renewing of your mind. Then you will be able to test and approve what God's will is – his good, pleasing and perfect will (Romans 12:2, NIV).

And when he comes, he will convict the world of its sin, and of God's righteousness, and of the coming judgment (John 16:8, NLT).

Make every day heavenly by renewing your mind to think heavenly and not worldly.

January 8

~ Living the moment ~

For you equipped me with strength for the battle; you made those who rise against me sink under me (Psalm 18:39, ESV).

A good mother strengthens her weakness in the Word. She clothes herself in the Word every day, so she can stand strong for her children through all the seasons. Even if she is a single mother she can do all things through Christ who strengthens her.

The Holy Spirit is the strength and the power from God that works within us. He will only reveal to us the powerful Word that He receives from God that will give us strength for the moment. His presence strengthens us for the present moment in which we are living.

God is our refuge and strength, an ever-present help in trouble (Psalm 46:1, NIV).

The joy of the Lord from the birth of your new day is your strength to live for the Lord for that moment.

January 9

~ *Life is empty without the Holy Spirit* ~

Consequently, you are no longer foreigners and strangers, but fellow citizens with God's people and also members of his household, built on the foundation of the apostles and prophets, with Christ Jesus himself as the chief cornerstone. In him the whole building is joined together and rises to become a holy temple in the Lord. And in him you too are being built together to become a dwelling in which God lives by his Spirit (Ephesians 2:19-22, NIV).

The house will never be a home without the presence of a mother, the house will feel empty; so it is with our life – it will feel empty without the presence of the Holy Spirit. Life will be empty when we don't provide a home to God's Spirit. A good mother knows that she was taken from within a man and was designed internally to be that house which must contain the Holy Spirit to build her family. For her house to be in order, she must be filled with the Holy Spirit to fully complete the man God has designed for her to marry.

Unless the Lord builds the house, the builders labor in vain. Unless the Lord watches over the city, the guards stand watch in vain. In vain you rise early and stay up late, toiling for food to eat – for he grants sleep to those he loves (Psalm 127:1-2, NIV).

A woman can only complete the man she marries when she has a complete life in Christ.

January 10

~ Child-like faith ~

Enter through the narrow gate. For wide is the gate and broad is the road that leads to destruction, and many enter through it. But small is the gate and narrow the road that leads to life, and only a few find it (Matthew 7:13-14, NIV).

The entrance and pathway to the kingdom of God is small and narrow so that a small child can easily walk through. This is why Jesus said, unless you become like little children, you will not enter the kingdom of God. Not only that, but little children don't carry worries, hatred, other issues and problems of the world. They focus on the joy and happiness of the moment. Every mother has at least travelled through that path of life with their little one enjoying their simple joy. That joy is the path of life. A good mother maintains this by keeping her children on that narrow road to continue the journey of life that leads to LIFE. No matter how much suffering she goes through, she knows that Jesus is waiting to share His glory with her.

The Holy Spirit is the kingdom of God within us, and when we are born again we will see the kingdom of God, and what a joy it is.

For the kingdom of God is not a matter of eating and drinking but of righteousness and peace and joy in the Holy Spirit (Romans 14:17, ESV).

Jesus replied, 'Very truly I tell you, no one can see the kingdom of God unless they are born again' (John 3:3, NIV).

Have a child-like faith and be filled with joy every day. Children are so full of joy and energy every day because they have many years to live through their lives. As a born-again child of God into the new life of Christ that is of eternity, we must be full of joy and energy because we have a long life of eternity in Christ.

January 11

~ Creating beautiful moments ~

Your word, Lord, is eternal; it stands firm in the heavens (Psalm 119:89, NIV).

A good mother already knows that God has made provision about all her concerns regarding the future of her household. She laughs at yesterday's memories that today remind her, and she smiles at her many tomorrows of the future.

Strength and dignity are her garments; she smiles about the future (Proverbs 31:25, ISV).

The devil cannot rob her present joy with any worries of life. She invests her time wisely in Word and prayer that the devil cannot rob her of enjoying the moment.

The Holy Spirit inside us is the provision to enjoy life towards eternity. Everything that we have in Christ is in Him. We just have to faithfully walk with Him and enjoy this inheritance of joy as we journey towards eternity with Him. The devil can't rob the joy and peace that you have found in the Holy Spirit. He has been defeated.

You make known to me the path of life; you will fill me with joy in your presence, with eternal pleasures at your right hand (Psalm 16:11, NIV).

Enjoy the ever-present presence of God that is all around you. The clouds' movement above you, the giggles of a baby, or the flowers that bloom in their seasons.

January 12

~ Obeying God's Word without delay~

Answer me when I call to you, my righteous God. Give me relief from my distress; have mercy on me and hear my prayer (Psalm 4:1, NIV).

When mother's don't respond quickly to their children, the children shout and constantly call their mother until they have been attended to. A good mother will always respond to her child's needs. Just as she is always hurries to obey God's Word, she also responds to her children's needs without any delay when they constantly bother her. Psalm 119:60 is her prayer.

I will hurry, without delay, to obey your commands (Psalm 119:60, NLT).

The Holy Spirit is right inside us and will always respond to our needs. We can constantly call on Him until He responds to us.

The parable of the widow who constantly calls on the judge who responds explains this. God, our righteous judge, will attend to us for justice when we call on Him. This is written in Luke 18:1-8.

The eyes of the Lord watch over those who do right, and his ears are open to their prayers (1 Peter 3:12, NLT).

God is never out of the network zone, keep calling and calling until you get hold of Him, and He responds to your call of need.

January 13

~ *Contentment* ~

Not that I speak in regard to need, for I have learned in whatever state I am, to be content: Philippians 4:11, (NKJV).

A good mother is content; she doesn't do impulse buying. She doesn't spend to impress people but would rather save that money than store something she will never use or that she doesn't need. The needs of her household come before hers. She makes an effort to spend 'ME TIME' with God in Word and prayer to increase her faith to add SELF-CONTROL. This is how she maintains her inner beauty which refreshes her demeanour.

> *For this very reason, make every effort to add to your faith goodness; and to goodness, knowledge; and to knowledge, self-control; and to self-control, perseverance; and to perseverance, godliness; and to godliness, mutual affection; and to mutual affection, love (2 Peter 1:5-7, NIV).*

The Holy Spirit within us produces His fruit of 'SELF-CONTROL' so we do not lose control. We control our SELF to be content. The more we receive and contain the WORD, the more we are content like a child.

> *But I have calmed and quieted myself, I am like a weaned child with its mother; like a weaned child I am content (Psalm 131:2, NIV).*

Fill your days with life from the Word of God and be content with what the day contains for you.

January 14

~ Be broken for God to mend ~

You prepare a table before me in the presence of my enemies. You anoint my head with oil; my cup overflows. Surely your goodness and love will follow me all the days of my life, and I will dwell in the house of the Lord forever (Psalm 23: 5-6, NIV).

Every one of us who lives has given a woman the name and title Mother. Everyone is born out of a woman. She is not just a mother; she strives each day to be a good mother. Every day, she sits down before God in Word and prayer with an empty cup for God to fill with His goodness so her household can drink from it and dissolve any evil around them. Some days, she brings herself as a broken cup to God and pours out all that is within her, so that God can touch, shape and mend her broken pieces into a beautiful new chapter. It's those times, when her heart is broken, that God is closer to her. She loves the comfort and closeness of God in her heartbroken moments.

The Holy Spirit is not only closer to us, but He is inside our heart. Because the flesh of Jesus has been broken, and His blood has been spilled for us, the Holy Spirit can now be closer to us by living inside us.

The Lord Jesus, on the night he was betrayed, took bread, and when he had given thanks, he broke it and said, 'This is my body, which is for you; do this in remembrance of me.' In the same way, after supper he took the cup, saying, 'This cup is the new covenant in my blood; do this, whenever you drink it, in remembrance of me. (1 Corinthians 11:23-25, NIV).

Bring together your broken pieces and give them to God; He will exchange it for His peace.

January 15

~ *Trusting God* ~

> *I will love You, O Lord, my strength. The Lord is my rock and my fortress and my deliverer; My God, my strength, in whom I will trust; My shield and the horn of my salvation, my stronghold. (Psalm 18:1-2, NKJV).*

Every child trusts their mother simply because she is always with them. A good mother wants her children to trust her, so that even in the dark days of life, she will always be there for them as their light to show them the way out. To be that light, she has to connect to the source of light, Jesus. When she spends time in Word and prayer, she not only remains connected, but she knows God in a personal way. She is always with God in His Word, so she has no problem trusting God.

The Holy Spirit within us is gifted to us by Jesus and He is alive in us. We can trust and rely that God is always with us through His Spirit and He will provide all we need at its time of need.

> *But I trust in you, Lord; I say, 'You are my God.' My times are in your hands; deliver me from the hands of my enemies, from those who pursue me (Psalm 31:14-15, NIV).*

Spend time every day with God in His Word and prayer to grow your trust in Him.

January 16

~ Love God, love people ~

Love the Lord your God with all your heart and with all your soul and with all your strength (Deuteronomy 6:5, NIV).

In order to provide love in the right way to her household, she remains connected in the righteous love of God. A good mother first loves the Lord God with all her heart, soul and strength. She shows it by using her strength, her flesh to spend quality time with God in His Word. Her soul, mind, will and emotion are renewed and refreshed by the Word. She has the mind of Christ (1 Corinthians 2:16). Her heart is now upright with God and is in the right place to provide love to her household.

The Holy Spirit is the love of God; in Christ Jesus, He produces the fruit of righteousness inside us, so we can show love towards anyone we know who has gone the wrong way.

Be completely humble and gentle; be patient, bearing with one another in love (Ephesians 4:2, NIV).

God gives us a new day every day with a new command. His new command is to love one another. Love one another every day. A new day, with a new command to love one another is to love God.

January 17

~ Smiling the glory of God ~

May the Lord bless you and protect you. May the Lord smile on you and be gracious to you. May the Lord show you his favour and give you his peace (Numbers 6:24-26, NLT).

A good mother's lifestyle is rooted in Numbers 6:24-26; every day she speaks the life of God's Word to her children so the Holy Spirit can make this Word come alive and live with her and her children. She hugs her children and says, 'May the Lord bless you and protect you. May the Lord smile on you and be gracious to you. May the Lord show you his favour and give you his peace.'

She is speaking blessings to her children each day. The Word which has become flesh has already blessed us with the Holy Spirit who protects us from the curses of this world. The Holy Spirit smiles at us with His eternal joy, and He is the greatest gift from Jesus by the grace of God.

God has shown us His favour and given us His peace through His Holy Spirit which was given to us by Jesus Christ.

> *The grace of the Lord Jesus Christ and the love of God and the fellowship of the Holy Spirit be with you all (2 Corinthians 13:14, ESV).*

Each and every day give someone smiles from the joy of the Holy Spirit.

January 18

~ *The reward of being loyal* ~

> *The one who has found a good wife has found what goodness is and obtained a delightful gift from the Lord (Proverbs 18:22, NET).*

A good woman will do anything to maintain her godly character of being loyal. Whoever God finds favour with, He will give this good woman as a gift to that man. She becomes a good wife to her husband, and a good mother to her children.

At this, she bowed down with her face to the ground. She asked him, 'Why have I found such favour in your eyes that you notice me – a foreigner?' Boaz replied, 'I've been told all about what you have done for your mother-in-law since the death of your husband – how you left your father and mother and your homeland and came to live with a people you did not know before. May the LORD repay you for what you have done. May you be richly rewarded by the LORD, the God of Israel, under whose wings you have come to take refuge. (Ruth 2:10-12, NIV).

Let the life of Ruth shape your character from being a good woman to a good mother. Her loyalty to God makes her loyal in her other relationships, and so she was given as a gift to a good man by God.

But Ruth replied, 'Don't urge me to leave you or to turn back from you. Where you go I will go, and where you stay I will stay. Your people will be my people and your God my God. (Ruth 1:16, NIV).

Because of her loyalty to Naomi, God has given her as a gift to Boaz. They became the mother and father of Obed, who is the grandfather of King David. From King David comes Jesus Christ our Messiah. Maintain your godliness character of a good woman, even after you become a wife and mother. The fruit of your womb will be blessed. Your children will shine the light of God in darkness where there is no light. They will be the light in whatever profession they choose in life.

The Father has given the Holy Spirit as a gift through what Jesus did. He is our loyal friend who will be with us until the end of time. The Holy Spirit is the love of Jesus in action. Nothing can separate us from God's love not even death (Romans 8:38-39). He is the eternal finished work of Jesus. The light in our life. We have to maintain our loyalty to Him by faithfully spending time with Him in the Word of God and in prayer.

Every day shape your character in the Word of God and find favour with God and people.

January 19

~ *Renewing your mind* ~

> *I appeal to you therefore, brothers, by the mercies of God, to present your bodies as a living sacrifice, holy and acceptable to God, which is your spiritual worship. Do not be conformed to this world, but be transformed by the renewal of your mind, that by testing you may discern what is the will of God, what is good and acceptable and perfect (Romans 12:1-2, ESV).*

Just as she changes her clothes into beautiful clean linens to wear, a woman also changes and renews her mind into beautiful clean thoughts that align with the Word of God. A good mother connects her earthly home chores by renewing her mind to make choruses in her heart that sing with the angels to the one who sits on the throne and rules in righteousness. She lives heaven on earth. Just as little children have singalong songs, she too sings along with her heart, praising God in whatever home chores she is doing.

The Holy Spirit is the living sacrifice of Jesus. God sacrificed Jesus, so His Spirit can live in us forever. Just like how a good mother lays down and sacrifices her life for her family. Our heavenly good Father sacrificed His life through His one and only Son, so He can live in us through His Spirit. Jesus lives in the Father, and we live in Jesus, and He lives in us in the Holy Spirit, whom we house.

> *On that day you will realize that I am in my Father, and you are in me, and I am in you (John 14:20, NIV).*

Each and every day be grateful and thankful for the life you are living. You live in Jesus in the Father's Holy Spirit and Jesus lives in the Father. You are alive and well in the God trinity. What more can you ask.

January 20

~ Sleeping through storms ~

> *But now the Lord my God has given me rest on every side, and there is no adversary or disaster (1 Kings 5:4, NIV).*

January 20 of 2020, Blessed (11 months' old then) was asleep when a big storm came. The thunder that it brought was so loud that it woke him up. I went and cuddled him and put him back to sleep.

When the thunder happened again he was disturbed but continued to sleep because this time I was comforting and cuddling him. This is what the Holy Spirit taught me: A good mother is always with her children during their storms, and no matter how bad that storm may be, the comfort she gives to her child gives the child assurance that they will be fine.

> *When Jesus woke up, he rebuked the wind and said to the waves, 'Silence! Be still!' Suddenly the wind stopped, and there was a great calm (Mark 4:39, NLT).*

The Holy Spirit is the comforter in our storms; when we hear His voice it calms our storm like water that puts out a fire. The Holy Spirit is the very presence of the Father and the Son and is always going to be with us to comfort us when we go through life's storms.

Just as I slept with Blessed and He was comforted through that storm, the Holy Spirit sleeps as Jesus slept through the storm within us. Jesus has finished the work and His Spirit is now resting in us. He has the power to calm our storm and comfort us as well.

> *And he said, 'My presence will go with you, and I will give you rest.' (Exodus 33:14, ESV).*
>
> *For just as we share abundantly in the sufferings of Christ, so also our comfort abounds through Christ (2 Corinthians 1:5, NIV).*

Sleep in peace through your storms in the night and wake up in joy in the morning, for this is a new day to walk victoriously in all that life has for you.

January 21

~ *Struggles* ~

> *But he said to me, 'My grace is sufficient for you, for my power is made perfect in weakness.' Therefore I will boast all the more gladly of my weaknesses, so that the power of Christ may rest upon me. For the sake of Christ, then, I am content with weaknesses, insults, hardships, persecutions, and calamities. For when I am weak, then I am strong (2 Corinthians 12:9-10, ESV).*

January 21 of 2020, while watering the garden, Blessed (11 months' old then) got his leg trapped and was struggling to release it. He struggled for some time then finally cried out for me to help him. This is what the Holy Spirit taught me: Every mother has struggles in any areas of their lives. They go into trials or some sort of temptation or even tests that continue their struggle. A good mother instantly cries out to God in her struggles. She doesn't let herself get stuck in a situation for a long time. She knows that God created her to be a helper to her husband and a guiding star for her children, and to help her husband she has to go back to the source of life who gave her that role.

> *No temptation has overtaken you that is not common to man. God is faithful, and he will not let you be tempted beyond your ability, but with the temptation he will also provide the way of escape, that you may be able to endure it (1 Corinthians 10:13, ESV).*

The Holy Spirit is our helper from God that Jesus promises to give to us. He lives inside us. He sees our struggles and feels our pain too, we just have to reach within us and cry out to Him for help. He is our inner strength when we are weak.

> *And I will ask the Father, and he will give you another advocate to help you and be with you forever—the Spirit of truth. (John 14:16-17, NIV).*

A woman was taken out from a man and she is her inner strength. Every mother is the inner strength of their husband completing their missing rib.

January 22

~ *Do everything as a worship unto God* ~

> *My mouth is filled with your praise, declaring your splendor all day long (Psalm 71:8, NIV).*

Every day she does the same house chores over and over again. A good mother does it with joy, knowing that every day in the throne room of God, He is worshipped in Spirit and in truth. Her everyday chores are done as a worship unto God. She serves her house from a heart of pure love.

> *God is spirit, and his worshipers must worship in the Spirit and in truth (John 4:24, NIV).*

The Holy Spirit produces the same fruit of His righteousness all the time, regardless of how many times we fail to make use of what He is producing. Producing the fruit of righteousness in our everyday living is a kingdom lifestyle.

> *But the fruit of the Spirit is love, joy, peace, patience, kindness, goodness, faithfulness, gentleness, self-control; against such things there is no law (Galatians 5:22-23, ESV).*

Let everything that you do today and every day be a worship unto God. Glorify God in everything you do.

January 23

~ seeking God's face ~

> *My heart says of you, 'Seek His face!' Your face, Lord, I will seek. (Psalm 27:8, NIV)*

A good mother seeks God's face in everything she does. This is the WORD of prayer she quotes from Psalm 63:1.

> *O God, you are my God; earnestly I seek you; my soul thirsts for you; my flesh faints for you, as in a dry and weary land where there is no water (Psalm 63:1, ESV).*

She looks forward to seeing Jesus revealing himself in whatever she does. The more she feeds her new life with the Word, the more the Word becomes her flesh, and that's how she sees Jesus in what she is doing. She knows what to do with any situations that arise in her house.

The Holy Spirit is the righteousness of Christ and we can only seek Him from within. The more we connect deeper into the Word with our strength, soul and spirit, the more easily we will find Him.

> *You will seek me and find me when you seek me with all your heart (Jeremiah 29:13, NIV).*

Keep seeking God every day until you find Him. When you find Him, worship Him until the end of your time when your flesh wears out and returns to where it came from.

January 24

~ Renew your mind in the Word of God ~

> *But if we walk in the light, as he is in the light, we have fellowship with one another, and the blood of Jesus His Son cleanses us from all sin (1 John 1:7, ESV).*

Whenever she does washing, she is reminded of how the blood of Jesus has washed away her sin and made her clean, just like those clothes she is washing which become clean.

> *Just think how much more the blood of Christ will purify our consciences from sinful deeds so that we can worship the living God. For by the power of the eternal Spirit, Christ offered himself to God as a perfect sacrifice for our sins (Hebrews 9:14, NLT).*

The Holy Spirit remains in us to keep us clean from inside out. The more we receive the Word into us and renew our mind in accordance with the Word, the cleaner we remain.

> *You are already clean because of the word I have spoken to you (John 15:3, NIV).*

Every time we renew our mind in the Word of God, there is washing and cleansing going on inside us.

January 25

~ New image in Christ ~

> *Humans can reproduce only human life, but the Holy Spirit gives birth to spiritual life (John 3:6, NLT).*

A good mother doesn't tell her children, 'You are just like your father always being angry and losing your temper'. She knows that after Adam sinned, he fathered a child in his own likeness (Genesis 5:3). We are all born in the image of a fallen man. A good mother looks at her new identity which is the image of Christ. And this is what her children are; they are the image of Christ. Her new image in Christ gives her the new character of Christ through the Holy Spirit inside her. Because she has a good heavenly Father, she ensures that she plays her role of being a good mother, so her children will inherit her good character. She has influence over her words and actions. When she speaks, her house abides by it; she makes sure that she walks her talk. She talks more to God in prayer so she can walk and live in love.

Just as a newborn baby is a gift to the parents, the Holy Spirit is gifted to us when we are born again. The Holy Spirit produces the character of Christ inside us, for us to reproduce it so we can become the image of Christ.

Since you have been born again, not of perishable seed but of imperishable, through the living and abiding Word of God (1 Peter 1:23, ESV).

We receive a new spirit and a new heart in this new life. We just have to renew our mind to think and act in its new way of living.

January 26

~ Fight the good fight of faith in the courtroom of heaven ~

Fight the good fight of the faith. Take hold of the eternal life to which you were called and about which you made the good confession in the presence of many witnesses (1 Timothy 6:12, ESV).

A good mother brings a life into a world where she knows that the god of the world will blind her children when they grow up, so he can steal them and kill them slowly until they are dead, and he knows he has destroyed them. She fights for her children in the courtroom of God. She fights the good fight of faith by listening and hearing the Word of God until she is heard in the highest court of heaven.

The Spirit of the Lord is on me, because he has anointed me to proclaim good news to the poor. He has sent me to proclaim freedom for the prisoners and recovery of sight for the blind, to set the oppressed free, (Luke 4:18, NIV).

The Holy Spirit resurrected the life of Jesus, so that Jesus can live again in us through Him. Jesus has come to give sight to the blind that the god of this world has blinded. He has destroyed the work of the devil which is death.

> *The reason the Son of God appeared was to destroy the devil's work (1 John 3:8, NIV).*

Each and every day celebrate your life, that Jesus has set you free from devil who has stolen you and blinded you. You can now see and come out from the path that leads to death and walk on the path of eternal life in the Holy Spirit.

January 27

~ *Storing the Word of God* ~

> *Likewise, every good tree bears good fruit, but a bad tree bears bad fruit. A good tree cannot bear bad fruit, and a bad tree cannot bear good fruit (Matthew 7:17-18, NIV).*

What takes place in our mind can come from outside or even from inside us. A good mother knows that she can control what comes into her, but she can't control what's happening outside of her. How she responds to what she wants inside her mind depends on what is inside her heart. The Word that she has received by faith and stored produces goodness.

> *'Blessed is the man who trusts in the Lord, whose trust is the Lord. He is like a tree planted by water, that sends out its roots by the stream, and does not fear when heat comes, for its leaves remain green, and is not anxious in the year of drought, for it does not cease to bear fruit.' (Jeremiah 17:7-8, ESV).*

If you always include chillies in all your cooking ingredients; you will either grow chillies or store them so you can easily reach for some to use. It's the same as with the Word of God; a good mother stores the Word of God to grow in it. Whenever she is in need, she reaches within her for the Word.

Her household is full of hope regardless of what season of life they are passing through.

The Holy Spirit produces the fruit of life, a life full of goodness from the Word of God we store within us. He is the storehouse of eternal life of love, joy and peace for us to use in our body, which is His house in which He resides. We are to reach within us and seek the Holy Spirit to reproduce His eternal life in our life.

> *I am the vine; you are the branches. Whoever abides in me and I in him, he it is that bears much fruit, for apart from me you can do nothing (John 15:5, ESV).*

God, who is good, has made a good day for you every day, invest goodness into it by overcoming any evil with good.

January 28

~ *Holy Spirit, the helper* ~

> *Nevertheless, I tell you the truth: it is to your advantage that I go away, for if I do not go away, the Helper will not come to you. But if I go, I will send him to you (John 16:7, ESV).*

The Holy Spirit is our personal assistant through our personal relationship with Christ, the Word that has become flesh. The devil went through the personal assistant of the first man, Adam, and deceived her. The father of lies, the devil, cannot deceive us because our personal assistant, the Holy Spirit, is the Spirit of truth, and He will tell us the truth that will set us free and expose the dark lies of the devil.

> *And I will ask the Father, and he will give you another Helper, to be with you forever, even the Spirit of truth, whom the world cannot receive, because it neither sees him nor knows him. You know him, for he dwells with you and will be in you (John 14:16-17, ESV).*

A mother is a personal assistant to her husband through their relationship of becoming one as flesh and having children. She is a good mother when she connects to the Holy Spirit to be her personal assistant, so she can be the good mother and wife that God designed her to be.

> *But the Helper (Comforter, Advocate, Intercessor—Counselor, Strengthener, Standby), the Holy Spirit, whom the Father will send in My name [in My place, to represent Me and act on My behalf], He will teach you all things. And He will help you remember everything that I have told you (John 14:26, AMP).*

Each day of your every day, let all the life issues of your life be handled by your personal assistant, the Holy Spirit.

January 29

~ *delighting in the Lord* ~

Delight yourself in the Lord, and he will give you the desires of your heart (Psalm 37:4, ESV).

Every mother has great plans for her children doing something great with their life. A good mother thinks and plans in the way God has designed her children's future and that is for them to enjoy life to the fullest in whatever their heart desires. The way to enjoy their heart's desire is to delight in the Lord. She leads her children in delighting in what the Lord delights. She teaches her children to understand the kindness, justice and righteousness of God on earth for that is what God delights in. God delightfully gives the desires of our heart when we delight in what He delights in.

> *This is what the Lord says: 'Let not the wise boast of their wisdom or the strong boast of their strength or the rich boast of their riches, but let the one who boasts boast about this: that they have the understanding to know me, that I am the Lord, who exercises kindness, justice and righteousness on earth, for in these I delight,' declares the Lord (Jeremiah 9:23-24, NIV).*

The Holy Spirit is the Spirit of understanding, who exercises the kindness, justice and righteousness of God on earth through us. This is what we should be proud of, to boast about and boost our actions; the kindness, justice and righteousness of God. When we action what God delights in His heart, He also actions the delights of our heart. Our actions put God to action.

> *For the Lord your God is living among you. He is a mighty saviour. He will take delight in you with gladness. With his love, he will calm all your fears. He will rejoice over you with joyful songs (Zephaniah 3:17, NLT).*

Seek and delight in the Lord and His righteousness all the days of your life, and all the desires of your heart will be given unto you.

January 30

~ *Holy, clean and washed by the cleansing of God's Word* ~

> *to make her holy and clean, washed by the cleansing of God's word (Ephesians 5:26, NLT).*

Every day she cleans the house and does it joyfully. She is reminded of how the blood of Jesus has cleaned her body to house His Holy Spirit.

> *If we confess our sins, he is faithful and just to forgive us our sins and to cleanse us from all unrighteousness (1 John 1:9, ESV).*

A good mother is grateful for the cleaning she does around her home, especially after seeing how the house is cleaned. She now understands that Jesus too is happy and celebrates with the angels when a sinner is cleansed by the blood.

The Holy Spirit glows the glory of God from within us when we keep His house clean by hearing and hearing the Word of God daily. The cleaning process starts taking place from inside and makes its way out. We begin to shine and others around us begin to see the changes in us. Jesus said in Matthew 23:26, to first clean the inside of the cup and the plate [it is necessary] so that the outside is also clean.

> *He saved us through the washing of rebirth and renewal by the Holy Spirit (Titus 3:5, NIV).*

> *You are already clean because of the word I have spoken to you (John 15:3, NIV).*

When the Word of God cleanses and changes you from inside, it starts showing outside with your actions.

January 31

~ Peace of God ~

> *You keep him in perfect peace whose mind is stayed on you, because he trusts in you (Isaiah 26:3, ESV).*

A good mother rests in Christ while she is working so hard. She puts to rest her 'old me' life by giving service to it with the fruit of the Holy Spirit. Every time her 'old self' wants to rise up against issues in her house, she feeds it with the fruit of the Spirit by renewing her mind and letting the peace of God reign over her 'old me'. In this way she is ruling and reigning with Christ in the heavenly realms.

> *Don't worry about anything, but pray about everything. With thankful hearts offer up your prayers and requests to God. Then, because you belong to Christ Jesus, God will bless you with peace that no one can completely understand. And this peace will control the way you think and feel. (Philippians 4:6-7, CEV).*

The Holy Spirit is the peace of God that Jesus gives in His Word not as the world gives. The Holy Spirit gives you the 'new me' life in

Christ to rule and reign with Christ. We can now have inner peace by renewing our mind to have the mind of Christ and walk with and be led by the Holy Spirit.

> *Peace I leave with you; my peace I give you. I do not give to you as the world gives. Do not let your hearts be troubled and do not be afraid (John 14:27, NIV).*

Put to rest everything that worries your soul and live in peace.

FEBRUARY

~ Baptism of the Holy Spirit ~

He who believes in Me, as the Scripture has said, out of his heart will flow rivers of living water.' (John 7:38, NKJV).

2 May 2020. The Lord showed me a public pool and a person going for a fresh shower after having a dip in the pool. This is what the Lord taught me. You see that person having a dip in the public pool is the same as how, when you received Jesus and got baptized, it was witnessed in public. To be baptized in the Holy Spirit is like going in for a second fresh cleansing. Jesus does the baptism of the Holy Spirit within you. This is where springs of fresh living water will flow within you. It's the same as having a wash in fresh, clean, flowing water after having a dip in a public pool. The fresh, living, flowing water baptism of the Holy Spirit is from Jesus within us.

> *John answered them all, 'I baptize you with water. But one who is more powerful than I will come, the straps of whose sandals I am not worthy to untie. He will baptize you with the Holy Spirit and fire (Luke 3:16, NIV).*

Jesus baptizes us in the Holy Spirit and The Holy Spirit brings the life of Christ to LIVE AGAIN in us. A spring of fresh living water flows from inside us so that we will never again be thirsty. We remain content and satisfied with life.

> *Jesus replied, 'Anyone who drinks this water will soon become thirsty again. But those who drink the water I give will never be thirsty again. It becomes a fresh, bubbling spring within them, giving them eternal life.' (John 4:13-14, NLT).*

God Himself baptized Jesus with the Holy Spirit after He was baptized by John.

> *When all the people were being baptized, Jesus was baptized too. And as he was praying, heaven was opened and the Holy Spirit descended on him in bodily form like a dove. And a voice came from heaven: 'You are my Son, whom I love; with you I am well pleased.' (Luke 3:21-22, NIV).*

Jesus said, 'I am in the Father, and you are in me, and I am in you' (John 14:20). Jesus is in the Father, and He is being baptized by the Father with the Holy Spirit. We are in Jesus and are baptized by Jesus with the Holy Spirit. Live that life of the fresh bubbling spring of eternal life of joy and peace in the Holy Spirit.

Each day of the month of February and EVERY DAY, let's renew our mind in the fresh Word of God making our FLESH become Word (John 1:14), so we can have the mind of Christ (1 Corinthians 2:16) and maintain our new heart and spirit.

> *And I will give you a new heart, and a new spirit I will put within you. And I will remove the heart of stone from your flesh and give you a heart of flesh (Ezekiel 36:26, ESV).*

> *The Word became flesh and made his dwelling among us (John 1:14, NIV). But we have the mind of Christ (1 Corinthians 2:16, NIV).*

February 1

~ We are the joy and pride of the Holy Spirit ~

Yes, you are our pride and joy (1 Thessalonians 2:20, NLT).

A good mother takes care of her household with joy and pride. Her children are her greatest joy, and she serves them with joy and pride. A full-time unpaid job done with love. Jesus is the joy and pride of God. The Holy Spirit confirmed this in the form of a dove and descended on Him, after He was baptized.

> *…and the Holy Spirit, in bodily form, descended on him like a dove. And a voice from heaven said, 'You are my dearly loved Son, and you bring me great joy.' Luke 3:22, (NLT).*

The Spirit of God that was upon Jesus now lives joyfully inside us, serving us with His fruit of righteousness full-time. God is love and His Spirit serves us pure love that comes with love, joy, peace, patience, kindness goodness, faithfulness, gentleness and self-control. We are the joy and pride of the Holy Spirit of God in Christ Jesus.

Every new day is another great opportunity to serve someone you love with joy and pride to the glory of God.

February 2

~ God speed ~

Yes, today, tomorrow, and the next day I must proceed on my way (Luke 13:33, NLT).

2 February 2020. While looking at today's date, 02.02.2020, and how this date can be read backwards, the Lord laid this interesting

piece in my heart. He showed me a train and said, 'Look at this train, after it arrives at its point of destiny it moves backwards to reach its next point of destiny.' A train only terminates at its point of destiny as scheduled. Today is a special day and date that from where you are, you are moving forward, and even when you go backwards, you will always arrive at your destiny with my schedule.

A good mother moves in the schedule of God and so she moves from destiny to destiny living a full life of abundance. She gets most of her strength from those ill thoughts that knock her down and try to make her go backwards. As long as God is the driver, she enjoys her Godspeed ride into the promised land.

It doesn't matter where you are placed or what age you have reached, the Holy Spirit inside you can take you from right where you are to where God wants you to be at 'God's speed'.

> *Put God in charge of your work, then what you've planned will take place (Proverbs 16:3, MSG).*

Every day, get into God's Word to travel at Godspeed. You will get your plans achieved at God's speed.

February 3

~Crying~

> *In my trouble I cried to the Lord, And He answered me (Psalm 120:1, NASB).*

A good mother attends immediately to her crying child that needs attention. She doesn't neglect them. She knows well how if she would cry to the Lord, He would be right there immediately with His presence giving her peace and comfort.

> *Remember your promise to me; it is my only hope. Your promise revives me; it comforts me in all my troubles (Psalm 119:49-50, NLT).*

When we can no longer talk in prayers, our body leaks our pain in tears from inside us as prayers. The Holy Spirit inside us sees it from within and comforts us with His fruit of peace.

> *You keep track of all my sorrows. You have collected all my tears in your bottle. You have recorded each one in your book (Psalm 56:8, NLT).*

> *Your eyes saw my unformed body; all the days ordained for me were written in your book before one of them came to be (Psalm 139:16, NIV).*

If today brings you pain and sorrow let your body and soul roll out your tears in your spirit. The Holy Spirit is just a breath away to take it and record it in His book.

February 4

~ *God will make a way* ~

> *In all your ways acknowledge him, and he will make straight your paths (Proverbs 3:6, ESV).*

A good mother always makes a way for her children through her prayers. Her prayers create the path of success for her children. She connects herself to the source of resources for her children to benefit.

God is always making a way for us too. His Spirit inside directs us to walk in the way that God made for us and Jesus Christ is the only way to that way that God made for us.

> *I will go before you. And make the crooked places straight;*
> *(Isaiah 45:2, NKJV).*

> *Jesus said to him, 'I am the way, the truth, and the life. No one comes to the Father except through Me.' (John 14:6, NKJV)*

Jesus Christ is the only way to the Father to make ways for us to achieve that day's dreams successfully.

February 5

~ *Be loving and respectful* ~

> *In the same way, you wives must accept the authority of your husbands. Then, even if some refuse to obey the Good News, your godly lives will speak to them without any words. They will be won over by observing your pure and reverent lives (1 Peter 3:1-2, NLT).*

A good mother respects her husband, the father of her children. Whatever she needs, she asks him kindly and in line with what he can provide. She doesn't ask him to do something he can't do. She receives the Word of God in Ephesians to become her flesh. The beauty of God's Word becoming her flesh attracts her husband to love her more.

A husband who works on making the Word of God become his flesh loves his wife the way he loves himself.

> *However, each one of you also must love his wife as he loves himself, and the wife must respect her husband (Ephesians 5:33, NIV).*

The Holy Spirit respects the Father, that He speaks to Him and intercedes according to the will of the Father. It's the language of love to which the Holy Spirit speaks and the very action God takes to protect His loved ones. Everything is done with love.

> *And he who searches our hearts knows the mind of the Spirit, because the Spirit intercedes for God's people in accordance with the will of God (Romans 8:27, NIV).*

Ask the Holy Spirit to pray for you for God's will to be done in your life every day.

February 6

~ Trusting God ~

> *But blessed are those who trust in the Lord and have made the Lord their hope and confidence. They are like trees planted along a riverbank, with roots that reach deep into the water. Such trees are not bothered by the heat or worried by long months of drought. Their leaves stay green, and they never stop producing fruit (Jeremiah 17:7-8, NLT).*

6 February 2020. After dropping off Angelilly (my five-year-old) at school I thought, 'okay, I just don't need to worry about her until school ends'. This is what the Holy Spirit taught me: A good mother brings and offers to God all the days of her household, and she doesn't worry about what the future holds for them, because she trusts the hands that are holding her future. When the hour of her needs arrives God will be there to meet it.

The Holy Spirit inside us constantly produces joy and peace that keeps us happy and free from worry about any life issues. The kingdom of God is not about worrying about the demands of the flesh that want to keep up with the standards of this fallen world. Rather, it is of joy and peace in the righteousness of the Holy Spirit (Romans 14:17).

> *Do not be anxious about anything, but in every situation, by prayer and petition, with thanksgiving, present your requests to God. And the peace of God, which transcends all understanding, will guard your hearts and your minds in Christ Jesus (Philippians 4:6-7 NIV)*

The more you spend time with God in His Word and in prayer, the more you will grow to trust Him.

February 7

~ *Bearing fruit* ~

> *'Your mother was like a vine in your vineyard planted by the water; it was fruitful and full of branches because of abundant water (Ezekiel 19:10, NIV).*

When something is not fruitful it has no purpose to exist. Jesus cursed the fig tree because it didn't produce any fruit to serve its purpose. Our purpose of Jesus is to produce the fruit of His Holy Spirit to serve others who needs it. This is the purpose where God has positioned us to live and serve in love. God has positioned every mother to be the steward of their home.

A good mother knows her position is given by God to serve Him through her house. As long as she sits in Word and prayer in that position, she will be producing good fruit. She may fail at times but she never gives up continuing to sit in Word and prayer.

> *I will take my post; I will position myself on the fortress. I will keep watch to see what the Lord says to me and how he will respond to my complaint (Habakkuk 2:1, CEB).*

Jesus has positioned the Holy Spirit within us to serve us in producing His character. He produces His good fruit at the same hour we invited Him into our heart.

> *We prove ourselves by our purity, our understanding, our patience, our kindness, by the Holy Spirit within us, and by our sincere love. We faithfully preach the truth. God's power is working in us. We use the weapons of righteousness in the right hand for attack and the left hand for defense (2 Corinthians 6:6-7, NLT).*

Each and every day, take your position in the Word and remain in it. Do not lose it to the temporary things of the world.

February 8

~ *Hungry for the Word* ~

> *Blessed are those who hunger and thirst for righteousness, for they will be filled (Matthew 5:6, NIV).*

8 February 2020. While making Angelilly's breakfast, she kept checking on me to see if I had finished making her breakfast because she was hungry. Her hunger causes her to get into that desperate situation to come to me constantly for her food. This is what the Holy Spirit taught me: A good mother is always hungry for the spiritual milk which is God's Word that she constantly goes to God. She wants to fill herself, so that she is able to serve and feed her hungry family. Man cannot live by bread alone but by every word that comes from God's mouth.

> *Like newborn babies, crave pure spiritual milk, so that by it you may grow up in your salvation (1 Peter 2:2, NIV).*

The Holy Spirit breathes into the Word of God so that it becomes alive to satisfy our hunger. The Word keeps us content as long as we are feeding on it, and the Holy Spirit breathes on it to make it alive. To be blessed is to remain hungry and thirsty for the righteous Word of God.

> *I am the Lord your God, who brought you up out of Egypt. Open wide your mouth and I will fill it (Psalm 81:10, NIV).*

Every day let God continue to feed you until you overflow from the goodness from the Word of God.

February 9

~ make the Word become your flesh ~

> *He makes my feet like the feet of a deer; he causes me to stand on the heights (Psalm 18:33, NIV).*

I remember looking around the house and thinking of putting away anything that looks harmful or is a threat of harm to my children. This is what the Holy Spirit taught me: A good mother puts away things that are a threat to her life or can destroy her house. She is mindful of building her home so she trains her feet and knees to step firmly over any stumbling blocks that are in her way.

> *Stand firm then, with the belt of truth buckled around your waist, with the breastplate of righteousness in place, and with your feet fitted with the readiness that comes from the gospel of peace (Ephesians 6:14-15, NIV).*

Her mind is set on being renewed in the Word all the time. Her new heart and spirit are overflowing with love to forgive her enemies. As she keeps building a home for the Holy Spirit to live in, the Word is becoming her flesh. She can only build a beautiful home for her family by building a home for the Holy Spirit first.

> *Unless the LORD builds the house, the builders labor in vain. Unless the LORD watches over the city, the guards stand watch in vain (Psalm 127:1, NIV).*

We become a threat to the kingdom of darkness when the Holy Spirit feels at home within us. The more we hear and hear the Word, the more the Holy Spirit lives and works upon the Word. The Word of God is sharper than any double-edged sword and is harmful to the kingdom of darkness.

> *Take the helmet of salvation and the sword of the Spirit, which is the Word of God (Ephesian 6:17, NIV).*

When we make the Word within us become flesh by putting it into action, we become a threat to the kingdom of darkness. The light and love from the Word of the Holy Spirit shines through our flesh.

The Word, the sword which is your flesh, is harmful to any evil that wants to come near you. The Word has become flesh (John 1:14).

February 10

~ *Rise up in the Word* ~

> *And these words that I command you today shall be on your heart. You shall teach them diligently to your children, and shall talk of them when you sit in your house, and when you walk by the way, and when you lie down, and when you rise (Deuteronomy 6:6-7, ESV).*

In raising her children a good mother teaches them about the Word of God. Everything she does in her house, she reminds them, is from God's Word and His goodness.

> *Train up a child in the way he should go; even when he is old he will not depart from it (Proverbs 22:6, ESV).*

The Holy Spirit inside teaches us the truth of life. Jesus did say, 'When I go the Spirit of truth will come and tell you everything about me.' In everything we do the Holy Spirit is within us to teach us the kingdom's lifestyle. It is the power of the Holy Spirit that raises the WORD who is Jesus to life, and He will raise us up in the Word that we contain.

> *If the Spirit of him who raised Jesus from the dead dwells in you, he who raised Christ Jesus from the dead will also give life to your mortal bodies through his Spirit who dwells in you (Romans 8:11, ESV).*

Rise and shine with your new day by raising yourself up in the Word of God.

February 11

~ *The joy of spreading the good news* ~

> *The man called his wife's name Eve, because she was the mother of all living (Genesis 3:20, ESV).*

The first woman was a wife and was given the name 'Eve' which means 'the mother of all living things'. Every living person is born with the nature of her disobedience. The Holy Spirit resolved that with the virgin birth of Jesus Christ.

For Mary to become a mother, the Holy Spirit had to go inside of Her to bring out the purity and value of a good mother. The devil works hard at targeting a woman, wife or mother as they can easily access and connect to the Holy Spirit in a more powerful way.

The Holy Spirit inside us is the good news of the resurrected life of Jesus. He is the living proof living in us that Jesus is no longer dead but is alive forever. Spread joy from the fruit of the Holy Spirit, as good news that Jesus is alive in you through the Holy Spirit.

A good woman or mother will always tell of the goodness of the life which she is living that Jesus resurrected. Matthew 28:5-9, tells us about the angel who told the women about the resurrection of Jesus, and to go tell others.

> *Tell every nation on earth, 'The Lord is wonderful and does marvelous things! (Psalm 96:3, CEV).*

It's always a woman's joy to spread good news even if it is still yet to happen.

February 12

~ Your name in Christ ~

> *'Do not be afraid, for I have ransomed you. I have called you by name; you are mine (Isaiah 43:1, NLT).*

It is mostly mothers who name their children. A good mother gives a good name to her children knowing that her child will become what the name says.

As mother to a one-year-old at the moment, I would call my child all the time to stop him from touching or doing something that can hurt him. God has also named us, and that is what His Spirit inside calls us each day to give direction to the way we go.

When you are aware of who you are in Christ, you hear the Holy Spirit voice because He is calling you by your name and leading you. And just as I call my child by his name to not do something that will hurt him, the Holy Spirit does the same to us. Or, like a fire alarm that keeps buzzing when it senses the danger of fire, the Holy Spirit starts calling us constantly when we start heading towards the path of death. The Holy Spirit is the life of Christ to give us life towards the path of life.

> *Listen to me, O coastlands, and give attention, you peoples from afar. The Lord called me from the womb, from the body of my mother he named my name (Isaiah 49:1, ESV).*

Every day God prepares a new day for us, and He calls us to it. It's called life. Jesus is the living LIFE, and to make our life live that LIFE, we have to stay connected with the Spirit of life, by spending time in Word and prayer.

February 13

~ Interrupting God ~

> *Keep watch over yourselves and all the flock of which the Holy Spirit has made you overseers. Be shepherds of the church of God, which he bought with his own blood (Acts 20:28, NIV).*

A good mother always has time for her children whenever they interrupt her busy schedule. She knows that Jesus was the busiest man who has ever lived, yet He has time for anyone who interrupts him for help.

Her family is what the Holy Spirit has given her to keep watch over, and she must respond to their needs when she is asked. She interrupts God first thing in the early morning in Word and prayer before she enters the schedule of her day with all the interruptions from her surroundings.

We can interrupt and talk to Jesus through the Holy Spirit anytime, anywhere and whenever the need arises. He is right inside us.

> *Let us then approach God's throne of grace with confidence, so that we may receive mercy and find grace to help us in our time of need (Hebrews 4:16, NIV).*

In your busy day today, take time out and be kind to someone who needs it, to the glory of God.

February 14

~ Dress up for the day ~

> *Do you not know that your bodies are temples of the Holy Spirit, who is in you, whom you have received from God? You are not your own; you were bought at a price. Therefore honour God with your bodies (1 Corinthians 6:19-20 NIV).*

A good mother always ensures that her children are clothed right. She dresses in a modest way showing a good example to her children. She teaches her children that they must respect their body as it houses the Holy Spirit.

****

I remember waking up one morning (it was 19 May 2020). The Lord put this beautiful word in my heart.

Being a full-time stay at home mum, I wake up anytime of the day and go with the flow of the day. This is what the Lord said, 'Rise up early and start well with your new day. Wash and dress up physically and spiritually, it's good for the mind, your soul. Dress up and be well presented to your day. It doesn't matter if you are not going somewhere special. You are doing it for the glory of the one who made this day for you. You are special and this day is especially being made for you. This is the day that the Lord has made for you to rejoice and be glad in it.'

****

This is what the Lord wants us all to do.

When you shower, let your heart make music and sing God's Word in 1 Corinthians 6:11. When you are getting dressed, clothe your mind in Romans 13:14 and Psalm 29:2. This is how you can maintain your new fresh beauty from inside and out.

> *Stand at attention! Dress your best to honor Him (Psalm 29:2, MSG).*
>
> *And I want women to be modest in their appearance. They should wear decent and appropriate clothing and not draw attention to themselves by the way they fix their hair or by wearing gold or pearls or expensive clothes. For women who claim to be devoted to God should make themselves attractive by the good things they do (1 Timothy 2:9-10, NLT).*

The Holy Spirit holds us in our body, His house where He resides, and clothes us in the righteous blood of Christ. The blood of Jesus is always there to cleanse us when we feel naked and exposed to the evil of this world.

> *How much more, then, will the blood of Christ, who through the eternal Spirit offered himself unblemished to God, cleanse our consciences from acts that lead to death, so that we may serve the living God! (Hebrews 9:14, NIV).*

> *Wash, put on perfume, and get dressed in your best clothes (Ruth 3:3, NIV).*

Every day rise, wash and dress up and present yourself happily to the day. Clothe yourself in the righteousness of Christ. Look good and feel good for the love of your life, Jesus.

February 15

~ A mother is the strength to her household ~

> *The wise woman builds her house, but with her own hands the foolish one tears hers down (Proverbs 14:1, NIV).*

A good mother knows that being the strength to the foundation of her household she will use that strength to build her house, and not destroy it. She sits in the Word of God to steer her life in that direction and stands in prayer to pray for peace upon all that she walks on.

> *How beautiful on the mountains are the feet of the messenger who brings good news, the good news of peace and salvation, the news that the God of Israel reigns! (Isaiah 52:7, NLT).*

The Holy Spirit is the power and strength of God that work within us to build us to be more Christ-like each day.

> *But you, dear friends, must build each other up in your most holy faith, pray in the power of the Holy Spirit, and await the mercy of our Lord Jesus Christ, who will bring you eternal life. In this way, you will keep yourselves safe in God's love (Jude 1:20-21, NLT).*

In order for the Holy Spirit to build us to be Christ-like, we have to take in by faith, the Word of God who is Jesus in flesh on a daily basis. The Word is Holy Spirit's building material to build our flesh into Word to become Christ-like.

February 16

~ A good mother leads ~

> *The Lord will guide you continually, giving you water when you are dry and restoring your strength. You will be like a well-watered garden, like an ever-flowing spring (Isaiah 58:11, NLT).*

A good mother guides her children on the right path that leads towards a great future. She seeks guidance from God's Word and prays for God's peace to confirm her decision. Oftentimes she sits in the Word waiting patiently for God to lead through His Spirit.

> *…to shine on those living in darkness and in the shadow of death, to guide our feet into the path of peace (Luke 1:79, NIV).*

The Holy Spirit lives inside us and speaks from within us to convict us of our wrongs and lead us back on track to travel the path of life.

> *The Lord says, 'I will guide you along the best pathway for your life. I will advise you and watch over you' (Psalm 32:8, NLT).*

Let the Holy Spirit lead you on the right path every day as you lead your children.

February 17

~ *Your purpose and true identity* ~

> *Before I formed you in the womb I knew you, before you were born I set you apart; I appointed you as a prophet to the nations (Jeremiah 1:5, NIV).*

The day you found the truth about yourself is the day you found who you are, your true identity.

A good mother helps her children to discover their purposes in life and guides them on that journey. She teaches her children about the Word of God in Jeremiah; about God having a purpose for them before they were born, and that God has planned a great future for bringing them into this world.

> *'For I know the plans I have for you,' declares the Lord, 'plans to prosper you and not to harm you, plans to give you hope and a future (Jeremiah 29:11, NIV).*

The Holy Spirit is the Spirit of truth and will tell you nothing but the truth to guide you on your journey of life in Christ. When you know the truth, the Word of God, you will be set free from the cunning lies of the devil (John 8:32).

That will be the day you will come to know your true identity and your purpose from the Spirit of truth.

> *But when he, the Spirit of truth, comes, he will guide you into all the truth. He will not speak on his own; he will speak only what he hears, and he will tell you what is yet to come (John 16:13, NIV).*

Every day speak the truth of God's Word into your life, that's your true identity.

February 18

~ A mother hears and responds in action ~

> *Does he who fashioned the ear not hear? Does he who formed the eye not see? (Psalm 94:9, NIV).*

To hear your child and to respond in action to what you hear are two different things. A good mother hears and hears the Word of God, and this places her in a better position to hear her children and respond in love to her child's needs. Faith comes by hearing and hearing the Word, and faith without action is dead. She actions her faith by responding in love towards her child's needs, after hearing them out.

If a child asks for something that is not beneficial for them, they will not receive it. She speaks with love so that her children can understand her love language.

> *Before they call I will answer; while they are still speaking I will hear (Isaiah 65:24, NIV).*

The Holy Spirit is the Spirit of God; He knows what good things God intends for you to have in life. He works on building and developing you in the Word, so that you mature and are ready to receive what He has in store for you.

> *But now to continue—the son who will receive his father's property is treated just like a slave while he is young, even though he really owns everything. While he is young, there are men who take care of him and manage his affairs until the time set by his father (Galatians 4:1-2, GNT).*

Keep hearing and hearing the Word on a daily basis, so the Holy Spirit can work on you to bring you to maturity.

To hear the Holy Spirit clearly, you have to hear and hear the Word of God. Faith comes from listening to and hearing the Word. Without faith it is impossible to please God, and faith without action is dead. Your faith is not alive if you don't live in obedience to the voice of the Holy Spirit, which you hear from the Word of God.

February 19

~ Lifted up ~

> *He sets on high those who are lowly, and those who mourn are lifted to safety (Job 5:11, ESV).*

A good mother will lift her children up when they feel down. No matter how grown up her children are, they are still her babies. She not only lifts her children up in prayers but she seeks the Word of God and speaks the light and truth from God's Word into their life.

The Holy Spirit brings into life the Word which we believe and receive into our spirit. He interceded on our behalf according to the will of the Father. This is how the Holy Spirit lift us up, so we do not lose hope in God. He lifts us up and our prayers to the Father by interceding for us.

> *Then the Spirit lifted me up and brought me into the inner court, and the glory of the Lord filled the temple (Ezekiel 43:5, NIV).*

Every new day speak the Word of God into your life to lift you to higher grounds where you are kept safe from the enemy's reach.

February 20

~ Hiding the treasures of God's Word in your heart ~

> *I have hidden your word in my heart that I might not sin against you (Psalm 119:11, NIV).*

Nothing much about how Mary raised Jesus is known because she kept everything in her heart. A good mother keeps everything beautiful in her heart. The safest place to keep the treasures of life is her heart. All the beautiful things in her life are stored in her heart and used as thanksgiving unto God to glorify Him. The secret to her walking a blameless life is storing the Word of God in her heart.

> *But Mary treasured up all these things and pondered them in her heart (Luke 2:19, NIV).*

The Holy Spirit is the beautiful gift from Jesus that is hidden in our heart. To know the mind of the Holy Spirit is to keep Him alive in your heart. God speaks His mind through the heart. You have a new heart and new spirit, continue to renew your mind in the Word to have the mind of Christ.

> *Those who live according to the flesh have their minds set on what the flesh desires; but those who live in accordance with the Spirit have their minds set on what the Spirit desires (Romans 8:5, NIV).*

Keep renewing your mind in the Word of God when the world of evil tries to pollute your thoughts.

February 21

~ Born again in the Spirit ~

> *But when the fullness of time had come, God sent forth His Son, born of woman, born under the law, to redeem those who were under the law, so that we might receive adoption as sons (Galatians 4:4-5, ESV).*

When God formed a woman out of a man, God removed again what He made within a man. The inner strength of a man was removed by God to create a woman. This explains why a man becomes weak around a woman. He doesn't have the strength to overcome the temptation of the attraction to other women.

> *Humans can reproduce only human life, but the Holy Spirit gives birth to spiritual life (John 3:6, NLT).*

Just as humans need the presence of our human parents, our spirit too cannot live without the Spirit of God that gave birth to our spirit. A woman gave birth to man in the flesh through conception, and God gives birth to man through His Spirit into our spirit, and we become a living soul. Just as Adam was conceived out of earth but only became a living soul when God breathed into Him and made him a living soul. Our soul becomes alive through the flesh and the spirit. What we feed most becomes our soul being. We only become alive by the Spirit of God giving life to our spirit to live. This is why Jesus wants us to be born again because we have been born from our parents out of the fallen generation of Adam. Once we are outside, we can be born again into the spirit. Jesus was perfect and sinless because His flesh was conceived by the Holy Spirit inside the womb of a virgin. He is the Word that has become flesh.

> *So it is written: 'The first man Adam became a living being' the last Adam, a life-giving spirit. The spiritual did not come first, but the natural, and after that the spiritual. The first man was of the dust of the earth; the second man is of heaven. As was the earthly man, so are those who are of the earth; and as is the heavenly man, so also are those who are of heaven. And just as we have borne the image of the earthly man, so shall we bear the image of the heavenly man (1 Corinthians 15:45-49, NIV).*

February 22

~ Giving birth ~

> *But the fruit of the Spirit is love, joy, peace, patience, kindness, goodness, faithfulness, gentleness, self-control; against such things there is no law (Galatians 5:22-23, ESV).*

The womb of a mother performs the role of developing a full life in NINE MONTHS after which the image of the baby becomes the likeness of the parents.

> *When Adam was 130 years old, he became the father of a son who was just like him—in his very image. He named his son Seth (Genesis 5:3, NLT).*

A good mother who is expecting a baby connects herself with the Holy Spirit in producing the nine fruit of the Spirit while she journeys through the nine months of her pregnancy. She looks forward with joy to receiving every new day. The birth of each brand new day brings her one day closer to giving birth to the brand new life she carries inside her body. It also brings her one day closer to receiving the great promises God has in store for her life and the life she is carrying within her.

The womb of the Holy Spirit also performs a role inside us to develop a full life of Christ when we produce the NINE FRUIT of the Spirit. We become Christ-like and walk and live in love just like our heavenly Father.

> *Imitate God, therefore, in everything you do, because you are his dear children. Live a life filled with love, following the example of Christ. He loved us and offered himself as a sacrifice for us, a pleasing aroma to God (Ephesians 5:1-2, NLT).*

Every day God gives you life to live for that day He made for you. Your day is your life you carry around, what you sow in your day you will reap in your life.

February 23

~ Influenced by God's Word ~

> *Take hold of my instructions; don't let them go. Guard them, for they are the key to life (Proverbs 4:13, NLT).*

A mother is an influence on her household. A good woman not only makes a good mother but also a good wife. She teaches herself to remain in the instruction of God's Word and she influences her husband to live by the command of God's Word. Every rule they set is based upon the rules of God's Word.

My son, obey your father's commands, and don't neglect your mother's instruction. Keep their words always in your heart. Tie them around your neck. When you walk, their counsel will lead you. When you sleep, they will protect you. When you wake up, they will advise you. For their command is a lamp and their instruction a light; their corrective discipline is the way to life (Proverbs 6:20-23, NLT)

The Holy Spirit influences us to live the Word of God, which is the breath of God, so that we are prepared to carry out the good work which Christ has made ready for us before the creation of the world.

All Scripture is God-breathed and is useful for teaching, rebuking, correcting and training in righteousness, so that the servant of God may be thoroughly equipped for every good work (2 Timothy 3:16-17, NIV).

Let the Word of God influence you in making everyday decisions for the choices you make in life.

February 24

~ Unconditional love ~

For as woman came from man, so also man is born of woman. But everything comes from God (1 Corinthians 11:12, NIV)

God designed every woman in the characters of the nine fruit of His Spirit during her nine months of pregnancy to make her become a loving mother. This happened when the Holy Spirit took His position in the womb of the virgin birth of Jesus Christ. The womb of a woman has been transformed to have a special place for the Holy Spirit in every woman who every day receives the Word of God gladly into her life.

A mother blindly loves her unborn child and looks forward to meeting them. Her love for her baby is unconditional. A good mother raises up her children in the nine fruit of the Spirit. She is forever grateful to God for giving her a new day to do it all over again in whatever areas she fails.

> *But women will be saved through childbearing—if they continue in faith, love and holiness with propriety (1 Timothy 2:15, NIV).*
>
> *But the fruit of the Spirit is love, joy, peace, patience, kindness, goodness, faithfulness, gentleness, self-control; against such things there is no law (Galatians 5:22-23, ESV).*

The Spirit who raised up Christ in resurrection is the same Spirit who lives inside us to raise us up in the new life of Christ. He is the Holy Spirit, the Spirit of Almighty God.

> *And if the Spirit of him who raised Jesus from the dead is living in you, he who raised Christ from the dead will also give life to your mortal bodies because of his Spirit who lives in you (Romans 8:11, NIV).*

We are raised to higher places when we obey the living Word of God and live in love by producing the fruit of the Holy Spirit to everyone around us.

February 25

~ *A mother's instincts* ~

When you look at a baby, it's just that: a body you can look at and touch. But the person who takes shape within is formed by something you can't see and touch—the Spirit— and becomes a living spirit (John 3:6, MSG).

Every mother's flesh and spirit bonds with their babies inside the womb. The bond is still there when the baby is born. This is why a mother has a special connection with the child through her instinct, which tells her if things are right or wrong with her children. A good mother connects her spirit to God's Spirit in God's Word. She needs God's Word to build her spirit to then build her child's spirit in the way God originally designed, so they can have life.

The mind governed by the flesh is death, but the mind governed by the Spirit is life and peace (Romans 8:6, NIV).

The Spirit of God was over the dark form of this earth to bring life into existence. He brought the universe into life by God's Word. God is a loving Father who nurtures us through Mother Nature in the Holy Spirit.

Now the earth was formless and empty, darkness was over the surface of the deep, and the Spirit of God was hovering over the waters. And God said, 'Let there be light,' and there was light (Genesis 1:2-3, NIV).

Each and every day breathe the life-giving breath of God's Word into your life.

February 26

~ Compassion ~

Jesus said, 'Father, forgive them, for they do not know what they are doing' (Luke 23:34, NIV).

A good mother is full of compassion. She understands the compassion Jesus has towards us. Jesus has so much compassion because He can see how we are blind and lost, not knowing what to do. This is how she sees all those who hurt her. She teaches her house to have delight in compassion as this is the key to forgiveness. She sits in Word and prayer with the Holy Spirit every day and is strengthened to action God's love by producing the fruit of the Holy Spirit.

> *Be kind and compassionate to one another, forgiving each other, just as in Christ God forgave you (Ephesians 4:32, NIV).*

Jesus is the love of God in action who lay down His life for us. The Holy Spirit is the love of Christ in action who raised the life that Jesus laid down. And we are the Holy Ghost's love in action when we produce His fruit of righteousness to serve everyone we come into contact with.

> *By this we know love, that he laid down his life for us, and we ought to lay down our lives for the brothers (1 John 3:16, ESV).*

You are the Holy Ghost's love in action when you produce His fruit of righteousness for every unrighteousness that gets in your way.

February 27

~ *Giving birth* ~

A woman giving birth to a child has pain because her time has come; but when her baby is born she forgets the anguish because of her joy that a child is born into the world. So with you: Now is your time of grief, but I will see you again and you will rejoice, and no one will take away your joy (John 16:21-22 NIV).

During the nine months God works through and prepares a woman for giving birth to a life. The Holy Spirit also works through and prepares us to be fully developed and matured in His NINE FRUIT to give birth to a Christ-like life. A good mother lays down her life and sacrifices it to raise her children to have a life in the Spirit. It's her desire to see her children inherit the joy and peace of the Holy Spirit. This is what she would love to see her children inherit before she goes to her heavenly home.

Humans can reproduce only human life, but the Holy Spirit gives birth to spiritual life (John 3:6, NLT).

The same Spirit that resurrected Jesus from life is inside us and He will give us life and power to be victorious over sin and death. The pains we go through are signs that we are about to give birth to new life and beginnings. Be strong and keep pushing until you give birth to it.

Just as a pregnant woman writhes and cries out in pain as she gives birth, so were we in your presence, LORD (Isaiah 26:17, NLT).

> *Weeping may last through the night, but joy comes with the morning (Psalm 30:5, NLT).*

A new day is born unto us to be joyful of and forget the night's pain and sorrow.

February 28

~ Filled with joy and life ~

> *So be happy with your wife and find your joy with the woman you married – pretty and graceful as a deer. Let her charms keep you happy; let her surround you with her love (Proverbs 5:18-19, GNT).*

Every mother always wants to see their children happy and full of joy and life. A good mother builds up happy and content children. She is then a happy wife living a happy life with a happy husband. For this to become a reality in her house, she is content by the Word of God contained within her. She fills up her heart with thanksgiving and gratitude.

The Holy Spirit is the joy and life of Christ inside us, and His joy is complete when we remain in love with Jesus by loving others.

> *If you keep my commands, you will remain in my love, just as I have kept my Father's commands and remain in his love. I have told you this so that my joy may be in you and that your joy may be complete. My command is this: Love each other as I have loved you (John 15:10-12, NIV).*

Every day is made with love by LOVE to fall in love with LOVE and remain in His love. Love is a person, He is God.

MARCH

~ Incomplete without God ~

> *For you have been born again, but not to a life that will quickly end. Your new life will last forever because it comes from the eternal, living Word of God (1 Peter 1:23, NLT).*

I was worried about Blessed (my one-year-old) whenever he was away from me even for just a short while. Even if only for a little while, every mother misses their children when they are not around, especially when they are babies. We mothers worry because we cannot see what our children are doing. All kinds of thoughts rush around into our minds. Is our child safe from harm? We miss them and feel incomplete. This is when the Holy Spirit moved closer and comforted me and taught me this: 'You see, you feel this way because as a mother, your children come from inside you. And so, you feel incomplete when they are away from you and not around you. The bonding of NINE MONTHS within you has made you become one with them. They are the love of your life. The same is the kingdom of God. God feels empty without you. You came out from God, and His bonding into one with you in the NINE FRUIT OF HIS RIGHTEOUSNESS is just like your NINE MONTHS bonding with your child from inside you. You are born out from a mother after nine months to be born again of the spirit. The Holy Spirit has to be inside you to produce His nine fruit of righteousness for you to reproduce to become Christ-like. God is complete when He sees himself in you just as you also feel complete having your child with you and doing what you would like to see them do.

God made the first man from outside and breathed into him His Spirit. The devil deceived him through the woman's disobedience. The last man, Jesus Christ, God made by breathing His Spirit into the womb of the woman to create from inside. She obeyed God and believe His Word from the angel though she was a virgin. She made herself available for God to use her womb. The womb of God, His Spirit entered the womb of a woman. This time the devil couldn't deceive her because the Spirit of truth was inside of her.

The Spirit of God has made me; the breath of the Almighty gives me life (Job 33:4, NIV).

Each day of the month of March and EVERY DAY, draw out the living Word of Life into you to attract the Holy Spirit more over your life from within. So you can conceive and produce the Word to become flesh when you action the nine fruit of the Spirit in your life. It's the same as when a mother gives birth to a life in her image after nine months; you also give birth to the image of Christ by producing the nine fruit of the Spirit.

****

March 1

~Comparing~

For you created my inmost being; you knit me together in my mother's womb.

I praise you because I am fearfully and wonderfully made; your works are wonderful, I know that full well (Psalm 139:13-14, NIV).

A good mother doesn't compare her children on how each develops; she understands that each of them is unique and wonderfully created by God.

> *But you are the ones chosen by God, chosen for the high calling of priestly work, chosen to be a holy people, God's instruments to do his work and speak out for him, to tell others of the night-and-day difference he made for you—from nothing to something, from rejected to accepted (1 Peter 2:9-10, MSG).*

God doesn't compare his creation; though the sun and moon both give light neither one is better than the other, they are both unique and wonderfully designed to perform from the strength God gave them. God gave the sun more strength to light up the day brighter, and the moon less strength to shine in the night. The night would be day if the moon had as much strength as the sun. One shines its light during the day and the other during the night. One of your children may perform well at school and the other in sport. That doesn't make one better than the other, they are simply different. The Holy Spirit inside us has different gifts for us to give service as a body of Christ, so we can work together accordingly as purposed by God.

> *There are different kinds of gifts, but the same spirit distributes them. There are different kinds of service, but the same Lord. There are different kinds of working, but in all of them and in everyone it is the same God at work (1 Corinthians 12:4-6, NIV).*

Instead of comparing yourself with someone, compliment them on their achievements and speak well of them. Each one of us is a unique creation of God to give Him glory in our own special way.

March 2

~Looking on and beyond the power of cross ~

Open the eyes of their hearts, and let the light of Your truth flood in. Shine Your light on the hope You are calling them to embrace. Reveal to them the glorious riches You are preparing as their inheritance (Ephesians 1:18, VOICE).

A good mother is her children's eye opener. She talks in a wise way that opens the eyes of her children to see and learn from around them so as to live a good life. She makes sure their view is from the cross of cavalry and the throne of grace, where Jesus is seated and glorifying the Father in what we do in His name. They see through the eyes of compassion and not condemnation.

The wise have eyes in their heads, while the fool walks in the darkness; (Ecclesiastes 2:14, NIV).

When the Holy Spirit says something to you He opens your eyes at the same time to see whatever it is. The Holy Spirit inside you gives you eyes to see from your mind and heart. The eyes of your mind are open and your lookout is from the throne room of God where Jesus is. Everything you see is good and beautiful. You see life the way God sees it and life is beautiful.

For God, who said, 'Let light shine out of darkness,' made his light shine in our hearts to give us the light of the knowledge of God's glory displayed in the face of Christ. (2 Corinthians 4:6, NIV).

> *Yet God has made everything beautiful for its own time. He has planted eternity in the human heart, but even so, people cannot see the whole scope of God's work from beginning to end (Ecclesiastes 3:11, NLT).*

Each and every day let the 'lookout' of your life be the Word of God. You will see that God made everything beautiful in its time.

March 3

~Contentment~

> *Keep your lives free from the love of money and be content with what you have, because God has said, 'Never will I leave you; never will I forsake you.' (Hebrews 13:5, NIV).*

A good mother appreciates and is grateful for everything she has. She is so content with what she holds that when someone gives her a gift she is even more thankful. Receiving Jesus as the gift from the father, the Holy Spirit as the gift from Jesus, and joy and peace as the gift from the Holy Spirit, she is filled with thanksgiving and praises all the days of her life.

She is focused on containing the Word that brings contentment and conquers the lust of this materialistic world.

The Holy Spirit we contain not only makes us content but gives us the indescribable joy that strengthens us to conquer the arrows of the enemy.

> *This day is holy to our Lord. Do not grieve, for the joy of the Lord is your strength.' (Nehemiah 8:10, NIV).*

Every day we have to be grateful and give thanks that an imperfect person like us now has the Holy Spirit who is the perfect gift from the perfect life of Jesus Christ.

March 4

~Inheritance ~

> *A good person leaves an inheritance for their children's children (Proverbs 13:22, NIV).*

A good mother invests her time in God for her children. She leaves an inheritance for her children by investing her time in God's Word and prayer. She makes sure that her children inherit righteousness, joy and peace in the Holy Spirit, before she leaves her body on earth and moves into living dead in Christ.

The Holy Spirit is the inheritance from God through what Jesus has done. When we receive Jesus, we inherit the Holy Spirit, the kingdom of God's righteousness that produces the fruit of righteousness. He is our promised land that God promised us in Jesus Christ.

> *For no matter how many promises God has made, they are 'Yes' in Christ. And so through him the 'Amen' is spoken by us to the glory of God (2 Corinthians 1:20, NIV).*

> *For the kingdom of God is not a matter of eating and drinking, but of righteousness, peace and joy in the Holy Spirit, (Romans 14:17, NIV).*

Every day seek God in His righteousness to inherit righteousness, joy and peace in the Holy Spirit.

March 5

~ You are the city of God ~

Never again will you be called 'The Forsaken City' or 'The Desolate Land.' Your new name will be 'The City of God's Delight' and 'The Bride of God,' for the Lord delights in you and will claim you as his bride (Isaiah 62:4, NLT).

A good mother is like a good city where her house dwells in joy and peace. She knows it's an honour to house the Spirit of the Almighty God. The Spirit that goes forth and creates something amazing out of nothing in the universe by the Word of God now resides in her. She contains inside of her nothing but the Word of God to cover all areas of her life. She is joyful, a holy city of God that the Lord delights in and claims as His bride. God has engraved her on His palms and her walls are before Him. Because she houses the Holy Spirit in the right way, her home lives in peace and joy. There may be storms against her house, but she is not afraid because she walks with God, and her walls are before Him.

See, I have engraved you on the palms of my hands; your walls are ever before me (Isaiah 49:16, NIV).

The Holy Spirit inside us can make amazing creations out of nothing; all we have to do is contain the Word of God. He can build us into a beautiful Holy City of God's delight from the Word we contain. We are the 'Holy City' of God in the holiness of the Holy Spirit because we house Him within us.

March 6

~ Walking in the right path ~

Your word is a lamp to my feet and a light to my path (Psalm 119:105, ESV).

A good mother watches over her child in prayer so her children don't go the wrong way and do the wrong things. She knows that even if her children do go astray, her prayers in the Word of God will shine light on that dark path and bring them back to the right direction.

Jesus intercedes for us, and the voice of the Holy Spirit always guides us so we walk in the righteousness of Christ, producing His fruit of righteousness.

> *Whether you turn to the right or to the left, your ears will hear a voice behind you, saying, 'This is the way; walk in it.' (Isaiah 30:21, NIV).*

We need the lamp of God's Word to light up our paths to walk through our every day.

March 7

~ The great I am is fighting for you ~

You shall not fear them, for it is the LORD your God who fights for you.' (Deuteronomy 3:22, ESV).

A good mother doesn't fight against her children when they choose the wrong path, she fights for them in prayer to bring them back on the right path. She knows her strength is not to be used on flesh or blood as they are not the enemy. She comes before God in stillness and calmness for God to fight for her.

Be still, and know that I am God (Psalm 46:10, ESV).

She uses that energy, strength and time to kneel before God. She knows that only God has the right way and when God fights for her, she will win the fight.

The Lord will fight for you; you need only to be still.' (Exodus 14:14, NIV).

The Holy Spirit inside us stops us from fighting against what we should be fighting for. What you are fighting against is what God is trying to use to bring His purpose through. Greater is He that is in us than He that is in the World.

He must become greater; I must become less.' (John 3:30, NIV).

The more you feed the Holy Spirit with the Word of God, the more He expands and becomes great in you. He becomes great and you become less.

March 8

~Being faithful with your patience ~

Be completely humble and gentle; be patient, bearing with one another in love (Ephesians 4:2, NIV).

A good mother has the patience to continually teach her children to listen to her until they become obedient and respond. Love is patient and she actions love by being patient. Every time her patience runs out she turns to the Word of God and replenishes herself.

The Holy Spirit is patient and that is His character. The Word of God is the same and never changes. The Holy Spirit reminds us of that same Word of God with so much patience until we can abide and be obedient to it. His aim is for us to remain connected to the Word, so we can produce His fruit through all seasons. When we remain in the Word, we also have access to anything we ask in Jesus' name.

> *If you remain in me and my words remain in you, ask whatever you wish, and it will be done for you (John 15:7, NIV).*

Keep abiding in the Word and have more patience to faithfully wait on God every day to meet your needs.

March 9

-Love and joy -

> *Let your father and mother be glad; let her who bore you rejoice (Proverbs 23:25, ESV).*

When you love a person so much, you talk about them. When you talk about them, you bubble with joy and your face lights up with life. Love gives joy and lights up life. A good mother loves her children and she talks about them to others with joy.

The Holy Spirit is the love from the life Jesus gave us. He lives inside us and loves to talk to us about Jesus. The Holy Spirit reveals

Jesus to us with much joy. We feel that love and joy when Jesus is revealed to us by the Holy Spirit.

> *which was not made known to people in other generations as it has now been revealed by the Spirit to God's holy apostles and prophets (Ephesians 3:5, NIV).*

Jesus who is LOVE of God flows out JOY when He is revealed to us by the Holy Spirit.

March 10

~ Reaping and sowing ~

> *Do not be deceived: God cannot be mocked. A man reaps what he sows (Galatians 6:7, NIV).*

A good mother knows the principles of sowing and reaping. She sows righteousness into her children because this is what she wants to reap from them. Just as farmers wait patiently for their seeds to grow, she waits patiently for her children to do the right things in life. God sent Jesus to save us from sin and do the right thing. He is waiting patiently for us to repent.

> *The Lord is not slow in keeping his promise, as some understand slowness. Instead he is patient with you, not wanting anyone to perish, but everyone to come to repentance (2 Peter 3:9, NIV).*

Jesus Christ is the righteousness of God. God sowed His righteous Son, so He can reap many righteous sons of the house. Sons who can constantly reproduce the fruit of righteousness from the Holy Spirit.

> *I put on righteousness, and it clothed me; my justice was like a robe and a turban (Job 29:14, ESV).*

Each day clothe yourself in the righteousness of Christ and remain in the holiness of the Holy Spirit. You are the righteousness of God in Christ and the holiness of God in the Holy Spirit. You are a son, a holy city where the Holy Spirit dwells.

March 11

~God preparing you for great things ~

> *May he give you the desire of your heart and make all your plans succeed (Psalm 20:4, NIV).*

A good mother intercedes for her children, seeking God in prayer for her every needs and for Him to make her children succeed in life. The Holy Spirit also prays for us to God in groans that is according to God's will. What happens is that we may pray for something else, but the Holy Spirit, being the Spirit of God, knows what God's will is for us. He talks to God about our desires and they work on what is best for us.

> *In the same way, the Spirit helps us in our weakness. We do not know what we ought to pray for, but the Spirit himself intercedes for us through wordless groans (Romans 8:26, NIV).*

God gives us what we need by bringing His desire into our desires and this is more than 100 times better than what we need. Then God combines his desires and our desires into one. It's the same as when preparing a recipe when you bake and you mix all the ingredients together into one and put it through the heat intensity to get the finished product. When God starts mixing His desires and will into ours, we do not like it. We wonder why things are not showing up the way we prayed and asked for. Many times we walk away from God's preparation and so we never receive the best desires of our heart that God has prepared.

God stirs our desires to become one mixture and puts it through his furnace. Although we walk through fire in life if we just wait patiently we will receive the desires of our heart.

Sometimes, when God is still working on us, the enemy will distract us, and we move away from God's work. This is where we have unanswered prayers and we do not get the desires of our heart. But if we patiently endure the suffering and pain, and delight in the Lord, thanking and praising Him in every situation, we will come out stronger and receive the best God has designed for us.

It's a long process, where one has to allow God to work inside them and prepare them to be stronger to give birth to the desire of their heart. When a mother is expecting a baby her body goes through dramatic changes to prepare her to give birth and bring life out of her. She often feels unwell and towards the last trimester, she experiences a lot of pain. These are the last stages before giving birth. When the time is almost here for you to give birth to the life God has for you, you will go through pain . And just like the expecting mother who is told to keep pushing to give birth, you too must keep pushing and pushing to give birth to what God has conceived in you. The Word, that you receive into you must become flesh. Whatever your heart desires, speak the Word of God upon it, and the Holy Spirit will conceive it and bring it into the physical realm.

You will conceive and give birth to a son, and you are to call him Jesus.

The angel answered, 'The Holy Spirit will come on you, and the power of the Most High will overshadow you. So the holy one to be born will be called the Son of God (Luke's 1:31, 35, NIV).

March 12

~Comforted and strengthened ~

In my distress I called to the Lord; I cried to my God for help. From his temple he heard my voice; my cry came before him, into his ears (Psalm 18:6, NIV).

A good mother is always available 24/7 for her child; she responds as soon as her child calls or cry out to her for help. Every day she connects herself to the Word of God to remain strong and comforted, so that she can pour out that strength to comfort her children when they cry out to her.

The Holy Spirit is available all the time within us; He is our helpline when we call out for help. He will gives us the strength to take us through or comfort us with His voice. Whatever He speaks into our heart gives us the strength and comfort we need.

If you love me, you will keep my commandments. And I will ask the Father, and he will give you another Helper, to be with you forever, even the Spirit of truth, whom the world cannot receive, because it neither sees him nor knows him. You know him, for he dwells with you and will be in you (John 14:15-17, ESV).

The more you know and receive God's Word as the truth, the more you will know the Holy Spirit. He is the one that brings to life the Word of God that you receive.

March 13

~ The mirror of God's Word ~

> *For the word of God is alive and active. Sharper than any double-edged sword, it penetrates even to dividing soul and spirit, joints and marrow; it judges the thoughts and attitudes of the heart (Hebrews 4:12, NIV).*

A good mother sees the beauty of her child's inner character and nourishes it to bloom; she fixes what needs to be fixed, she is her child's mirror to the soul. She tells her child what things can destroy life and what things can build their life. The Word of God is life, and only the Word of God can build life.

> *Listen, my son! Listen, son of my womb! Listen, my son, the answer to my prayers! (Proverbs 31:2, NIV).*

The Word of God is a mirror that shows our inner beauty of who we are in Christ and guides us on the right path. The Word of God nourishes our beauty from inside to outside. The Holy Spirit inside us reflects back how we look inside when we receive into us the Word. This is why the Bible is the only book that can read your heart and soul when you read it to strengthen your flesh.

> *And we all, who with unveiled faces contemplate the Lord's glory, are being transformed into his image with ever-increasing glory, which comes from the Lord, who is the Spirit (2 Corinthians 3:18 NIV).*

Every day look into the mirror of God's Word and fix what needs to be fixed.

March 14

~God's eyes are watching over you ~

> *For the eyes of the Lord run to and fro throughout the whole earth, to give strong support to those whose heart is blameless toward him (2 Chronicles 16:9, ESV).*

One day, on 18 July, (2019), I met up with a lady friend whose child hangs out with Angelilly, my four-year-old. Even while we were busy chatting our eyes continued to roam around every movement our children made.

This is what the Holy Spirit taught me; the kingdom of God is like this. God's eyes roam around watching over us. He may be receiving all the worship and praise from His Holy ones or running the universe and keeping it in balance but His eyes are on you. A good mother's eyes are always on her child even when she is busy doing house chores. God wants to keep an eye on you from inside you where He is, and so He sent His only Son to come into the world to die for you. He can now live in you with the new resurrection life of His Son through His Holy Spirit.

> *Therefore, if anyone is in Christ, the new creation has come: The old has gone, the new is here! (2 Corinthians 5:17, NIV).*

You are the apple of God's eyes. His eyes are on you watching over you, to prevent you from harm. Whatever happens in your life that you may not understand is God protecting you from harm.

March 15

~Adoption ~

And behold, I am with you always, to the end of the age (Matthew 28:20, ESV).

A good mother never leaves her children but stays by their side until the end of her days. They may no longer live and be with her but they live inside of her. She carries them in her heart.

If she is not in a better position to provide for her child, she gives them up for adoption, so the child has the chance of a good and better life.

God decided in advance to adopt us into his own family by bringing us to himself through Jesus Christ. This is what he wanted to do, and it gave him great pleasure (Ephesians 1:5, NLT).

God also wants to be with us until the end of time. And so He gave His only Son to us that through Him, He can adopt us into His family, and give us an abundant life full of goodness.

Keep your lives free from the love of money and be content with what you have, because God has said, 'Never will I leave you; never will I forsake you.'(Hebrews 13:5, NIV).

God is now always with us through His Holy Spirit so that not even death will separate us from Him. He adopted us into His family and He will never leave us nor forsake us.

March 16

~Seeing Jesus, the light ~

The Lord gives sight to the blind, the Lord lifts up those who are bowed down, the Lord loves the righteous (Psalm 146:8, NIV).

A good mother gives sight to her children knowing how lost they can be in making decisions. She does it in love. She speaks kindly and with patience. She is that light in the house giving sight to her household to make right decisions when they are in darkness. To be a good light she connects daily in Word and prayer to the source of light. She regularly seeks God in His Word to see Jesus, the light.

No one lights a lamp and then puts it under a basket. Instead, a lamp is placed on a stand, where it gives light to everyone in the house. In the same way, let your good deeds shine out for all to see, so that everyone will praise your heavenly Father (Matthew 5:15-16, NLT).

Jesus came and gave sight to us so we can see the light. He is the light. We now have His Holy Spirit inside us, and His voice not only opens our ears to hear but our eyes to see the light and follow the path to eternal life.

Open the eyes of their hearts, and let the light of Your truth flood in. Shine Your light on the hope You are calling them to embrace. Reveal to them the glorious riches You are preparing as their inheritance (Ephesian 1:18, VOICE).

When our ears and eyes are open we will see Jesus. We see Jesus, the light of the Word, when we hear the voice of the Holy Spirit revealing Him.

March 17

~God never fails ~

Let us hold fast the confession of our hope without wavering, for he who promised is faithful (Hebrews 10:23, ESV).

A good mother never gives up on her children, she keeps loving them unconditionally, even when they fail in life. She understands that she has failed God but God has never failed her in His promises.

Not one word of all the good promises that the Lord had made to the house of Israel had failed; all came to pass (Joshua 21:45, ESV).

God loves us unconditionally and He never fails us through His Spirit who gives us life to live life again and again every day.

His mercies are renewed every morning to renew us to live our new Christ-like life.

The steadfast love of the Lord never ceases; his mercies never come to an end; they are new every morning; great is your faithfulness (Lamentation 3:22-23, ESV).

The Holy Spirit is the unconditional love of God in the finished work of Jesus Christ.

March 18

~A new way ~

We can make our own plans, but the Lord gives the right answer (Proverbs 16:1, NLT).

A good mother has something new for her children all the time, she thinks of good new plans and the future of her children. When things don't go the way she wants, she understands that God's ways and thoughts are much higher and better than hers. She looks forward to receiving that great plan and future that God is taking her house into. All she can do is wait on God in His Word and prayer to see what God will do.

> *'For my thoughts are not your thoughts, neither are your ways my ways,' declares the Lord. 'As the heavens are higher than the earth, so are my ways higher than your ways and my thoughts than your thoughts (Isaiah 55:8-9, NIV).*

The Holy Spirit inside us makes the same Word of God that has plans and a future for us renewed all the time. When we mess up the steps we take He creates a new path again because of the great many new plans He has in mind for us.

> *Forget the former things; do not dwell on the past. See, I am doing a new thing! Now it springs up; do you not perceive it? I am making a way in the wilderness and streams in the wasteland (Isaiah 43:18-19, NIV).*

Every day God wakes you up again because He has a plan for you to live for today that will bring changes for tomorrow.

March 19

~Cleanliness~

> *Create in me a clean heart, O God, and renew a right spirit within me (Psalm 51:10, ESV).*

While cleaning the kitchen after the mess from cooking, the Holy Spirit reminded me that such is how the kingdom of God works. A good mother doesn't get upset about her children making a mess in the house after playing with their toys; she cleans up and tidies up the mess. She is reminded from the mess her children make that if it wasn't for the mercy and grace of God, her life would be a mess. You see, you were in a great mess, but when you accept Jesus, His blood cleanses you from your sin. His Spirit comes and lives in you and keeps cleansing you when you ask.

> *First clean the inside of the cup and the plate, that the outside also may be clean (Matthew 23:26, ESV).*

The Holy Spirit inside you works on the Word you receive into you to cleanse you from the mess and scars that man speaks into your life.

> *You are already clean because of the word I have spoken to you (John 15:3, NIV).*

If you abide in the Word and spend time in the Word every day you are cleansed.

March 20

~Perfect love drives out fear ~

> *There is no fear in love. But perfect love drives out fear, because fear has to do with punishment. The one who fears is not made perfect in love (1 John 4:18, NIV).*

A good mother doesn't fear what seasons of the year she will face. She is always wrapping her household in God's perfect love which drives out fear. She spends time in Word and prayer clothing her family in God's perfect love.

When it snows, she has no fear for her household; for all of them are clothed in scarlet (Proverbs 31:21, NIV).

The fruit of the Holy Spirit is love which He produces within us and this drives out fear.

For we know how dearly God loves us, because he has given us the Holy Spirit to fill our hearts with his love (Romans 5:5, NLT).

For God gave us a Spirit not of fear but of power and love and self-control (2 Timothy 1:7, ESV).

When life drives us through seasons of fear, the Holy Spirit drives us out of that fear. He steers us well from the inside so we don't go off track.

March 21

~ The joy in the storm ~

You will show me the way of life, granting me the joy of your presence and the pleasures of living with you forever (Psalm 16:11, NLT).

She loves living life so she leaves out of her life anything that is negative. With so much joy in her heart that her face bursts into smiles, she looks forward to tomorrow and all the days of her life. She is that good mother who is keeping strong for her house. The light from God's Word shines out the inner strength that she built from the storms she walked through. She is well experienced in knowing

God is already there for her even before she gets there. She raises her head up with smiles and laughs out loud at her coming days.

> *She is clothed with strength and dignity; she can laugh at the days to come (Proverbs 31:25, NIV).*

We are the dwelling place of the Holy Spirit. He clothes us with His strength and joy to walk through our storms with joyful sounds of gratefulness, so we can come out stronger and wiser.

We are clothed with the strength and power of the Holy Spirit within us, that we can sing and laugh with joy.

> *Splendor and majesty are before him; strength and joy are in his dwelling place (1 Chronicles 16:27, NIV).*

Every day seek God's joy in His Word to strengthen you to walk through your storms with a joyful heart.

March 22

~ Treasures ~

> *But Mary treasured up all these things and pondered them in her heart (Luke 2:19, NIV).*

A good mother holds her heart to God, in gratefulness and praises, thanking God for His goodness in her life. Every good thing God has done for her, she takes into her heart and praises God right there . God used Mary to mother her child because she had a heart that was always praising and trusting God. The life of how she raised Jesus as a child was kept in her heart, and she communicated with God with praise and prayer from her heart.

> *Then he went down to Nazareth with them and was obedient to them. But his mother treasured all these things in her heart (Luke 2:51, NIV).*

The Holy Spirit is the very treasure of Jesus. The abundant life of Jesus is in the Holy Spirit who resides in us. We can have access to the Holy Spirit at any time, all the time.

> *My goal is that they may be encouraged in heart and united in love, so that they may have the full riches of complete understanding, in order that they may know the mystery of God, namely, Christ, in whom are hidden all the treasures of wisdom and knowledge (Colossians 2:2-3, NIV).*

Every day lay into your heart the Word of God and make it your heart's treasure. The Holy Spirit will keep it safe from any mould or rust. Even thieves can't break in to steal it. Where your treasure is, there your heart will be also.

March 23

~Relationships~

> *Life does not consist in an abundance of possessions (Luke 12:15, NIV).*

A good mother knows that her blessings are not material things but her relationships with her children and spouse. So, whenever her children ruin that new household item she just bought, she doesn't make it hard on her children but speaks and teaches them to be extra careful with things. She wants to enjoy the presence of her children and watch them grow and bloom in God's presence.

> *Christ bought us with His blood and made us free from the Law. In that way, the Law could not punish us. Christ did this by carrying the load and by being punished instead of us. It is written, 'Anyone who hangs on a cross is hated and punished.' Because of the price Christ Jesus paid, the good things that came to Abraham might come to the people who are not Jews. And by putting our trust in Christ, we receive the Holy Spirit He has promised (Galatians 3:13-14, NLV).*

God didn't buy us with gold but with the priceless blood of His Son so we can be in a relationship with Him. We may be concerned about asking God for material things but He is more interested in pouring out His Holy Spirit within us to experience a relationship of pure joy and happiness. The joy and happiness we thought we would gain from the material things of this world is temporary. God wants to give us more than we could ever imagine. He wants us to have a solid relationship with Jesus and receive the joy and peace of the Holy Spirit.

> *And hope does not put us to shame, because God's love has been poured out into our hearts through the Holy Spirit, who has been given to us (Romans 5:5, NIV).*

Each and every day seek righteousness first in your relationship with God and His kingdom, and all other relationships in your life will always go right.

March 24

~ The home ground of God ~

> *This is the day that the Lord has made; let us rejoice and be glad in it (Psalm 118:24, ESV).*

A good mother is joyful every day; even when there are storms, she smiles. She knows that her joy gives a positive energy to her children that everything is under control. She wakes up in the morning and says, 'This is the day the Lord has made for me', to remind her that there may be evil all around.

> *But as for me and my house, we will serve the Lord.'*
> *(Joshua 24:15, ESV).*

And the joy of the Lord is my strength to keep my house strong in God.

The Holy Spirit within you gives you joy and that is your strength to make it through each day.

> *This day is holy to our Lord. Do not grieve, for the joy of the Lord is your strength (Nehemiah 8:10, NIV).*

You are the house of the Holy Spirit, and as you and your house serve the Lord, the Holy Spirit will feel right at home. You are taking him to his home ground. It's the same as when someone comes and lives with you from another country and you take him in and then go back with him to his country. Jesus came and lived with us and died, then rose again and is now back where He came from. His Spirit has come to live with us because of what He did. When we keep cheerfully receiving into us the Word of God, we become the home ground for the Holy Spirit to breed life into us.

> *Now therefore may it please you to bless the house of your servant, so that it may continue forever before you. For you, O Lord God, have spoken, and with your blessing shall the house of your servant be blessed forever (2 Samuel 7:29, ESV).*

When we worship God we will find ourselves in another atmosphere. We are in the home ground of the Holy Spirit. After worship we come out a different person with so much love, joy and peace within us.

March 25

~ Time ~

At the right time, I, the Lord, will make it happen (Isaiah 60:22, NLT).

A good mother is like an alarm clock who reminds you in advance so that you won't be late but on time. Time is her best friend; she is loyal and faithful to time. She makes time to faithfully seek God in His Word. She understands that Jesus himself is time. Jesus told the Samaritan woman, 'A time is coming and the time is here now.' Jesus himself is time and He is here now.

Yet a time is coming and has now come when the true worshipers will worship the Father in the Spirit and in truth, for they are the kind of worshipers the Father seeks (John 4:23, NIV).

For he says, 'In the time of my favour I heard you, and in the day of salvation I helped you.'

I tell you, now is the time of God's favour, now is the day of salvation (2 Corinthians 6:2, NIV).

The Holy Spirit is the alarm clock of God keeping you alert to keep praying, and not to give up because when the time is right God will bring it to pass.

> *For it is time to seek the Lord, till He comes and rains righteousness on you (Hosea 10:12 NKJV).*

When we commit ourselves to time and faithfully do something, we will see great results over time.

March 26

~Apple of His eye ~

> *for he who touches you touches the apple of His eye (Zechariah 2:8, NKJV).*

A good mother is gentle and kind but her eyes are always watchful over her children; if you hurt them she will confront you. She prays the Word of Psalm 17:8, and tells God,

> *Keep me as the apple of your eye; hide me in the shadow of your wings.*

We are also the apple of God's eye; if someone touches us they touch the pupil of God's eyes, and God will fight on our behalf. The Holy Spirit inside us is the eye of God watching over us, giving us light and sight to see the way Jesus sees things.

> *Your eye is like a lamp that provides light for your body. When your eye is healthy, your whole body is filled with light (Matthew 6:22, NLT).*

Wear the lens of the eyes of Jesus every day in His Word, so you can see situations the way God sees.

March 27

~ Cheerful ~

The minute I said, 'I'm slipping, I'm falling,' your love, God, took hold and held me fast. When I was upset and beside myself, you calmed me down and cheered me up (Psalm 94:18-19, MSG).

A good mother always cheers up her children when they feel down, she cheers them to rise up and move forward. She even cheers her children on when they have made little progress in life. While she cheers herself in the Word of God, she makes a better cheerleader for her house.

The Holy Spirit inside us produces the joy from His Love towards us to give us a purpose to live for that day He made for us.

> *This is the day that the Lord has made; let us rejoice and be glad in it (Psalm 118:24, ESV).*

And also, the hero of faith in the clouds of witnesses cheers for us to complete the race of our faith.

> *Do you see what this means—all these pioneers who blazed the way, all these veterans cheering us on? It means we'd better get on with it. Strip down, start running— and never quit! No extra spiritual fat, no parasitic sins (Hebrews 12:1, MSG).*

Wake up to your new day every day and cheer yourself up in the Word of God all through the day.

March 28

~ *The blaming game* ~

'Don't hurt your friend, don't blame your neighbor; despise the despicable (Psalm 15:3-4, MSG).

A good mother doesn't shift the blame when something wrong happens in her household, she takes responsibility for finding a solution just as Abigail did. Abigail took the blame for her foolish husband and made peace with King David. The story of this whole scenario can be found in the book of 1 Samuel 25.

> *David said to Abigail, 'Praise be to the LORD, the God of Israel, who has sent you today to meet me. May you be blessed for your good judgment and for keeping me from bloodshed this day and from avenging myself with my own hands. Otherwise, as surely as the LORD, the God of Israel, lives, who has kept me from harming you, if you had not come quickly to meet me, not one male belonging to Nabal would have been left alive by daybreak.' Then David accepted from her hand what she had brought him and said, 'Go home in peace. I have heard your words and granted your request.' (1 Samuel 25:32-35, NIV).*

> *Arise, for this matter is your responsibility. We also are with you. Be of good courage, and do it.' (Ezra 10:4, NKJV).*

When the blame took place in the garden after the fall of man. God took the responsibility of finding the solution, and He sent the power of His Spirit to conceive the Word to make it flesh. The Word became flesh and saved us from the curse that was put on us. The man blamed the woman and the woman blamed the serpent.

The Holy Spirit is now inside us and He produces the fruit of righteousness for us to use instead of blaming. We produce the fruit of kindness to someone who is unkind to us.

> *Now then, please swear to me by the Lord that you will show kindness to my family, because I have shown kindness to you. Give me a sure sign (Joshua 2:12, NIV).*

Instead of putting blame on someone for being unkind to us we should serve them the fruit of kindness.

March 29

~Righteous blood of Jesus ~

> *...pray without ceasing (1 Thessalonians 5:17, ESV).*

A good mother never gives up on her children in prayer no matter how rebellious they become. She knows that the power of the blood of Jesus can do anything. She continues to pray for the blood of Jesus to cleanse her house and to cover them all.

God never gave up on us. He purchased us with the blood of Jesus, and until now He has never given up on us because He knows we can be made right with Him with the power of the Blood.

> *...but God shows his love for us in that while we were still sinners, Christ died for us (Romans 5:8, ESV).*

The Holy Spirit inside us is the righteous Spirit of God from the purchase made by the righteous blood of Jesus. He is always patient with us when we are rebellious. He convicts to bring us back to the path of righteousness. The blood of Jesus is multitasked, it can wash away your sin and protect you from all sickness, diseases and evil in this fallen world. The blood of Jesus can do anything and everything to save you and set you free.

> *I have taught you in the way of wisdom; I have led you in right paths (Proverbs 4:11, NKJV).*

Every new day wake up and walk upright with God in producing the fruit of His righteousness.

March 30

~Praying ~

> *The Lord will conquer your enemies when they attack you. They will attack you from one direction, but they will scatter from you in seven! (Deuteronomy 28:7, NLT).*

A good mother watches over her loved ones every day in her household and makes sure of everyone's well-being. She uses preventive measures in her house to prevent them from getting into trouble. She stays connected to the Holy Spirit in God's Word, and she can sense in her spirit if trouble will occur. God doesn't slumber; He watches over your life.

> *He will not let your foot slip—he who watches over you will not slumber; (Psalm 121:3, NIV).*

The Holy Spirit inside you knows your every move and will warn you should you face any troubles. He will warn you to quickly pray to destroy the work of the dark forces.

> *The reason the Son of God appeared was to destroy the devil's work (1 John 3:8. NIV).*

God will work in you when you pray; every day pray and pray to keep God working in you.

March 31

~Hero of faith)

> *I would be disobeying the Lord if I stopped praying for you! I will always teach you how to live right (1 Samuel 12:23, CEV).*

A good mother prays endlessly for her household; even when she doesn't see results she keeps praying. She may not see the harvest of the fruit of her prayer and die, but she dies as a hero of faith and joins the clouds of witness to cheer for the loved ones she has left behind.

> *All these people were still living by faith when they died. They did not receive the things promised; they only saw them and welcomed them from a distance, admitting that they were foreigners and strangers on earth (Hebrews 11:13, NIV).*

> *Therefore, since we are surrounded by such a huge crowd of witnesses to the life of faith, let us strip off every weight that slows us down, especially the sin that so easily trips us up (Hebrews 12:1, NLT).*

Jesus came and died and is our hero of faith. We receive Him into our life by faith, and He lives in us through His Spirit. Jesus is now alive through the Holy Spirit, and because He lives we can live again.

> *Soon the world will no longer see me, but you will see me. Since I live, you also will live (John 14:19, NLT).*

Fight the good fight of faith every day so you can die as a hero of faith.

APRIL

~ Making God happy ~

> *Make your face shine on your servant and teach me your decrees (Psalm 119:135, NIV).*

29 April 2020. While teaching Angelilly (my five-year-old) her spelling of dictionary words I realized how happy I felt when she knew how to use those words in the right vocabulary according to their definitions.

This is what the Holy Spirit taught me: When you know the Word of God and know how to use it in the right way as defined by God, you make God happy. The Word of God is the truth and when you live and walk in the truth of God's Word, He is happy.

> *Nothing makes me happier than to hear that my children live in the truth (3 John 1:4, GNT).*

A good mother defines her true identity and worth in what the Word of God says of her. She doesn't look into the beauty of the world to maintain her beauty, she looks into the Word of God to maintain and keep her beauty, so she can shine the light from God's Word out into the dark world. She wants to grow closer and deeper with the Holy Spirit, so she empties and breaks herself at the feet of Jesus and fills herself with the Word of God. God is closer to the brokenhearted.

> *The Lord is close to the brokenhearted and saves those who are crushed in spirit (Psalm 34:18, NIV).*

She knows that to attract the Holy Spirit more and more, she has to fill herself with the Word of God. Her prayers are filled with praises, thanksgiving and songs from her heart, this is the evidence of her being filled with the Holy Spirit.

> *Don't be drunk with wine, because that will ruin your life. Instead, be filled with the Holy Spirit, singing psalms and hymns and spiritual songs among yourselves, and making music to the Lord in your hearts. And give thanks for everything to God the Father in the name of our Lord Jesus Christ (Ephesians 5:18-20, NLT).*

To be that good woman and mother every day all through the month of April and all the days of your life, make yourself attractive to the Holy Spirit and be broken at the feet of Jesus and fill yourself in Him, in His Word.

The woman with the alabaster jar was broken at the feet of Jesus by pouring her brokenness onto Jesus through what her heart loves. The perfume was the source of her living. She poured it over Jesus and Jesus said her many sins are forgiven, and that what she did was beautiful.

> *'Leave her alone,' said Jesus. 'Why are you bothering her? She has done a beautiful thing to me' (Mark 14:6 NIV).*

This is how you will attract the Holy Spirit to move deeper into becoming one with your spirit.

> *But whoever is united with the Lord is one with him in spirit (1 Corinthians 6:17, NIV).*

Each day of the month of April and EVERY DAY, show everyone around you that you are filled with the Holy Spirit, and start singing psalms, hymns and spiritual songs making music in your heart to the Lord. Be full of thanksgiving to God in everything, whether good or bad, because all things God works for goes to those that love Him.

****

April 1

~ *Wisdom* ~

> *She opens her mouth with wisdom and the teaching of kindness is on her tongue (Proverbs 31:26, ESV).*

A good mother is wisdom of God, she is that voice of light that enters every path that her child takes and gives godly instructions. She takes her wisdom from the mouth of God in His Word so that when she opens her mouth her words are wisdom.

> *Christ is the power of God and the Wisdom of God (1 Corinthians 1:24, NLT).*

The Holy Spirit is the Spirit of wisdom from God that speaks the voice of God, so we walk in the righteousness of God. Wisdom is a timely Word and it is Jesus. When you speak a timely message to someone, you heal them. Jesus is the healer.

> *Listen as Wisdom calls out! Hear as understanding raises her voice! On the hilltop along the road, she takes her stand at the crossroads. By the gates at the entrance to the town, on the road leading in, she cries aloud, (Proverbs 8:1-3, NLT).*

Keep connecting to the Word every day, so that the Holy Spirit can voice out into your voice the wisdom to live happily ever after all the days of your life. No amount of money can buy that joy from hearing the voice of the Holy Spirit clearly.

April 2

~ Spiritual blessings ~

> *Praise be to the God and Father of our Lord Jesus Christ, who has blessed us in the heavenly realms with every spiritual blessing in Christ (Ephesians 1:3, NIV)*

On 2 April 2020, I was thinking about some gifts I have for friends, and how to get them delivered to them in another country. This is what the Holy Spirit taught me: Your spiritual blessings are all in the spiritual realm; it is you, yourself, that will bring it to you in the physical world. But for that to happen you have to declare that God's Word is yours and communicate in prayer constantly until you receive it. Be ready for any battles that will become a hindrance to your blessings being delivered. Fight your battles with faith. Faith comes from listening to and hearing the Word, so keep listening and hearing the Word while you are battling in the courtroom of heaven.

For an effective and fast delivery when posting your gift to another country there is an extra cost so it can be delivered in a quicker and safer way. Fasting is a price to pay to have your spiritual blessings delivered to you quicker. Fasting makes your flesh weak and your spirit stronger. Your flesh becomes weak and your spirit becomes strong and willing to enter the spiritual realm and receive God's will for your life. Your spiritual blessing is in Christ.

> *The spirit is willing, but the flesh is weak (Matthew 26:41, NIV).*

A good mother has great plans for her children after she has given birth to them in the physical realm. To equip her children for a great future and be successful, she makes many sacrifices along their journey. She seeks God's wisdom and direction in His Word, and prayer to lead her to all that God has in store.

Jesus did it too. He delivers to us His Spirit into our spirit in the spiritual realm. The Holy Spirit is now inside us, and His voice directs and leads us to receiving all that Christ paid and sacrificed for us to have.

> *Led by the Lord, they were as sure-footed as wild horses, and never stumbled. As cattle are led into a fertile valley, so the Lord gave his people rest. He led his people and brought honor to his name (Isaiah 63:13-14, GNT).*

This is a new day for you to live and enjoy to the fullest the life for which Christ has already paid. Forgive yourself and forgive others that need your forgiveness. Enjoy your freedom in your new life in Christ.

April 3

~ *The joy of life* ~

And the believers were filled with joy and with the Holy Spirit (Acts 13:52, NLT).

A good mother is full of joy and she runs her household cheerfully. She laughs at her coming days. Every day she sits under the shelter of God's Word to trade her sorrows, pains and worries with joy from the fruit of the Holy Spirit. Jesus said, if you abide in me you will produce fruit. The Holy Spirit abides in the Word of God who is Jesus. He produces joy and this is also what a good mother produces when she abides in the Word of God.

She is clothed with strength and dignity; she can laugh at the days to come (Proverbs 31:25, NIV).

When the Holy Spirit starts living inside us we will start experiencing the joy of life. When we are feeling sad and empty about life, it is because our life is designed to be filled with the Spirit of God. Jesus said He will complete our joy when we receive Him.

So with you: Now is your time of grief, but I will see you again and you will rejoice, and no one will take away your joy (John 16:22, NIV).

That joy from the Holy Spirit when Jesus is revealed completes us. We are no longer sad now that we can see Jesus again.

April 4

~ *Consulting God first* ~

But first let's consult the Lord (1 Kings 22:5, GNT).

A good mother always consults the Lord in prayer before she makes any significant decision for her house. She houses the Holy Spirit, and whatever decision she makes can affect her relationship with the Holy Spirit. Even though the Holy Spirit knows every movement of her thoughts and choices, she still needs to consult Him because He makes the final decision.

We humans make plans, but the Lord has the final word. We may think we know what is right, but the Lord is the judge of our motives. Share your plans with the Lord, and you will succeed (Proverbs 16:1-3, CEV).

> *You have searched me, Lord, and you know me. You know when I sit and when I rise; you perceive my thoughts from afar. You discern my going out and my lying down; you are familiar with all my ways. Before a word is on my tongue you, Lord, know it completely (Psalm 139:1-4, NIV).*

The Holy Spirit will only tell us what He hears from the father. He will not say anything of His own. He is the Spirit of truth, and He will only speak the truth to us even if it hurts. Even if you are the victim of a battle that has left you broken, if the Holy Spirit asks you to take that first step to reach out and forgive, obey His voice.

> *But when he, the Spirit of truth, comes, he will guide you into all the truth. He will not speak on his own; he will speak only what he hears, and he will tell you what is yet to come (John 16:13, NIV).*

Speak the truth of God's Word into your life every day so the devil cannot deceive you with his lies.

April 5

~ Feeding and storing the Word of God ~

> *His divine power has given us everything we need for a godly life through our knowledge of him who called us by his own glory and goodness (2 Peter 1:3, NIV).*

A good mother always prepares food for her household in advance. When they are hungry there is food for them. As long as she feeds herself in the spiritual food and stores the Word of God in her spiritual house, her house never runs out of physical food.

A good household is the result of being fed by a good mother.

> *She gets up before dawn to prepare breakfast for her household and plan the day's work for her servant girls (Proverbs 31:15, NLT).*

The Holy Spirit produces the fruit of righteousness all the time, so we can access it any time the need arises. Where they are unkind people we produce the fruit of kindness towards them. We must only feed from what the Holy Spirit produces within us. He produces His fruit of righteousness for us to feed and become full and strong. When we are full we refuse to be fed from any unrighteous table as Daniel did. When we are strong we have the strength to tear down any unrighteousness that wants to trap us.

> *Daniel made up his mind to eat and drink only what God had approved for his people to eat. And he asked the king's chief official for permission not to eat the food and wine served in the royal palace (Daniel 1:8, CEV).*

Each day wake up to your new day and feed yourself in the Word before the schedules of the day distract you.

April 6

~ *The right path* ~

> *Whether you turn to the right or to the left, your ears will hear a voice behind you, saying, 'This is the way; walk in it.' (Isaiah 30:21, NIV).*

A good mother is like the steering wheel of the car; she steers steadily and ensures she is in the right lane all the time. Whether her household turns to the left or right she is that voice that says 'this is the way to walk'. She steers in the right direction because she sits on the seat of the council of God's Word.

> *Your word is a lamp for my feet, a light on my path (Psalm 119:105, NIV).*

The Holy Spirit is the voice of God that produces the fruit of righteousness inside us, so that we can walk in it to be made right with God. He is the light to see through when darkness comes our way. It doesn't matter if we make a wrong decision in life and turn to the wrong path. God is a loving Father, full of patience, and waiting for us to obey the conviction of the Holy Spirit and return back to Him. He will welcome you back with open arms and put you back on the right track.

> *You are merciful, Lord! You are kind and patient and always loving (Psalm 145:8, CEV).*

God's mercies are new every day to make you that new creation in Christ and walk in the right path.

April 7

~ You are the garden of God ~

> *Abide in me, and I in you. As the branch cannot bear fruit by itself, unless it abides in the vine, neither can you, unless you abide in me (John 15:4, ESV).*

A good mother who loves gardens does her gardening as a worship unto God. She connects this physical chore to what God's Word speaks of her life. She is reminded that her heavenly Father is her gardener who works on her to grow her into a fruitful child so that others can enjoy her fruit.

> *Every branch in me that does not bear fruit he takes away, and every branch that does bear fruit he prunes, that it may bear more fruit (John 15:2, ESV).*

The Holy Spirit produces the fruit of the characters of Jesus Christ not only for us to enjoy but share with others to enjoy as well. And to also serve those that cause difficulties in our lives.

> *But the fruit of the Spirit is love, joy, peace, patience, kindness, goodness, faithfulness, gentleness, self-control; against such things there is no law (Galatians 5:22-23, ESV).*

The difficult people that we come across in our path of journey are those who need the fruit of the Holy Spirit from us.

April 8

~ *Feeling at home* ~

> *I am a stranger on earth; do not hide your commands from me (Psalm 119:19, NIV).*

A good mother always prepares the best for her visitor making them feel at home for their small visit. She provides the best she has in the house. Not only does she open the door of her home, she also opens the door of her heart with the actions of her hands. She is that woman who always opens herself up to receive the Word of God into her heart and, like a flower, she is open and beautiful from inside out.

> *Your beauty, within and without, is absolute, dear lover, close companion (Song of Solomon 7:6, MSG).*

> *He said, 'If I have found favour in your eyes, my lord, do not pass your servant by. Let a little water be brought, and then you may all wash your feet and rest under this tree. Let me get you something to eat, so you can be refreshed and then go on your way—now that you have come to your servant.' 'Very well,' they answered, 'do as you say.' (Genesis 18:3-5, NIV).*

The Holy Spirit inside us feels at home when we open the door of our heart and receive the Word of God and abide in it. When He feels at home, He makes us feel at home too with His peace in our hearts . The love of God is poured out into our hearts through the Holy Spirit, and we feel loved and belong. The love of God is His hospitality that His Spirit gives to us to enjoy during our short stay on earth. God is LOVE and inside Him is love, joy, peace, patience, kindness, goodness, faithfulness, gentleness and self-control which He pours into our hearts through the Holy Spirit.

> *And hope does not put us to shame, because God's love has been poured out into our hearts through the Holy Spirit, who has been given to us (Romans 5:5, NIV).*

The more we open up to God in hunger in His Word, the more He will continue to pour himself into us and our cup will start to overflow.

April 9

~ Light ~

> *'I am the light of the world. If you follow me, you won't have to walk in darkness, because you will have the light that leads to life.' (John 8:12, NLT).*

A good mother fills her life with Jesus' LIFE, His Word that has become flesh. She knows that for her to give life to her children she has to fill herself with LIFE to serve them.

The Holy Spirit is the life of Jesus that lights up our life. The Holy Spirit lights up our life even when it passes through the dark hours.

> *The Spirit gives life; the flesh counts for nothing. The words I have spoken to you—they are full of the Spirit and life (John 6:63, NIV).*
>
> *I may walk through valleys as dark as death, but I won't be afraid. You are with me, and your shepherd's rod makes me feel safe (Psalm 23:4, CEV)*

Though you walk through the darkest valley, the light from your flesh from the Word that has become flesh will flash its light, and you will not fear any evil.

April 10

~ Every scar has a story ~

> *As he spoke, he showed them the wounds in his hands and his side. They were filled with joy when they saw the Lord! (John 20:20, NLT)*

Every mother has a scar that has a story. It can be an inner pain that has left a scar on her heart, or a physical pain that leaves a scar on her flesh. Any mother can bring a life into this world naturally or through C-section. A good mother lays down her life and sacrifices her time, or resources, to bring this life into the world.

Let that C-section scar be a reminder that Jesus also has scars to show us, that He went through pain that leaves Him with scars, so we can be born again into His life that He laid down.

The Holy Spirit can now live inside us and gives us a new life, a born-again life from what Jesus did.

> *Jesus replied, 'Very truly I tell you, no one can see the kingdom of God unless they are born again.' John 3:3, (NIV).*

Your scar from yesterday will be a beautiful story for today to heal someone's pain.

April 11

~ Inheriting the kingdom of righteousness ~

> *Father, if you are willing, take this cup from me; yet not my will, but yours be done (Luke 22:42, NIV).*

A good mother is always willing to submit her will to the will of God. She understands that a will becomes effective through death. She inherits the kingdom's blessings through the death of Jesus. It was the will of the Father that Jesus died, so that she can inherit all that belongs to Him. When we accept Jesus into our lives, we receive the Holy Spirit, the great inheritance through the death of Jesus. The Holy Spirit is the Kingdom of God that produces joy and peace, which is the inheritance we receive from the death and resurrection of Jesus Christ.

> *For the kingdom of God is not a matter of eating and drinking, but of righteousness, peace and joy in the Holy Spirit, because anyone who serves Christ in this way is pleasing to God and receives human approval. Romans 14:17-18, (NIV).*

The flesh is weak, but the spirit is willing to receive the will of God from His Spirit.

April 12

~ *Rise up in your new life* ~

The wise woman builds her house (Proverbs 14:1, NIV).

A good mother builds her home by building her character in the Holy Spirit. The enemy that can stop her from building that Holy Ghost-like character is her SELF. She demolishes that old temple and raises up her new temple in the body of Christ. Her old temple was demolished when Jesus finished the work on the cross, and her new temple came into being when Jesus was raised from the dead by the power of the Holy Spirit. Because of this wonderful work of Jesus, she is able to rise up to what every day has in store for her and walk victoriously and joyfully into it.

> *Jesus answered them, 'Destroy this temple, and I will raise it again in three days.'*
>
> *They replied, 'It has taken forty-six years to build this temple, and you are going to raise it in three days?' But the temple he had spoken of was his body. After he was raised from the dead, his disciples recalled what he had said. Then they believed the scripture and the words that Jesus had spoken (John 2:19-22, NIV).*

Her victory over her old self is from feeding her old self with the fruit of the Holy Spirit. The Holy Spirit raised Jesus from dead and He lives inside us to raise and build us up in the new life of Jesus.

> *And if the Spirit of him who raised Jesus from the dead is living in you, he who raised Christ from the dead will also give life to your mortal bodies because of his Spirit who lives in you.(Romans 8:11, NIV).*

Each and every day feed your 'old self' with the fruit from the Tree of Life which is your new life in Christ.

April 13

~ *Living in Christ* ~

> *In peace I will both lie down and sleep; for you alone, O Lord, make me dwell in safety (Psalm 4:8, ESV).*

God rested on the seventh day after He finished His work. Jesus finished God's work on the cross. And we are now to rest in Christ in the Holy Spirit. A good mother rests in Christ; she lives her life in Christ and that is where she finds rest. She focuses not on her life and the troubles that pour out of that life, but instead she focuses on receiving new insights on the Word of God to enjoy her new life in Christ.

> *All things have been committed to me by my Father. No one knows the Son except the Father, and no one knows the Father except the Son and those to whom the Son chooses to reveal him (Matthew 11:27, NIV).*

The Holy Spirit is Jesus' gift to us to enjoy the finished work of the cross. The work of the Holy Spirit in producing His fruit of righteousness in us will be finished on Earth on the day Christ returns to take us home to be with Him for eternity. The Holy Spirit is getting us ready to live in that place Christ is preparing.

> *There has never been the slightest doubt in my mind that the God who started this great work in you would keep at it and bring it to a flourishing finish on the very day Christ Jesus appears.(Philippians 1:6, MSG).*

Control yourself to be controlled by God so you can find complete rest in God.

April 14

~ Clothed in the righteous blood of Jesus ~

> *When it snows, she has no fear for her household; for all of them are clothed in scarlet (Proverbs 31:21, NIV).*

A good mother always ensures that her children have clothes available for all seasons and through all seasons. She is well prepared on time. Scarlet represents the blood of Jesus. She clothes her household in the blood of Jesus. She also clothes herself in the Word of God that she bears fruit throughout every season.

> *Oh, the joys of those who do not follow the advice of the wicked, or stand around with sinners, or join in with mockers. But they delight in the law of the Lord, meditating on it day and night. They are like trees planted along the riverbank, bearing fruit each season. Their leaves never wither, and they prosper in all they do (Psalm 1:1-3, NLT)*

The Holy Spirit inside us is available all the time to clothe us in the righteous blood of Christ.

> *And to clothe yourselves with the new nature, which was created according to God's image in righteousness and true holiness (Ephesians 4:24, ISV).*

The fruit of righteousness that the Holy Spirit produces is available all the time for us to dress ourselves and also clothe others in need.

April 15

~ Unplanned child ~

> *My frame was not hidden from you when I was made in the secret place, when I was woven together in the depths of the earth. Your eyes saw my unformed body; all the days ordained for me were written in your book before one of them came to be (Psalm 139:15-16, NIV).*

If you think you are having an unplanned child, remember that Mary, the mother of Jesus never planned to have a child; it was God's plan. Every child born into this world is planned by God and has a purpose in their life to serve according to their call. A good mother not only sacrifices her body to feed and nourish the life she brings into this world; she invests her time in prayer and Word, that they will have life in the LIFE of God's Word for whatever calling God has designed for them.

God planned for the birth of His Son, Jesus. At the right time He sent forth His angel and the Holy Spirit to carry out the plan. The Holy Spirit conceived the spoken Word released from God by the angel in the womb of Mary. When we take in the Word of God, the Holy Spirit conceives the Word, so we produce a Christ-like character in our life.

> *The angel answered, 'The Holy Spirit will come on you, and the power of the Most High will overshadow you. So the holy one to be born will be called the Son of God (Luke 1:35, NIV).*

Each and every day, receive the Word of God into you, and give birth to the life of Jesus everywhere you go in your actions.

April 16

~ Every day is a gift of life ~

Whatever is good and perfect is a gift coming down to us from God our Father, who created all the lights in the heavens. He never changes or casts a shifting shadow. (James 1:17, NLT).

16 April 2020. Angelilly (my five-year-old daughter) asked me, 'What if you take back the gift you gave me?' She was referring to a colour book that I gave her as a gift. She said that because sometimes I tell her if she is not being good I will take away the nice stuff I gave her until she behaves well.

This is what the Holy Spirit taught me and reminded me of God's love. Every mother loves her children and gives them gifts to surprise them and make them happy. They can also remove it from their children as a way to discipline them when they misbehave.

A good mother first of all builds her children's character in good morals, and when they are faithfully being good, polite, respectful and kind, she rewards them with a gift for their faithfulness. When they misbehave she doesn't take that gift from them as she knows they rightfully earned it at that time.

For God's gifts and his call can never be withdrawn (Romans 29:11, NLT).

God loved us so much, and has given Jesus to us as a gift, and He will never take that back from us. That is what the perfect love of

God is all about. The love that understands how imperfect we are yet keeps giving us good and perfect gifts.

We need Jesus in our life to move us away from our bad way of living. The Holy Spirit is the perfect and best gift to receive from Jesus when we receive him as a gift from God.

> *So if you sinful people know how to give good gifts to your children, how much more will your heavenly Father give good gifts to those who ask him (Matthew 7:11, NLT).*

Every day is a gift of life from God to use and draw out LIFE from His living Word, so we can live a life of abundance in fullness.

April 17

~ *Growing closer to God* ~

> *No longer do I call you servants, for the servant does not know what his master is doing; but I have called you friends, for all that I have heard from my Father I have made known to you (John 15:15, ESV).*

A good mother has a personal one-on-one relationship with all her children to bring them closer to her. Apart from being a mother who serves them with love she becomes a close dear friend so as to understand them well. She makes them feel special when she understands them individually. She knows what their weaknesses and strengths are. She loves how much closer she is to Jesus with her relationship in the Holy Spirit. She sees all her imperfections in the perfect mirror of God's Word and strengthens against her weaknesses in the perfect Word of God.

Jesus wants us to have this personal relationship with Him so His Holy Spirit can be closer to us. Draw closer to God and He will draw closer to you.

> *But very truly I tell you, it is for your good that I am going away. Unless I go away, the Advocate will not come to you; but if I go, I will send him to you.*
>
> *But when he, the Spirit of truth, comes, he will guide you into all the truth. He will not speak on his own; he will speak only what he hears, and he will tell you what is yet to come (John 16:7,13, NIV).*

Every day is one more day closer to God when we faithfully spend time with Him in His Word.

April 18

~ *Becoming rich in Jesus* ~

> *And my God will meet all your needs according to the riches of his glory in Christ Jesus (Philippians 4:19, NIV).*

A good mother seeks to be rich in Jesus and so she digs continuously, and invests more on spending time in God's Word that has become flesh. She doesn't have to worry about her needs as they have already been met by Jesus.

God meets all her needs in the glorious riches of Jesus. All her needs and her house are already being provided for on the path of righteousness through which God leads her.

The Holy Spirit is the glorious riches of Jesus; we just have to use His fruit in both our difficult and good times. Our richness is the fruit of the Righteousness from the Holy Spirit and is only shown when it is used on difficult people in challenging situations.

> *I no longer have a righteousness of my own, the kind that is gained by obeying the Law. I now have the righteousness that is given through faith in Christ, the righteousness that comes from God and is based on faith (Philippians 3:9, GNT).*

The glorious riches of God are in Jesus, and this is in the Holy Spirit that is given to us by Jesus.

April 19

~ *Plan and future* ~

> *For I know the plans I have for you,' declares the Lord, 'plans to prosper you and not to harm you, plans to give you hope and a future (Jeremiah 29:11, NIV).*

A good mother isn't afraid for the future of her children. She understands God's great plan and future for her children. She smiles into tomorrow knowing that mercy and goodness will follow her all the days of her life, as long as she is connected daily to the Holy Spirit in Word and prayer for her children.

> *She is clothed with strength and dignity; she can laugh at the days to come (Proverbs 31:25, NIV).*

The gift of the Holy Spirit was the great plan and future that God had for us when He gave Jesus to us. Do not grieve the Holy Spirit. Be grateful with a heart overflowing with thanksgiving to the Father, thanking Him for Jesus. Because of Jesus, we can now have the Holy Spirit to live inside us giving us access to His fruit from the Tree of Life.

You become my delicious feast even when my enemies dare to fight. You anoint me with the fragrance of your Holy Spirit; you give me all I can drink of you until my heart overflows. So why would I fear the future? For your goodness and love pursue me all the days of my life. Then afterward, when my life is through, I'll return to your glorious presence to be forever with you! (Psalm 23:5-6, TPT).

Every day plant yourself in the Word, grow in the love of God, and bear fruit in the fruit of the Spirit.

April 20

~ Fruitful in prayer ~

Know therefore that the Lord your God is God; he is the faithful God, keeping his covenant of love to a thousand generations of those who love him and keep his commandments (Deuteronomy 7:9, NIV).

A good mother is a hero of faith, she keeps praying for and believing in a great future for her children's life even when she doesn't see anything. She knows that God is the God of generation, and even if her children don't see it, her children's children will see the fruit of it. This is how a good mother prays; she kneels down and breaks herself into this Word of God. She says this word as a prayer for her house and everyone with whom she has contact.

> *And so, from the day we heard, we have not ceased to pray for you, asking that you may be filled with the knowledge of his will in all spiritual wisdom and understanding, so as to walk in a manner worthy of the Lord, fully pleasing to him: bearing fruit in every good work and increasing in the knowledge of God; being strengthened with all power, according to his glorious might, for all endurance and patience with joy; giving thanks to the Father, who has qualified you to share in the inheritance of the saints in light (Colossians 1:9-12, ESV).*

The Father believes in His Son and sent Him to us who accomplish what the Father called Him to do. The Father can now have many sons through the gift of the one and only Son that He gave.

> *Real love isn't our love for God, but his love for us. God sent his Son to be the sacrifice by which our sins are forgiven (1 John 4:10, CEV).*

The Holy Spirit with His fruit of righteousness is the fruit from the finished work of Jesus. Jesus loves us and died for us to bring peace and joy through the Holy Spirit inside us. Being a son we can now inherit the kingdom of God of righteousness, peace and joy in the Holy Spirit.

> *For the kingdom of God is not a matter of eating and drinking, but of righteousness, peace and joy in the Holy Spirit, (Romans 14:17, NIV).*

Right out from the righteous love of God in Jesus, flows joy and peace.

April 21

~ We are Holy Spirit's love in action ~

But the fruit of the Spirit is love, joy, peace, patience, kindness, goodness, faithfulness, gentleness, self-control; against such things there is no law (Galatians 5:22-23, ESV).

A good mother is the Holy Spirit's love in action by producing His fruit. She pours this unconditional love upon her children and all in her care. She is the comforter, the strength, and courage to her children. The love of God is found in action in the fruit of His Spirit. Jesus is God's love in action who He sent into the world.

The Holy Spirit is Jesus' love in action who lives inside us and produces His fruit of righteousness. We are the Holy Spirit's love in action on whom He served His fruit within us to serve from inside out as a body of Christ.

I will comfort you there like a mother comforting her child.' When you see this happen, you will celebrate; your strength will return faster than grass can sprout (Isaiah 66:13-14, CEV).

Jesus has gifted us with the Holy Spirit who is freely available to give us His fruit to action. The Holy Spirit comforts us with His fruit of righteousness to comfort those that need it.

April 22

~ Battles ~

Now if we are children, then we are heirs—heirs of God and co-heirs with Christ, if indeed we share in his sufferings in order that we may also share in his glory. I consider that our present sufferings are not worth comparing with the glory that will be revealed in us (Romans 8:17-18, NIV).

A good mother remains faithful throughout her battles of storms in life. She knows that she will receive her rewards after she walks through the battles. She stands her feet on the Word of God and on His promises.

God will reward each of us for what we have done (Romans 2:6, CEV)

Jesus suffered in His body and from his suffering comes the reward of the Holy Spirit who the father has given to us. When we put to death our fleshly desires our body suffers, but we are rewarded because we begin to walk in the Spirit who is the reward from Christ.

Therefore, since Christ suffered in his body, arm yourselves also with the same attitude, because whoever suffers in the body is done with sin. As a result, they do not live the rest of their earthly lives for evil human desires, but rather for the will of God (1 Peter 4:1-2, NIV).

Fight your everyday battles of flesh in the Spirit. To be victorious make peace with your enemies, with the Love from the fruit of the Spirit. Let them be them, and you be Christ-like by serving them the love of Christ in the Holy Spirit.

April 23

~ Faith of a dog ~

Even the dogs eat the crumbs that fall from their master's table (Matthew 15:27, NIV).

A good mother has the faith of a dog, no matter how she gets treated and hurt in life, she will continue to follow the Word of God, and where it leads her to her next destiny.

She is the voice that fights for her children and family. She has the same loyalty as a dog. No matter how harshly a master treats his dogs they will always remain loyal. She follows the Word of God no matter how hard life knocks her down. God is looking for a loyal person like that to call home.

> *For the eyes of the Lord run to and fro throughout the whole earth, to show Himself strong on behalf of those whose heart is loyal to Him (2 Chronicles 16:9, NKJV).*

> *The woman came and knelt before him. 'Lord, help me!' she said. He replied, 'It is not right to take the children's bread and toss it to the dogs.' 'Yes it is, Lord,' she said. 'Even the dogs eat the crumbs that fall from their master's table.' Then Jesus said to her, 'Woman, you have great faith! Your request is granted.' And her daughter was healed at that moment (Matthew 15:25-28, NIV).*

The Holy Spirit is the loyal voice of Jesus that constantly speaks to us to lead us in the right direction. Even when we are unfaithful, He is always faithful. His voice keeps following and convincing us to get back to the right path.

> *My sheep listen to my voice; I know them, and they follow me. I give them eternal life, and they shall never perish; no one will snatch them out of my hand (John 10:27-28, NIV).*

God is loyal to us every day. He never stops giving us a new day to live a new life every day.

April 24

~ Fighting and conquering the enemy ~

> *Be sober-minded; be watchful. Your adversary the devil prowls around like a roaring lion, seeking someone to devour (1 Peter 5:8, ESV).*

A good mother knows that when she is about to achieve something great for her household the enemy roars to her in all directions but because she rides on the lion of Judah, she roars back, and silences the enemy with the blood of Jesus. She uses her energy and strength from God to focus on bringing her dream to come to pass rather than wasting it on fighting with the flesh and blood that get in her way.

> *The wicked flee when no one pursues, but the righteous are bold as a lion (Proverbs 28:1, ESV).*

The Holy Spirit is the power of God, the strength of Jesus Christ through whom we can do anything. The fruit of the Holy Spirit energizes and strengthens us to cope with what is being thrown at us. If unkindness is given to us, it must be returned with kindness from the fruit of the Holy Spirit.

> *I can do all things through Christ who strengthens me (Philippians 4:13, NKJV).*

Every day remind yourself that with the power from God's Word, you have the strength of the lion of Judah that can rip open the mouth of the devil from any lies he invents in your mind.

April 25

~ *Hope in the Word of God* ~

> *Everything's falling apart on me, God; put me together again with your Word (Psalm 119:107, MSG).*

A good mother always seeks God first when her world falls apart. Her hope and faith are found in the love she has for God's Word.

Her prayer is Psalm 119:107,

> *Everything's falling apart on me, God; put me together again with your Word.*

The Holy Spirit is the kingdom of God that exists inside us. He is the Faith that we gain from hearing the Word of God; our only HOPE when our world is falling apart. He is the gift from the LOVE of God through Jesus Christ.

> *…remember that at that time you were separate from Christ, excluded from citizenship in Israel and foreigners to the covenants of the promise, without hope and without God in the world (Ephesians 2:12, NIV).*

> *And now these three remain: faith, hope and love. But the greatest of these is love (1 Corinthians 13:13, NIV).*

It's all because of God's love that we can have a solid faith to keep our hope alive in this fallen world.

April 26

~ *Do not compare yourself with others* ~

let's just go ahead and be what we were made to be, without enviously or pridefully comparing ourselves with each other, or trying to be something we aren't (Romans 12:6, MSG).

A good mother doesn't compare herself and her children to other mothers and their children. She compares herself and her children to what the Word of God says and tries to live accordingly to the Word of God.

She speaks Psalm 119:5-6,

Oh, that my actions would consistently reflect your decrees!

Then I will not be ashamed when I compare my life with your commands.

The Holy Spirit, the power of God working in you does not want you to be like others. He helps you to live by what God originally designed for you. You have a unique gift to grow and glow in the likeness of Christ to give God glory in your original strength and beauty.

God has given each of you a gift from his great variety of spiritual gifts. Use them well to serve one another. Do you have the gift of speaking? Then speak as though God himself were speaking through you. Do you have the gift of helping others? Do it with all the strength and energy that God supplies. Then everything you do will bring glory to God through Jesus Christ. All glory and power to him forever and ever! Amen (1 Peter 4:10-11, NLT)

Each and every day compare your life to what God says about your life and live that life God designed in you for His glory.

April 27

~ *Good fruit* ~

> *Only take care, and keep your soul diligently, lest you forget the things that your eyes have seen, and lest they depart from your heart all the days of your life. Make them known to your children and your children's children— (Deuteronomy 4:9, ESV).*

A good mother teaches the goodness of God to her children and children's children. In order to do it in love she builds her faith in the goodness of God's WORD. She breathes the air of God in 2 Peter 1:5-7 to breathe out to her children.

> *For this very reason do your best to add goodness to your faith; to your goodness add knowledge; to your knowledge add self-control; to your self-control add endurance; to your endurance add godliness; to your godliness add Christian affection; and to your Christian affection add love (2 Peter 1:5-7, GNT).*

The Holy Spirit within us is the goodness of God. He is the Spirit of Jesus, the Tree of Life who produces the fruit of goodness so we can share it to all with whom we come in contact.

> *The seeds of good deeds become a tree of life; a wise person wins friends (Proverbs 11:30, NLT).*

Each and every day nourish the Tree of Life within you in Word and prayer and bloom the fruit of goodness from the seeds of good deeds.

April 28

~ Friend of God ~

I am a friend to all who fear you, to all who follow your precepts (Psalm 119:63, NIV).

A good mother becomes her children's friend. She shares and takes part in all the affairs of her children. Friends tell secrets, and in doing so there is nothing her children can hide from her.

She grows herself in the Word every day and asks the Holy Spirit to take their relationship into friendship.

The Holy Spirit is our close friend who reveals to us the secrets of the treasures of the kingdom of God. Jesus gave us His Spirit when we obeyed and received His Word into us.

You are my friends if you do what I command you. No longer do I call you servants, for the servant does not know what his master is doing; but I have called you friends, for all that I have heard from my Father I have made known to you (John 15:14-15, ESV).

If you belong to Christ, then you are Abraham's seed, and heirs according to the promise (Galatians 3:29, NIV).

Abraham was a friend of God, and we are now a friend of God because we are the seed of Abraham from Jesus. We are now friends with the Holy Spirit through Jesus.

April 29

~ Eternal life ~

For God so loved the world that he gave his one and only Son, that whoever believes in him shall not perish but have eternal life (John 3:16, NIV).

Just as Jesus came down to earth in the flesh to represent God's family a good mother loves her family so much that she represents her household every day and offers herself to God on behalf of her family. She sacrifices her SELF to God, so that her family can live a good life all the time. A good mother glorifies God through the sacrifice and service she provides for her household. It's her desire to see that what God promises her through Isaiah 44: 3-4 must come to pass in her house.

For I will pour water on the thirsty land, and streams on the dry ground; I will pour out my Spirit on your offspring, and my blessing on your descendants. They will spring up like grass in a meadow, like poplar trees by flowing streams (Isaiah 44:3-4, NIV).

The Holy Spirit is the good Spirit of God that represents God the good Father and God the good Son inside us. He is the very promise of all God's promises that we received in the finished work of Jesus Christ, the Son. He gives us eternal life to our perishing life.

April 30

~ *Build your universe with God's Word* ~

Do not let any unwholesome talk come out of your mouths, but only what is helpful for building others up according to their needs, that it may benefit those who listen. And do not grieve the Holy Spirit of God. (Ephesians 4:29-30, NIV).

A good mother knows that her words create her universe to live. Out of the mouth of God came His words and the universe was built. He spoke and built and said AND IT WAS GOOD. Words that come out of her mouth create a universe for her and her house to live. If she thinks negatively towards others then she will obviously start speaking negatively towards them, which then creates a negative atmosphere for her to live in. She builds herself in the Word and focuses speaking blessings into those with whom she comes into contact. She speaks the goodness of God upon their lives.

The Holy Spirit actions God's Word. When God spoke, His Spirit brought into creation the spoken Word of God. The Holy Spirit lives in us, and we have to declare and build God's Word into our life for Him to breathe life into the Word and bring it to flesh.

The words I have spoken to you—they are full of the Spirit and life (John 6:63, NIV).

Each and every day, speak and declare the Word of God into your life of what God says of you. God alone in His righteousness has the right to have the final say in your life.

MAY

~ A mother's role as a teacher to her children ~

1 May 2020. While doing home schooling, I was reading the dictionary vocabulary words with Angelilly, my five-year-old. I thought to myself. We will read it together up to the letter 'E' as that is what I have taught her so far and she is knowledgeable about it.

This is what the Holy Spirit taught me: So is the kingdom of God. God will not allow temptation that is beyond your capabilities, and He will find a way out for you if you fall into temptation.

> *The temptations in your life are no different from what others experience. And God is faithful. He will not allow the temptation to be more than what you can stand. When you are tempted, he will show you a way out so that you can endure (1 Corinthians 10.13, NLT).*

God will never allow you to sit any of His tests about which you are not knowledgeable. Just as I limit my teaching of Angelilly to her knowledge, so does God only allow tests into your life according to your knowledge of Him; the more you know God, the more difficult your test will be. Job sat through a difficult test because of his knowledge of God and he didn't sin.

> *In all this Job did not sin with his lips (Job 2:10, NKJV).*

A good mother may fall into temptation but she looks to the cross, the exit door out from her temptation. Evil was defeated at the cross.

She allows herself to sit in the Word of God, so the Spirit of knowledge can fall heavily on her and increase her knowledge of God. It's in her test that she practises the Word of God and sits faithfully until her test is done and dusted.

> *But the Lord is faithful, and he will strengthen you and protect you from the evil one (2 Thessalonians 3:3, NIV).*

A good mother teaches her house the prayer Jesus taught her disciples. She seeks God in His Word every day for daily strength, which is the daily bread, and to be protected from evil and not be led into temptation. She is not stressed out with her debts if there are any, because Jesus teaches her to pray for that too. Say the Lord's Prayer each day for the month of May, and EVERY DAY with your house faithfully.

This, then, is how you should pray:

> *Our Father in heaven, hallowed be your name, your kingdom come, your will be done, on earth as it is in heaven. Give us today our daily bread. And forgive us our debts, as we also have forgiven our debtors. And lead us not into temptation, but deliver us from the evil one (Matthew 6:9-13, NIV).*

May 1

~ *To serve and not to be served* ~

And the Word became flesh, and dwelt among us, and we saw His glory, glory as of the only begotten from the Father, full of grace and truth (John 1:14, NASB).

To give God glory is to serve in love, serving people their needs. If you are in a position to do so then do it with the knowledge that you are doing this for the love of God. A good mother serves her household with love and doesn't complain when she is not appreciated, as she knows that by serving her house with love she is doing it as an act of love towards God. She gives glory to God daily through her daily task. Jesus said I came to serve and not to be served. Jesus is now serving us through the fruit of the Holy Spirit produced inside us.

When we take a servant's heart, God's glory is shown.

> *He said to Me, 'You are My Servant, Israel, In Whom I will show My glory.' (Isaiah 49:3, NASB).*

When you live a life to serve without expecting to be served you will never be disappointed.

May 2

~ God's right timing ~

> *Put it in writing, because it is not yet time for it to come true. But the time is coming quickly, and what I show you will come true. It may seem slow in coming, but wait for it; it will certainly take place, and it will not be delayed. (Habakkuk 2:3, GNT).*

A good mother is like an alarm clock: she wakes her house up a little early on time so they are ready and not late for the day. She ensures that everything is prepared before she wakes them up. In order to be that fully charged alarm she first charges herself in the Word of God, to be the alarm to remind her of all the promises in the abundant life of Jesus.

The Holy Spirit is God's clock inside us. He has the perfect timing that God appoints for us and so he prepares us each day by guiding us to walk on the right path to the destiny God purposed for us at the right time. At the right time, His alarm will come on, and this is when we will know that we have received what we were prepared for.

> *At the right time, I, the Lord, will make it happen (Isaiah 60:22, NLT).*

Write down what you want God to do for you. Delight in the Lord every day in His Word, that He is preparing you to receive in the right timing you desire.

May 3

~ *Distraction* ~

> *And when he comes, he will convict the world of its sin, and of God's righteousness, and of the coming judgment (John 16:8, NLT).*

A good mother removes anything in her household that could distract her children from becoming the person they are meant to be. Distraction is harmful to them. She receives into her the Word of God to keep her on track of becoming a godly mother. Nothing in this world can distract her godly motherly role as long as her mind is aligned and renewed in the Word of God all the time.

The Holy Spirit within us will always prompt us to go away from something that can cause destruction or disturbance in our life. He will also remove anything in our life that could be a distraction to live the purpose God created us for.

> *I am saying this for your benefit, not to place restrictions on you. I want you to do whatever will help you serve the Lord best, with as few distractions as possible. (1 Corinthians 7:35, NLT).*

Every day connect to God first in Word and prayer before the disturbing demands of the world show up.

May 4

~ Wisdom ~

> *He grants a treasure of common sense to the honest (Proverbs 2:7, NLT).*

The wisdom of common sense comes only from God. A good mother is sensitive in her spirit to the Spirit of wisdom so that when she speaks, it is wise. She draws it out by seeking God and being knowledgeable of God's Word and what God says of her. Her goodness to her household is reflected in her actions of kindness and patience. She not only speaks kindness into her house but she actions it.

> *She speaks with wisdom, and faithful instruction is on her tongue (Proverbs 31:26, NIV).*

The Holy Spirit is God's Spirit of wisdom, and He faithfully produces kindness inside the house in which He resides. Faithfulness and kindness are two of His fruit of righteousness.

> *The Spirit of the LORD will rest on him – the Spirit of wisdom and of understanding, the Spirit of counsel and of might, the Spirit of the knowledge and fear of the LORD (Isaiah 11:2, NIV).*

> *Love is patient, love is kind. It does not envy, it does not boast, it is not proud (1 Corinthians 13:4, NIV).*

Wisdom is a timely word that is full of kindness and has the patience to heal you with time.

May 5

~ *Dreams and visions* ~

Where there is no vision, the people perish: but he that keepeth the law, happy is he (Proverbs 29:18, KJV).

A good mother always has dreams and visions for her children so they can live life to the fullest and not go astray. She dreams what God dreams for her children by doing what God says in His Word for her life and her household.

The Holy Spirit within us enables us to dream dreams and see vision. He works from inside us. Without dreams and visions people wander off and go astray.

And afterward, I will pour out my Spirit on all people. Your sons and daughters will prophesy, your old men will dream dreams, your young men will see visions (Joel 2:28, NIV).

Thanks to Jesus' sacrifice, God has now poured His Holy Spirit into us once and for all to live inside us forever. We can dream big dreams and see great visions, and make it happen in Jesus' name by the power of the Holy Spirit.

May 6

~ *Storing* ~

Do not store up for yourselves treasures on earth, where moths and vermin destroy, and where thieves break in and steal. But store up for yourselves treasures in heaven, where moths and vermin do not destroy, and where thieves do not break in and steal. (Matthew 6:19-20, NIV)

I was thinking of how I want to store up things, so that when I need it I can just go and get it. This is what the Holy Spirit taught me: A good mother stores within her the Word, her faith, and when she needs it she just reaches from within her to release it.

The Holy Spirit inside us is the storehouse and power from which God's treasure is stored. Jesus is the treasure of God's knowledge in the Holy Spirit.

> *That their hearts may be encouraged, having been knit together in love, and attaining to all the wealth that comes from the full assurance of understanding, resulting in a true knowledge of God's mystery, that is, Christ himself, in whom are hidden all the treasures of wisdom and knowledge (Colossians 2:2-3, NASB).*

Focus on building up your faith account with the Word, you will need it for every important transaction you want to make in your life.

May 7

~ *Unconditional love of God* ~

> *This is how God showed his love among us: He sent his one and only Son into the world that we might live through him (1 John 4:9, NIV).*

A good mother has not seen her baby in the womb yet she has a love that is unconditional. She accepts everything about the life of the baby as it is when the baby is born. This is how God showed his love among us. He loves and accepts us even while we are sinners.

> *But God showed his great love for us by sending Christ to die for us while we were still sinners (Romans 5:8, NLT).*

He sent his one and only Son into the world that we might live through Him. The very nature of God, the Father, is shown through the Son in flesh. And that very nature is now given to us through the Holy Spirit who lives inside us. No one can see the Holy Spirit inside us but they can see Him in the love we give to each other.

> *No one has ever seen God; but if we love one another, God lives in us and his love is made complete in us (1 John 4:12, NIV).*

We show God who we can't see that we love Him by loving the good and bad people He has allowed into our lives.

May 8

~ *Jesus, the pilot of your life* ~

> *Choose my instruction instead of silver, knowledge rather than choice gold, for wisdom is more precious than rubies and nothing you desire can compare with her (Proverbs 8:10-11, NIV).*

A good mother is the pilot of her household. She knows that to skilfully take her household through their journey of life, she has to get instruction from the Holy Spirit, the same way a pilot gets instruction from the tower operator to skilfully fly the plane to its destiny. To reach the destiny for her family depends on following the voice and instruction of the Holy Spirit. When we are in Christ, we take the pilot's position, and the Holy Spirit is our helper, the co-pilot. He takes instruction only from what Jesus wants us to know to become like Him.

> *But when he, the Spirit of truth, comes, he will guide you into all the truth. He will not speak on his own; he will speak only what he hears, and he will tell you what is yet to come (John 16:13, NIV).*

Jesus is the pilot and His Spirit is the co-pilot, the helper that Jesus promises to give you. They will take you safely to your destiny even through the storms.

May 9

~ God's purpose ~

> *But the plans of the LORD stand firm forever, the purposes of his heart through all generations (Psalm 33:11, NIV).*

A mother lives because of her children, and a good mother not only lives for her children but makes sure her children have a purpose to live. She seeks the Word of Life that defines their purpose and ensures that her children live the purpose and calling that God designed for them to become.

The Holy Spirit lives inside us because Jesus is ALIVE. Jesus lives in us through His Spirit and because He lives we can live. We have LIFE and a purpose.

> *Before long, the world will not see me anymore, but you will see me. Because I live, you also will live (John 14:19, NIV).*

> *For I know the plans I have for you,' declares the LORD, 'plans to prosper you and not to harm you, plans to give you hope and a future (Jeremiah 29:11, NIV).*

Mothers have the strength and hope to face tomorrow because of their children's future.

May 10

~ Gifts ~

> *Every good and perfect gift is from above, coming down from the Father of the heavenly lights, who does not change like shifting shadows (James 1:17, NIV)*

I was thinking about the gifts that I bought, and how I would get them to the people for whom I bought them as they all live in another country. This is what the Holy Spirit taught me about God giving us gifts from where He is. You see, a good wife is a gift from the Lord to his husband, and she becomes a good mother to their children. It doesn't matter what race, skin colour, language or tribe we come from, God sent His one and only Son as a gift, and He bought us with His precious priceless blood.

> *The one who has found a good wife has found what goodness is, and obtained a delightful gift from the Lord (Proverbs 18:22, NET).*

She is a good mother who trains and brings up her children in the fear of the Lord. Children are a good and perfect gift from above, and they need the perfect Word of God to guide them in this imperfect world that they have entered.

> *Children are a gift from the Lord; they are a reward from him (Psalm 127:3, NLT)*

Jesus is our gift from the Father. The Holy Spirit is our gift from Jesus. There are different kinds of gifts that the Holy Spirit distributes to us.

The Holy Spirit gives us these different kinds of gifts to each of us to serve the different parts of the body of Christ. Different kind of work is done but it is the same God working differently because we are all unique and special in our own way with the gifts given to us to glorify God.

> *There are different kinds of gifts, but the same Spirit distributes them. There are different kinds of service, but the same LORD. There are different kinds of working, but in all of them and in everyone it is the same God at work. Now to each one the manifestation of the Spirit is given for the common good (1 Corinthians 12:4-7, NIV).*

Discover your gift from the Holy Spirit within you and offer it to whoever is in your contact that needs it. This is how you will be living the purpose that God called you to live.

May 11

~ God of generations).

> *You, Lord, reign forever; your throne endures from generation to generation (Lamentations 5:19, NIV).*

A mother who constantly prays for her children moves God to work throughout her life. She is a good mother to her children, and a good child to her good Father. God crowns her with blessings from generation to generation. He is the God of generation.

The Holy Spirit's fruit is goodness and He is the Spirit of God gifted to us through the gift of God's Son, Jesus Christ. The same Spirit of God that lives in us also is living in our children and will also be living in our children's children for many generations to come. The Holy Spirit also prays to God on our behalf like a good mother.

> *In the same way, the Spirit helps us in our weakness. We do not know what we ought to pray for, but the Spirit himself intercedes for us through wordless groans. And he who searches our hearts knows the mind of the Spirit, because the Spirit intercedes for God's people in accordance with the will of God (Romans 8:26-27, NIV).*

Each and every day choose a scripture and meditate and pray about it. That is praying in the mind of Christ, the will of God.

May 12

~ A time for everything ~

And when he comes, he will convict the world of its sin, and of God's righteousness, and of the coming judgment (John 16:8, NLT)

A good mother only has good things to speak about her children, regardless of how messed up her child may be at the moment. She knows there is a time for everything, and that all those bad things in her household will pass through when its season is over. All she does is walk in the counsel of God's Word with prayers.

The Holy Spirit is all about good news and will only tell you good things to do or remind you of the goodness of God. When you go astray He will convince you that what you did is wrong, so you can get back on the track of righteousness.

> *There is a time for everything, and a season for every activity under the heavens: (Ecclesiastes 3:1, NIV).*

There is season for everything going all around you that you may not like but the good God is in control. In every season throughout all seasons, He is working only for the good of those who love Him.

May 13

~ *Start new and fresh* ~

> *If we confess our sins, he is faithful and just and will forgive us our sins and purify us from all unrighteousness (1John 1:9, NIV)*

Do not let someone's bad intention and bitterness rob you of your goodness, keep being you. God is faithful because even we fail him with our wickedness and ungratefulness, He remains faithful. He is waiting patiently for us to go back to and have a fresh start. A good mother is faithful, she keeps remaining as a mother doing everything a good mother does even when she is not appreciated for it.

God is so good that He shows His faithfulness through His Spirit that gives us life. Even when we don't appreciate God for being alive, He never removes His Spirit from us. He still gives us a new day to live, breathe and move in Him.

> *For in him we live and move and have our being (Acts 17:28, NIV).*

> *The steadfast love of the Lord never ceases; his mercies never come to an end; they are new every morning; great is your faithfulness (Lamentations 3:22-23, ESV).*

Every morning of each day ask God for His mercy over your physical and spiritual house to start new and fresh.

May 14

~ *The Spirit of Truth* ~

> *But when he, the Spirit of truth, comes, he will guide you into all the truth. He will not speak on his own; he will speak only what he hears, and he will tell you what is yet to come (John 16:13, NIV)*

I remember always trying to quieten my daughter whenever she was saying things that are not right. This is what the Holy Spirit taught me: A good mother shuts up the voice of the accuser, Satan devil, with the truth from God's Word. Because she sits in the truth of God's Word, she knows every time the devil twists the truth to lie to her. She has the Holy Spirit inside of her, the Spirit of truth.

Jesus is the way, the truth and the life. He lives inside us through the Holy Spirit. Whatever darkness of lies the devil blows towards us, the Spirit of truth and light will expose it.

> *I have come into the world as a light, so that no one who believes in me should stay in darkness (John 12:46, NIV).*

Every day tell yourself the truth about what God's Word says of you; it will set you free from any lies the devil tries to invent in your life.

May 15

~ Storing the essentials ~

> *When it snows, she has no fear for her household; for all of them are clothed in scarlet. (Proverbs 31:21, NIV)*

It is up to the woman of the house to get supplies in to keep in storage. A good mother stores all the essentials that her household needs and provides them through all seasons. This is what I learnt from the outbreak of COVID-19, the flu that broke out in Wuhan, China and affected everyone globally. The world went into lockdown except for the move of essential workers. A good mother locks herself in her house and stores up the essentials of heaven to meet her essential needs on earth. She locks the door of her house to shut out any evil with the blood of Jesus and opens her heart where resides the Holy Spirit, to constantly receive into her the Word of Life.

> *Go to the ant, you sluggard; consider its ways and be wise! It has no commander, no overseer or ruler, yet it stores its provisions in summer and gathers its food at harvest (Proverbs 6:6-8, NIV).*

The Holy Spirit brings life to God's Word that we have stored inside to meet our daily needs as they arise. Keep storing the Word as it is LIFE to our life to live. The Holy Spirit is essential to our everyday movements and living.

The Spirit gives life; the flesh counts for nothing. The words I have spoken to you—they are full of the Spirit and life (John 6:63, NIV).

The Word of life is the only essential to our life to meet all the other of life's needs.

May 16

~ Right track ~

God is within her, she will not fall; God will help her at break of day (Psalm 46:5, NIV).

I was at my daughter's school in preparation for their kindies next year and the teachers were showing us this beetle toy. It was programmed to walk in a path to its destiny. The Holy Spirit spoke to my heart and said that in the same way we can always program our self in God's Word before we start our day.

A good mother wakes up before dawn each day and prepares herself before she begins her day. She prepares herself to serve her household in the fruit of righteousness. Even if she goes off track, she comes back because she has programmed herself.

The Holy Spirit produces the fruit of righteousness and He is the voice that keeps us on the path of righteousness. Just as our flowing blood is the path that transports what we take in to all parts of our body, so is the blood of Jesus sinless and righteous. It is the path that transports the Word of God we take into us and calls out to us to remain on the path of righteousness.

> *Whether you turn to the right or to the left, your ears will hear a voice behind you, saying, 'This is the way; walk in it.' (Isaiah 30:21, NIV).*

Each and every day programme yourself to remain in the righteous Word of God.

May 17

~ *God's right timing* ~

> *You see, at just the right time, when we were still powerless, Christ died for the ungodly (Romans 5:6, NIV).*

I have a beautiful bracelet watch and wanted to reset the time but then realized after putting the right hour that it was not ticking. It just stayed in that hour. The Holy Spirit taught me this. You see, a good mother is a moving time, just like when you are at the right hour but it's not working, any woman or mother always see herself as being right all the time. Only a good woman and mother who walks in the righteousness of God will move in the right direction at all times. Your bracelet watch was put at the right hour but it was not working because it needs a new battery. Only when God gives a new heart and new spirit to a mother will she be that good mother who will be charged and connected well to His Spirit.

> *At the right time, I, the LORD will make it happen (Isaiah 60:22, NLT).*

The Holy Spirit works on God's time and makes everything happen with the right timing. He is the 'right time' of God working inside us to charge us fully in the righteousness of God.

> *I tell you, now is the time of God's favour, now is the day of salvation (2 Corinthians 6:2, NIV).*

> *The eyes of all look to you, and you give them their food at the proper time (Psalm 145:15, NIV).*

Each and every day put yourself right in God's Word and seek His kingdom and righteousness to meet all your needs at the right time.

May 18

~ *Pay evilness with goodness* ~

> *Do not repay anyone evil for evil. Be careful to do what is right in the eyes of everyone. If it is possible, as far as it depends on you, live at peace with everyone (Romans 12:17-18, NIV)*

I was trying to talk about some people treating me badly, and the Holy Spirit taught me this. Though someone may have done wrong or been bad to you, it's not God's image to talk about how bad and wrong it is, as God is already working on it for your good. For you to talk about it only creates a bad atmosphere for yourself to live in. You wouldn't like to live in a place where it is full of smelly stuff, so don't talk about it. A good mother always speaks about the good things in her household. She sees the good in every bad thing that happens to her. She knows for all things God is working for her good, and she must always focus on the good things in life.

The Holy Spirit produces His righteous fruit of goodness in our life in all seasons. You have been bought at a higher price already to produce this fruit of righteousness in all the seasons of your life. Your priceless value is shown when you produce the fruit of goodness in seasons where evil surrounds you.

> *And we know that in all things God works for the good of those who love him, who have been called according to his purpose (Romans 8:28, NIV).*

> *Make good use of every opportunity you have, because these are evil days (Ephesian 5:16, GNT).*

In each and every day there will always be some evil, so make the most of every day with the goodness of the Holy Spirit inside you.

May 19

~ *True friend* ~

> *And the believers were filled with joy and with the Holy Spirit (Acts 13:52, NLT).*

A good mother is a great companion and true friend. She entertains her children with fun things to do. She comforts and strengthens her children when they are sad and rejoices with them when they are joyful. She celebrates every small success and achievement that her child achieves. She finds her joy and strength in the Word of God every day.

> *You spoke to me, and I listened to every word. I belong to you, Lord God Almighty, and so your words filled my heart with joy and happiness (Jeremiah 15:16, GNT).*

The Holy Spirit is a great companion, always enjoying the new life we achieve in Christ, and is the joy in our lives. When we are sad He also comforts and strengthens us to carry on.

> *But let all my true friends shout for joy, all those who know and love what I do for you.*
>
> *Let them all say, 'The Lord is great, and he delights in the prosperity of his servant.' (Psalm 35:27, TPT)*

Today is the day that the Lord has made to rejoice and be glad in Him for the strength He gives to us every day.

May 20

~There is something good in every day~

But as for you, brethren, do not grow weary in doing good. 2 Thessalonians 3:13, (NKJV).

I know every mother does that all the time, every time. They try to do something but if they see something is not right, they put that thing back in its right place. I was trying to shower, and on my way to the bathroom I noticed a lot of stuff lying around the house that was not in its right place, so I began putting them back where they belonged. This is what the Holy Spirit taught me: A good mother always makes things right and puts them in order. Before she does something, if she notices something is not right, she sorts that out first. The world would be in a mess if there were no good mothers around. These are women who pray without ceasing because they want to see the righteousness of God in everything.

The Holy Spirit is the righteousness of God, and He is within us to ensure that we are productive in producing the fruit of righteousness. He convicts us when something is not right and gives us the strength we need to do the right things.

> *For the kingdom of God is not a matter of eating and drinking, but of righteousness, peace and joy in the Holy Spirit, because anyone who serves Christ in this way is pleasing to God and receives human approval (Romans 14:17-18, NIV).*

Find something good in your every new day and do it as a worship unto God for the day.

May 21

~ *You are safe under God's watch* ~

> *May the Lord keep watch between you and me when we are away from each other (Genesis 31:49, NIV).*

I was watching Blessed, then at eight months' old, carefully. He was at the crawling stage where he could just grab anything to hold onto and stand. I tried to ensure he would not lose balance and fall. I did that because there were times when I was not fast enough to prevent him from harm. This is what the Holy Spirit taught me:

A good mother keeps careful watch over her children so they do not harm themselves. And even if she is physically not present she keeps her children safe in her heart by praying to God for them.

God keeps watch over us through His Spirit within us, and even when we are sleeping like the dead, we wake up safely to a new day. God doesn't slumber or sleep; He is so watchful over us all the time. He is our present help at all times.

> *God is our refuge and strength, an ever-present help in trouble (Psalm 46:1, NIV).*
>
> *My help comes from the Lord, the Maker of heaven and earth. He will not let your foot slip – he who watches over you will not slumber; Indeed he who watches over Israel will neither slumber nor sleep (Psalm 121:2-4, NIV).*

You are the apple of God's eye and He watches over you all the time so that you are not harmed in a way that will bring about your demise. You have a call on your life to live the purpose God designed for you. Appreciate the life He gives you every day.

May 22

~ Joy and peace in the righteousness of the Holy Spirit ~

> *For the kingdom of God is not a matter of eating and drinking, but of righteousness, peace and joy in the Holy Spirit, (Romans 14:17, NIV).*

A good mother fills herself in the Word of God first before she serves her house. She constantly fills her cup, so it can overflow to everyone all around her. Before she sleeps, she fills herself with peace from the Word of God, so she can wake up in joy to a new day and start her day in the Word and prayer.

The Holy Spirit awakens our spirit every day to serve His fruit of righteousness into our spirit. But it is really up to us to decide to fill our heart by having communion with Him or rush off to do what our flesh desires.

> *This is why it is said: 'Wake up, sleeper, rise from the dead, and Christ will shine on you. 'Be very careful, then, how you live—not as unwise but as wise, making the most of every opportunity, because the days are evil. Therefore do not be foolish, but understand what the Lord's will is. Do not get drunk on wine, which leads to debauchery. Instead, be filled with the Spirit, (Ephesians 5:14-18, NIV).*

Arise in joy and celebrate the gift of life in the brand new day God has given to you to live again.

May 23

~ The sword of the Spirit ~

> *Take the helmet of salvation and the sword of the Spirit, which is the word of God (Ephesians 6:17, NIV).*

I know of most mothers who do that and I do that more often. We talk and we always have something to talk about all the time because there's always a household member who is just not doing little things right in the house. A good mother has the voice of a sword that she uses to keep her house in order. That demanding and commanding voice is to bring peace and maintain peace in her house. God is familiar with her voice because she talks to Him all the time. She is also familiar with hearing God's voice. She fails many times, and this is why she needs an unfailing God.

The Holy Spirit feels at home when you know how to master the art of using the sword of the Spirit, which is the Word. Only when you become matured in the Word do you become a son and are able to manage the art of using the sword of the Spirit. He feels at home because of the peace. A house becomes a home when there is peace.

> *Therefore repent; or else I am coming to you quickly, and I will make war against them with the sword of My mouth (Revelation 2:16, NASB).*

There is always sunshine and rainbows after a storm, and there is always peace after a war.

> *For he himself is our peace, who has made us both one and has broken down in his flesh the dividing wall of hostility by abolishing the law of commandments expressed in ordinances, that he might create in himself one new man in place of the two, so making peace, and might reconcile us both to God in one body through the cross, thereby killing the hostility (Ephesians 2:14-16, ESV).*

Take the sword of the Holy Spirit and use it within you to make peace with your old SELF.

May 24

~ *Doing great things* ~

> *Don't compare yourself with others. Just look at your own work to see if you have done anything to be proud of.*

> *You must each accept the responsibilities that are yours. (Galatians 6:4-5, ERV)*

A good mother doesn't compare herself with other mothers. She conquered her weaknesses to be better and work on improving herself. Jesus said, 'You will do greater things even greater than I because I am going to the Father.' Jesus goes to the Father and the Holy Spirit comes to us to do greater things inside us.

> *Very truly I tell you, whoever believes in me will do the works I have been doing, and they will do even greater things than these, because I am going to the Father. (John 14:12, NIV).*

A good mother keeps her house in order through her prayers, and so great things happen. She knows that greater is He that is in her than He that is in the world.

The Holy Spirit inside us through Christ who is with the Father is too great and does great things through us. Jesus is in the Holy Spirit when we receive Him, and the Holy Spirit is in the Father. He is God's Spirit. When we receive Jesus, we receive everyone, the God family.

> *But you belong to God, my dear children. You have already won a victory over those people, because the Spirit who lives in you is greater than the spirit who lives in the world (1 John 4:4, NLT).*

Every day is your day to walk in victory over everything that comes your way. You belong to the God family.

May 25

~ *You need the Holy Spirit to help you* ~

You do not have because you do not ask God (James 4:2, NIV).

25 May 2020. I asked Angelilly (my five-year-old) to put on her shoes so that I could take her to school. She was taking forever, so I went over to help her do it quickly. This is what the Holy Spirit taught me:

You see, many times you do not ask God to help you in what you are doing. You pray but you never ask Him to actually help you do it with you. If you had asked Him to help you, then many things that take you so long to do would have been done by now.

A good mother always asks the Holy Spirit to help her. She is so grateful that Jesus has helped her by providing a helper to support her all the time. Just as she is always available for her children to help them, 24/7, she can always seek the Holy Spirit all the time any time; He is always available 24/7 to help her.

Jesus said, 'He will give us the Holy Spirit to help us.'

> *Whatever you ask in my name, this I will do, that the Father may be glorified in the Son (John 14:13, ESV),*

> *But very truly I tell you, it is for your good that I am going away. Unless I go away, the Advocate will not come to you; but if I go, I will send him to you (John 16:7, NIV).*

The Holy Spirit lives in us and is our helper. He is a gentleman; His fruit is gentleness. He will only help us if we ask Him to. He will not force himself to do something we haven't asked Him to do. Every day let's ask God to help us in everything we want to do. He will help us through people or anyone who is in a better position to help us. The little things in our life matter to him. In the same way that we ask some members of our household to help us do this and that, we can also ask the Holy Spirit to help us do this and that. We are the house in which He lives and He will definitely help out.

> *If any of you lacks wisdom, let him ask God, who gives generously to all without reproach, and it will be given him (James 1:5, ESV).*

Ask God to give you the Spirit of wisdom to help you do everything concerning life.

May 26

~ Connecting to God ~

> *Remain in me, as I also remain in you. No branch can bear fruit by itself; it must remain in the vine. Neither can you bear fruit unless you remain in me (John 15:4, NIV).*

While I was charging my laptop I realized that it was not charging. I checked the connection of the charger to make sure that the power points were put firmly and right on the connector. This is what the Holy Spirit taught me: You see, a good mother is like that, she ensures that she is rightly connected to God's Word as she is the main supplier of power and energy to her household. God's Word is God's power that will constantly supply her with power. This is why she remains in Jesus, the Word that has become flesh.

The Holy Spirit is God's power working inside us to keep our spirit connected to Him. As long as we remain in Christ by abiding in His Word, we are connected to the Holy Spirit, and we are fully charged.

> *Now to him who is able to do immeasurably more than all we ask or imagine, according to his power that is at work within us, (Ephesians 3:20, NIV).*

Each and every day, fully connect and remain charged in God's Word.

May 27

~ *Pray without ceasing* ~

> *Rejoice always, pray without ceasing, give thanks in all circumstances; for this is the will of God in Christ Jesus for you (1 Thessalonians 5:16-18, ESV).*

I was thinking of taking an advance if my budget didn't make it through the month, and this is what the Holy Spirit taught me: You see, a good mother prays in advance for all her needs instead of taking an advance. She prays for all kinds of request. She prays in the spirit on all occasions with all kinds of prayers and requests. She prays without ceasing.

> *In the same way, the Spirit helps us in our weakness. We do not know what we ought to pray for, but the Spirit himself intercedes for us through wordless groans. And he who searches our hearts knows the mind of the Spirit, because the Spirit intercedes for God's people in accordance with the will of God. Romans 8: 26-27, NIV).*

The Holy Spirit prays for us in a language that God Himself understands. He sees each and every one of our thoughts for our future needs and worries in advance. You are His house of prayer to be a prayer warrior and not a stored house of worries.

> *Do not be like them, for your Father knows what you need before you ask him (Matthew 6:8, NIV).*

> *You know when I sit and when I rise; you perceive my thoughts from afar. You discern my going out and my lying down; you are familiar with all my ways. Before a word is on my tongue you, Lord, know it completely (Psalm 139:2-4, NIV).*

God knows what we will think about even when we haven't thought about it yet. Our thoughts are so precious to Him that He thinks about it all the time.

May 28

~ *Forgiveness* ~

> *Get rid of all bitterness, rage and anger, brawling and slander, along with every form of malice. Be kind and compassionate to one another, forgiving each other, just as in Christ God forgave you (Ephesians 4:31-32, NIV).*

A good mother always walks on the path of forgiveness. She understands that forgiveness is simply the act of changing your attitude towards the offender; it's moving from a desire to harm towards an openness to be at peace. She is in the business of peacemaking, not harming. The life of Abigail shows that kind of good mother.

The Holy Spirit inside us is the assurance that Jesus has cleansed and forgiven us with His precious blood. The love of God is freely moving inside us to go out and forgive someone who needs it.

> *Bear with each other and forgive one another if any of you has a grievance against someone. Forgive as the Lord forgave you (Colossians 3:13, NIV).*

When you forgive, you release yourself from being imprisoned by someone's mistake.

May 29

~ Control your SELF with the self-control fruit of the Spirit ~

> *Better a patient person than a warrior, with self-control than one who takes a city (Proverbs 16:32, NIV).*

A good mother is full of the self-control fruit of the Holy Spirit. This fruit controls her house to be in order even when she is losing it. She controls her SELF to stay under the influence of God's Word and bear the fruit of self-control.

The Holy Spirit's fruit of self-control, controls our SELF to not go astray. His voice steers and controls us to walk in the righteousness of God.

There are signs of growth and development when a good mother keeps her home in control by allowing the Holy Spirit to control her. She serves the self-control fruit of the Holy Spirit to build her home.

> *Under Christ's control the whole body is nourished and held together by its joints and ligaments, and it grows as God wants it to grow (Colossians 2:19, GNT).*

Each and every day control your SELF to not give in to any temptations or bad habits.

May 30

~Patience~

> *Love is patient, love is kind. It does not envy, it does not boast, it is not proud. It does not dishonor others, it is not self-seeking, it is not easily angered, it keeps no record of wrongs. (1 Corinthians 13:4-5, NIV).*

A good mother loves unconditionally; even if she is upset about a situation, it lasts only for a short time. She is full of patience and that causes her to be slow to anger. She fills up her patience by patiently and faithfully waiting on God to fulfil His promises to her.

One of the characters of the Holy Spirit is patience and as long as you fill yourself in the Word, you are filled in the Spirit and full of patience. The love of God in Christ through the Holy Spirit produces patience. Because God loves us so much, He is patiently waiting for us to return to Him before He returns for us.

> *The LORD is not slow in keeping his promise, as some understand slowness. Instead he is patient with you, not wanting anyone to perish, but everyone to come to repentance (2 Peter 3:9, NIV).*

Rise up to your day and fuel it with patience. Distribute it to anyone with whom you come into contact that needs it.

May 31

~ Your joy will be complete ~

But be very careful to keep the commandment and the law that Moses the servant of the Lord gave you: to love the Lord your God, to walk in obedience to him, to keep his commands, to hold fast to him and to serve him with all your heart and with all your soul. (Joshua 22:5, NIV).

A good mother serves her household with love. She makes sure that joy flows out from that love she actions towards her children. It makes her happy to see her children happy and so whatever she does, it is to make her children happy. Happy children, happy mother. She finds her happiness in Word and prayer.

The Holy Spirit is Love, and out of love flows joy which is one of His fruit. It is God's joy to see that we are joyful, for only then will His joy be complete.

I have told you this so that my joy may be in you and that your joy may be complete. (John 15:11, NIV).

Every new day is made with love by LOVE to love and be loved. To rejoice and be glad in the day that LOVE made. God is love.

JUNE

~ Cleaning your children's ears ~

> *Anyone with ears to hear must listen to the Spirit and understand what he is saying to the churches (Revelation 2:29, NLT)*

I clean my children's ears when I notice dirt in the entry to their ears. I believe this is what all the mothers do. This is what the Holy Spirit taught me: Every time you clean your children's ears remember that the shape of the ears has the shape of the handle of a cup. Your cup of the overflowing blessings will come from listening and hearing the Word of God. That is where faith comes from. A cup is lifted up by its handle that has the shape of an ear; you will be lifted up when your ears have been listening and hearing the Word of God. Also, when you put the two ears together, they form the shape of a heart. You have to keep listening and hearing the Word of God until it gets into your heart and shapes up your heart in love.

To maintain the position of a good woman or that good mother, you have to work on sharpening yourself in the Word of God to make your ears sharp to hearing the voice of the Holy Spirit so you can obey it. The Holy Spirit is a close friend. A friend sharpens a friend.

> *As iron sharpens iron, so a friend sharpens a friend (Proverbs 27:17, NLT).*

The Holy Spirit can only do His work of sharpening when we take in the Word of God. He works upon the Word of God to breathe life into it.

> *The Spirit gives life; the flesh counts for nothing. The words I have spoken to you—they are full of the Spirit and life (John 6:63, NIV).*

Because the Holy Spirit does the sharpening, the Word of God becomes alive and active and is even sharper than any two-edged sword.

> *For the Word of God is living and active, sharper than any two-edged sword, piercing to the division of soul and of spirit, of joints and of marrow, and discerning the thoughts and intentions of the heart (Hebrews 4:12, ESV).*

> *Whoever has ears, let them hear what the Spirit says to the churches. To the one who is victorious, I will give the right to eat from the tree of life, which is in the paradise of God (Revelation 2:7, NIV).*

A good mother understands that wherever she is, God planted her there. She nurtures herself in Word and prayer, so she can have ears that hear what the Spirit is saying. What she hears is actually eating from the Tree of Life. The Holy Spirit is the LIFE from the Tree of Life, which is Christ Jesus. He is the life of Christ, and He produces the fruit of righteousness from the Tree of Life.

Each day of the month of June and EVERY DAY, open your ears to listening and hearing the Word of God. This is where faith comes from. It comes from hearing and hearing the Word.

> *So then faith comes by hearing, and hearing by the Word of God (Romans 10:17, NKJV).*

Then store and hide the Word in your heart, it will pour out its light of truth that you will not sin.

I have hidden your word in my heart that I might not sin against you (Psalm 119:11, NIV).

****

June 1

~ Cheerful ~

If it is serving, then serve; if it is teaching, then teach; if it is to encourage, then give encouragement; if it is giving, then give generously; if it is to lead, do it diligently; if it is to show mercy, do it cheerfully. Love must be sincere. Hate what is evil; cling to what is good (Romans 12:7-9, NIV).

A good mother cheerfully does her act of services in her house. She is not worried about life's concerns as she knows how to get onto her knees and burden God with her worries. She is not afraid of the future because her heavenly Father controls her earthly future.

She is clothed with strength and dignity; she can laugh at the days to come (Proverbs 31:25, NIV).

The joy of the Lord gives her strength to laugh through all her days without fear and worry because she can do all things through Christ who strengthens her.

The Holy Spirit is the strength and power of God within us that produces joy for us to enjoy in our relationship with God the Father and Jesus the Son. The Holy Spirit is in charge and in control of every movement around us. We are to remain charged and connected to Him to go with His flow.

> *He gives strength to the weary and increases the power of the weak (Isaiah 40:29, NIV).*

Let no other relationship steal your joy in your relationship with the Father, Son and the Holy Spirit.

June 2

~ *Eternal life* ~

> *…and you are of Christ, and Christ is of God (1 Corinthians 3:23, NIV).*

A good mother is all love, she treats all her children's friends like her own and makes them feel they belong in her home. To belong is to be loved. The kingdom of God belongs to children. The kingdom of God, Jesus, is now residing inside her. She houses the Holy Spirit, the kingdom of the righteousness and Holiness of God. The living kingdom inside her draws children into her presence and all she has to do is welcome them and make them feel they belong. When they feel belonged, they feel loved.

> *But Jesus called them to him, saying, 'Let the children come to me, and do not hinder them, for to such belongs the kingdom of God.' (Luke 18:16, ESV).*

The Holy Spirit within us is the life and love of God through Jesus. When we have a personal relationship with Jesus, He becomes the head of our body in which we house His Holy Spirit. The Holy Spirit feels at home in our body when Christ becomes the head. God gave Jesus to us that we may have eternal life which is the Holy Spirit. Jesus is a child of God, and He belongs to the kingdom of God. Jesus belongs to us, for we house the Holy Spirit, the kingdom of God's righteousness that Jesus gave us.

> *For the wages of sin is death, but the free gift of God is eternal life in Christ Jesus our Lord (Romans 6:23, NIV).*

You have eternal life when you have the Holy Spirit living inside you and revealing who Jesus is.

June 3

~ Freedom ~

> *So Christ has truly set us free. Now make sure that you stay free, and don't get tied up again in slavery to the law (Galatians 5:1, NLT).*

When you love someone you let them do what they love to do and don't force them to do what they don't like to do. A good mother allows her children to choose what careers they would enjoy doing and not force them to do what she wants. She keeps them in God's will by praying for them.

The Holy Spirit is the love of Christ in action. Jesus came and gave us freedom from the slavery of sin, so we can live in His kingdom and be slaves to righteousness.

> *You have been set free from sin and have become slaves to righteousness (Romans 6:18, NIV).*

The old life in us is slave to sin and the new life in Christ is slave to righteousness. The wages of sin is death, and the wages of righteousness is eternal life in Christ Jesus. The Holy Spirit is the eternal life of Christ in us.

> *Now the Lord is the Spirit, and where the Spirit of the Lord is, there is freedom (2 Corinthians 3:17, NIV).*

Allow your loved ones to do what they would love to do. The kingdom of God is made out of love, where there is freedom.

June 4

~ A homemaker and not a home wrecker ~

> *Every wise woman builds up her household, but the foolish one tears it down with her own hands (Proverbs 14:1, ISV).*

A good mother works every day in her house to make it a home. She is a homemaker not a home wrecker to another home where she can steal the father of that house. She dedicates herself to building a better temple for the Holy Spirit to dwell within her, so that she will know how to build her house where her family can feel at home.

Your body is the house of the Holy Spirit and He works inside you all the time to prepare you to meet Christ where you will be at home with Him. The Holy Spirit builds you up in His fruit of righteousness, so you become the righteousness of God in Christ.

> *Celebrate God all day, every day. I mean, revel in him! Make it as clear as you can to all you meet that you're on their side, working with them and not against them. Help them see that the Master is about to arrive. He could show up any minute! (Philippians 4:4-5, MSG).*

Celebrate each day joyfully to meet the Master. Keep celebrating each day as it also brings you one day closer to meeting your Master.

June 5

~ Evil around us ~

And lead us not into temptation, but deliver us from the evil one. (Matthew 6:13, NIV).

Evilness is like a virus that is in the air all around us, and anyone can easily catch it if they allow themselves to keep in touch with it. The evil around us can only be overcome when we apply goodness. The goodness we apply may not completely remove evil as it will still be around us but it makes us victorious over evil. Women are the strength of their household and when they play with evil they burn down their house. A good mother is always good regardless of what kind of evil she comes into contact with. She spends time in Word and prayer every day. Goodness and mercy follow her all the days of her life as she dwells in the house of the Lord forever.

> *Even though I walk through the darkest valley, I will fear no evil, for you are with me; your rod and your staff, they comfort me. You prepare a table before me in the presence of my enemies. You anoint my head with oil; my cup overflows. Surely your goodness and love will follow me all the days of my life, and I will dwell in the house of the LORD forever (Psalm 23:4-6, NIV).*

The Holy Spirit inside us is God's goodness in action through the flesh of Jesus who, by the power of the Holy Spirit, conquered death and victoriously walked out of the grave. The Holy Spirit is now living inside us producing His fruit of righteousness for us to reproduce and conquer every evil around us or within us.

> *Don't let evil conquer you, but conquer evil by doing good (Romans 12:21, NLT).*

Every time the fruit of the knowledge of good and evil wants to raise its voice, we must silence it with the fruit of the Holy Spirit.

June 6

~ Love your enemies ~

> *Do not seek revenge or bear a grudge against anyone among your people, but love your neighbor as yourself. I am the Lord (Leviticus 19:18, NIV).*

A good mother not only teaches her children to be good to those that are good to them, but also to those that wrong them, and she also shows them how to do it. She reads Matthew 5:44-48 with her children, and they pray together for those that hurt them. She even gives gifts to her enemies to show her children that God's perfect love, Jesus, was also given to us as a gift. Children imitate parents' actions.

> *But I tell you, love your enemies and pray for those who persecute you, that you may be children of your Father in heaven. He causes his sun to rise on the evil and the good, and sends rain on the righteous and the unrighteous. If you love those who love you, what reward will you get? Are not even the tax collectors doing that? And if you greet only your own people, what are you doing more than others? Do not even pagans do that? Be perfect, therefore, as your heavenly Father is perfect (Matthew 5:44-48, NIV).*

You become perfect like your Father when you keep loving everyone that doesn't deserve your love like your enemies who curse you.

Only God's perfect love and gift, Jesus, can remove our curse. The one who has removed the curse with His love has asked us to love those that curse us with His love.

The Holy Spirit is the gift of Jesus to us. We open up that gift and release out His perfect love to the hurting and the ones that hurt us.

> *If your enemy is hungry, give him bread to eat, and if he is thirsty, give him water to drink, for you will heap burning coals on his head, and the Lord will reward you (Proverbs 25:21-22, ESV).*

Each and every day, release out the goodness of God that flows out from the gift of love to your enemies.

June 7

~ *Nourished in God's Word* ~

> *...since you have been born again, not of perishable seed but of imperishable, through the living and abiding Word of God; (1 Peter 1:23, ESV).*

The conscious mind is the gardener planting seeds, and the subconscious mind is the garden, fertile soil germinating the seed. What we constantly take into our conscious mind becomes our subconscious mind, and we produce the fruit of it naturally.

A good mother is like that conscious mind always doing things for her children, trying to plant them on the right path to their destiny. Prayer and the Word of God is where her source of strength flows from. Her children are her subconscious mind, and she speaks the

Word of Life from God's Word to nourish their lives and make them become that fertile soil, so the seed of God's Word can grow.

The Holy Spirit is the Spirit of God who is our gardener; we are His garden that He lives in to work. He nourishes us with Christ who is the Word, so we can stand strong and prosper through every season.

> *I am the true vine, and my Father is the gardener. He cuts off every branch in me that bears no fruit, while every branch that does bear fruit he prunes so that it will be even more fruitful. (John 15:1-2, NIV)*

Every day be that garden of God where He will visit you in fellowship in the morning and evening. He is to be praised from the rising of the sun to the setting of the sun. Keep on receiving into you the Word of God into your conscious mind to make it your subconscious mind.

June 8

~ The joy of hearing the voice of the Holy Spirit ~

A good wife is her husband's pride and joy... (Proverbs 12:4, GNT).

A good mother is a gift to anyone with whom she comes into contact, and whoever she is in touch with. She is her husband's pride and joy. When she opens her mouth, her words bring out beautiful surprises that light up her children's face. There are no bad or hurtful words in her speech.

The Holy Spirit is our gift from Jesus, and when we hear the voice of Jesus through Him, we light up in the delights of joy. It's God's joy to see us light up in joy. It's His voice that gives us the strength to continue to follow Him. The joy of the Lord is my strength.

> *This day is holy to our Lord. Do not grieve, for the joy of the Lord is your strength. (Nehemiah 8:10, NIV).*

The joy of receiving the most precious gift is from hearing the voice of Jesus giving light to our paths through the Holy Spirit inside us.

June 9

~ Our friend, Holy Spirit ~

A friend loves at all times (Proverbs 17:17, ESV).

A good mother treats her child like a friend, she understands that friends stick closer. So to be closer to and understand her child, she treats her like a treasured friend. She then tells her secrets to her child, and the child also does the same and opens up easily to her. A good mother's close friend is the Holy Spirit with whom she enjoys His company in Word and prayer.

> *A man of many companions may come to ruin, but there is a friend who sticks closer than a brother (Proverbs 18:24, ESV).*

The Holy Spirit is a friend when we hang out with Him constantly in His Word. He will reveal to us the secret of the kingdom of God. Jesus no longer sees us a servant but a friend, and a friend knows every movement and secret of his friend.

> *No longer do I call you servants, for the servant does not know what his master is doing; but I have called you friends, for all that I have heard from my Father I have made known to you (John 15:15, ESV).*

Every day grow closer to the Holy Spirit by spending time with Him in the Word. The Word of God attracts the Holy Spirit to come closer to you, and work upon the Word.

June 10

~ Building up in the righteousness of God ~

> *The wise woman builds her house, but with her own hands the foolish one tears hers down (Proverbs 14:1, NIV).*

Love is when you make time and give it to someone. You see, God is present with us 24/7 because He makes a new day and gives it to us. He makes time. When someone gives you their time, they are actually present with you. God is ever present with us; it is us who do not acknowledge His everyday presence.

A good mother works 24/7; she sacrifices her time and lays it down for her children. Everything she does is to meet her children's needs and comfort. She doesn't waste her time talking and minding about other people's lives because she is busy minding and building her house up in the righteousness of God.

> *For the kingdom of God is not a matter of eating and drinking, but of righteousness, peace and joy in the Holy Spirit, because anyone who serves Christ in this way is pleasing to God and receives human approval (Romans 14:17-18, NIV).*

The Holy Spirit is what Jesus gave us to house when we become the righteousness of God in Christ. He builds us up in His fruit of righteousness.

> *As you come to him, the living Stone—rejected by humans but chosen by God and precious to him— you also, like living stones, are being built into a spiritual house to be a holy priesthood, offering spiritual sacrifices acceptable to God through Jesus Christ (1 Peter 2:4-5, NIV).*

Love, joy and peace are the most beautiful precious stones of the Holy Spirit on which a good mother builds her home.

June 11

~ Christ-like mind is child-like character ~

> *And he said: 'Truly I tell you, unless you change and become like little children, you will never enter the kingdom of heaven (Matthew 18:3, NIV).*

A good mother makes God a priority in her home. She has a learning heart to allow her children to teach her of the kingdom of God with their characters. She teaches her children the Word of God while her children naturally teach her the kingdom lifestyle of God and how to live the faith with the belief of a child.

> *Whoever humbles himself like this child is the greatest in the kingdom of heaven (Matthew 18:4, ESV).*

The Holy Spirit is the faith in action of God's love, Jesus. The humble life of Jesus as a child of God and the kingdom of righteousness now lives in us. He is the Holy Spirit. He makes the Word of God we receive into us become alive to live in us. In the Holy Spirit, we have a Christ-like mind with a child-like character.

> *For, 'Who has known the mind of the Lord so as to instruct him?' But we have the mind of Christ. 1 Corinthians 2:16, NIV).*

Faith comes from listening and hearing the Word, and faith without action is dead. Without faith it is impossible to please God.

> *So also faith by itself, if it does not have works, is dead (James 2:17, ESV).*

Jesus is the faith in action, the Word that becomes flesh. His finished work is LIFE.

June 12

~ A servant heart ~

For no word from God will ever fail. (Luke 1:37, NIV)

Of all the virgins available and no matter how committed they were to God, He chose Mary to use her womb.

> *And Mary said, "Behold, I am the servant of the Lord; let it be to me according to your word." (Luke 1:38, ESV).*

It's that humble position Mary has, and God used her. Jesus even said I come to serve and not to be served. Because of her servant heart, her womb was used by God. Jesus also had a servant heart that wants to serve and not to be served. As a good mother it is now our role to serve our children and teach them to serve and not to be served when they are old enough to serve. When you serve, you action, and children follow examples. A good mother serves her children, knowing that she is serving the Lord through the service she provides to her children.

> *Slaves, obey your masters in all things. Do not obey just when they are watching you, to gain their favour, but serve them honestly, because you respect the Lord. In all the work you are doing, work the best you can. Work as if you were doing it for the Lord, not for people. Remember that you will receive your reward from the Lord, which he promised to his people. You are serving the Lord Christ (Colossians 3:22-24, NCV).*

Jesus is still serving us through His Spirit within us. The same Holy Spirit who conceived eternal life in a virgin servant girl's womb is inside us. He is serving us eternal life through His fruit of righteousness. The fruit of the Holy Spirit is our inheritance from God through the finished work of Jesus.

June 13

~ Meet Jesus and get connected to the Holy Spirit ~

> *Do not be like them, for your Father knows what you need before you ask him (Matthew 6:8, NIV).*

A good mother always has things in order, and on time ready for her children when the need arises. Therefore, her house is not in need, and she doesn't worry about what food to eat or drinks to drink. She builds her home in what her heavenly Father says in Matthew 6:8.

The Holy Spirit we house in us meets our need at the time we need it. And so, we are told not to worry about anything in life because the Holy Spirit is LIFE.

> *Therefore I tell you, do not worry about your life, what you will eat or drink; or about your body, what you will wear. Is not life more than food, and the body more than clothes? (Matthew 6:25, NIV).*

You are the body of Christ, and your life is hidden in His LIFE, so do not worry about the needs of your body. The Holy Spirit you house in your body is the LIFE, and HE will meet all the needs of your life.

> *And my God will meet all your needs according to the riches of his glory in Christ Jesus (Philippians 4:19, NIV).*

As long as you meet and connect well with the Holy Spirit through Jesus, He will meet all your needs. He has with Him the abundant life of Jesus.

June 14

~ *Be filled with the Holy Spirit* ~

> *Don't be drunk with wine, because that will ruin your life. Instead, be filled with the Holy Spirit, (Ephesians 5:18, NLT).*

A good mother has a prayer kind of life like Hannah. She takes her deepest aches to God, and moans and groans in prayer to Him. Her spirit talks like a drunkard that only God understands her special needs. She is drunk in the spirit with special needs that only God can understand.

> *Hannah was in deep anguish, crying bitterly as she prayed to the Lord (1 Samuel 1:10, NLT).*

The Holy Spirit also moans and groans on our behalf to God. He takes our cries and aches of needs to God in a way that only God can understands. It's this kind of spirit attitude that brings answered prayers. The kind that moves God.

> *In the same way, the Spirit helps us in our weakness. We do not know what we ought to pray for, but the Spirit himself intercedes for us through wordless groans (Romans 8:26, NIV).*

Every day drink the Word like wine and be filled in the Holy Spirit, then voice out your prayer in aches and pain like Hannah.

June 15

~ Sustaining life ~

> *He will renew your life and sustain you in your old age. For your daughter-in-law, who loves you and who is better to you than seven sons, has given him birth. (Ruth 4:15, NIV).*

Every mother sustains life in their unseen womb. A good mother will continue to sustain her children's life in the goodness of God, after she brings them into this world. She connects her life, and the little life of her child to the Word of life. She speaks that life from God's Word into the child. Man cannot live by bread alone but every Word that comes out of God's mouth.

> *Jesus answered, 'It is written: Man shall not live on bread alone, but on every word that comes from the mouth of God.' (Matthew 4:4, NIV).*

The Holy Spirit is the life of Christ unseen inside us. When we hear and hear the Word of God and receive it into us, the Holy Spirit brings the Word to life and sustains our life in the goodness of God. We become more like Christ each day.

> *It is the Spirit who gives life; the flesh is no help at all. The words that I have spoken to you are spirit and life (John 6:63, ESV).*

Keep listening and hearing, and receiving the Word of God into you, so the Holy Spirit can bring it to LIFE for you to live in.

June 16

~ *A broken – crushed spirit* ~

> *The spirit of a man will sustain him in sickness, But who can bear a broken spirit? (Proverbs 18:14, NKJV).*

When a good mother's health fails, her house starts to crash as there is no more flow of goodness. There is no more order in the house. She knows that she is the strength of her household, and her house has no strength to stand strong. Even in her sick bed she clings onto the Word of God, her rock of refuge. She is still grateful because it's during these hard and challenging days that she sees God giving her the strength, to continue to see the gift of a new day. All she whispers is Psalm 73:26.

> *My flesh and my heart may fail, but God is the strength of my heart and my portion forever. (Psalm 73:26, NIV).*

When the Holy Spirit no longer resides within us, there is no life and light in us. We live a ruined broken life. Our spirit is crushed and broken.

> *The Lord is near to the brokenhearted and saves the crushed in spirit (Psalm 34:18, ESV).*

It's during such hard times that we draw closer to God and seek His Word to heal us. God draws closer to us and strengthens and comforts us with His Spirit.

June 17

~ Making time for God ~

So teach us to number our days that we may get a heart of wisdom (Psalm 90:12, ESV).

A good mother makes time for God in her busy schedule. She will never say she has no time for prayer or Word. It is her life. She knows God made time for her. She also creates time for God in Word and prayer every day when God gives her all 24 hours of a day.

My times are in your hand; (Psalm 31:15, ESV).

Strength and dignity are her clothing, and she laughs at the time to come (Proverbs 31:25, ESV).

We are now living in the times of the Holy Spirit. He is the time and movement of Jesus within us. The Holy Spirit is the Spirit of wisdom, and wisdom is the timely word. He is our closest friend.

You can trust what your friend says, even when it hurts. But your enemies want to hurt you, even when they act nice (Proverbs 27:6, ERV).

A word of faith that heals up a wound at that moment is wisdom.

June 18

~ Image of love ~

I pray that from his glorious, unlimited resources he will empower you with inner strength through his Spirit. Then Christ will make his home in your hearts as you trust in him. Your roots will grow down into God's love and keep you strong (Ephesians 3: 16-17, NLT).

18 June 2020. Little Angelilly, gave me a little leaf that has the shape of love. She said, 'Mom, here is a love leaf for you.' This is what the Holy Spirit taught me: A good mother knows that to have the appearance and features of love, she must action love. When she actions love, she portrays the image of Christ. The beauty of life comes from the love of God in Christ, everything is beautiful with love and blooms well in love. Even at the times she doesn't receive love from her husband, the eternal love of God she receives inside her blooms beautifully and deeply from inside out.

But we don't need to write to you about the importance of loving each other, for God Himself has taught you to love one another. (1 Thessalonians 4:9, NLT).

The Holy Spirit inside us is the love of God. The Holy Spirit produces the characters of Jesus, which are the fruit of righteousness for us to reproduce and become the image of Christ, the love of God. Jesus is the visible love of God in action outside of us. He has gone back to the Father, so the Holy Spirit can come to us. The Holy Spirit is the visible love of God in Christ inside us that the world doesn't see and know.

> *The Spirit will show you what is true. The people of this world cannot accept the Spirit, because they don't see or know him. But you know the Spirit, who is with you and will keep on living in you (John 14:17, CEV).*

Be grateful every day, that you have what the world doesn't have and cannot give. You have what the Word of God can give, and that is the Holy Spirit.

June 19

~ *Giving God glory through acts of service* ~

> *After removing Saul, he made David their king. God testified concerning him: 'I have found David son of Jesse, a man after my own heart; he will do everything I want him to do.' (Acts 13:22, NIV).*

A good mother occupies the highest position of God's love in His heart. She is the woman after God's heart. Like King David, who was the man after God's heart because he always brought his broken heart to God, she too is always before God, with every broken piece stored within her heart, so God has made her the woman after His own heart. God is close to the brokenhearted.

> *The Lord is close to the brokenhearted and saves those who are crushed in spirit (Psalm 34:18, NIV).*

We are the slaves of righteousness which Jesus serves through the fruit of righteousness in the Holy Spirit. Jesus said, 'I came to serve and not to be served.' He is now serving us through the fruit of the Holy Spirit produced inside us. When we take the servants heart, God's glory is shown.

> He said to Me, 'You are My Servant, Israel, In Whom I will show My glory.' (Isaiah 49:3, NASB).

We were drawn closer to God at the cross where Jesus was broken for us. He cried out to God with a broken heart. We are the very reason Jesus offered a broken heart to the Father. Because of this, God is not only closer to us but is inside us through His Spirit.

> The Word became flesh and made his dwelling among us. We have seen his glory, the glory of the one and only Son, who came from the Father, full of grace and truth (John 1:14, NIV).

The Holy Spirit reveals to us, the glory of God, when we receive insights of who Jesus is in our lives.

Each and every day, spend time in Word and ask the Holy Spirit to reveal to you who Jesus is in your everyday living.

June 20

~ New creation in Christ ~

> Therefore, if anyone is in Christ, the new creation has come: The old has gone, the new is here! (2 Corinthians 5:17, NIV).

A good mother is creative in making her own new construction from the bad blocks that have been thrown onto her. She builds a strong foundation of her home on all those bricks of life's hardships. As long as she knows how to worship God in Spirit and truth, she is able to take hold of all those thoughts and make them obedient to Christ. She renews her mind to have the mind of Christ, so she can build her new image of the new creation in Christ Jesus.

> *We demolish arguments and every pretension that sets itself up against the knowledge of God, and we take captive every thought to make it obedient to Christ (2 Corinthian 10:5, NIV).*

> *For, 'Who has known the mind of the Lord so as to instruct him?' But we have the mind of Christ (1 Corinthians 2:16, NIV).*

The Holy Spirit breathes new life into our life. He gives us a new heart and a new spirit so we can live that new life. We just have to renew our mind all the time to live that new life. All we have to do is breathe into ourselves Psalm 51:10.

> *Create in me a pure heart, O God, and renew a steadfast spirit within me (Psalm 51:10, NIV).*

Every new day is a new opportunity to be renewed in the Word of God again and create and develop the image of Christ within us.

June 21

~ *Loving a rebellious child* ~

> *But God demonstrates his own love for us in this: While we were still sinners, Christ died for us (Romans 5:8, NIV).*

A good mother accepts her children regardless of how rebellious they may become in life. She loves them unconditionally and constantly tries to take them out of any mess they are in. From inside she gave birth to them and loves them regardless of how messed up they can be. She sees them the way she prayed for them. God sees and accepts you in the righteousness of Christ; He sees you as everything Christ laid down His life for; He sees you as victorious, a conqueror, and that you even have the power of authority. God sees you through what Christ paid for you, and not what you used to be.

The Holy Spirit inside you is the proof of the transaction that Jesus made. God loves you through the love Jesus laid down even while you were a sinner, and He loves you more and more through the Holy Spirit who produces the fruit of His love inside you, which you reproduce.

> *And hope does not put us to shame, because God's love has been poured out into our hearts through the Holy Spirit, who has been given to us (Romans 5:5, NIV).*

Remind yourself all the time that you are the righteousness of God in Christ, and the Holiness of God in the Holy Spirit. You are worth more than any price tag in this world.

June 22

~ Resting in God ~

> *Come to me, all you who are weary and burdened, and I will give you rest (Matthew 11:28, NIV).*

When you rest in God, you are resting from any worries of life. You are relaxing and enjoying your rest. When you sit on a lounge to rest, you do not do any physical work, you just sit and relax. Just say to yourself that the lounge is God you are resting on, you feel comfy, and the lounge is in your house, so you feel at home, and it belongs to you so you feel belonged. When you feel belonged you feel loved. It is the same with God; when you rest in God, He comforts you from your weariness and burdens. You feel at home, you feel belonged and complete because you house the Spirit of the Almighty.

Any child who comes home first wants to know before anything else if mother is at home. When Mom is at home, they feel at peace and relaxed. They get the comfort of just knowing that their mother's presence is there. A good mother provides that right atmosphere for her children because she carries the presence of God, and her home is heaven on earth.

> *The Lord replied, 'My Presence will go with you, and I will give you rest.' (Exodus 33:14, NIV).*

The Holy Spirit is the very presence of God that lives inside us. We carry the presence of God through the Holy Spirit. We feel loved, belonged, at peace and full of joy resting in our body that houses the Holy Spirit. He lives and works through us to get to others with whom we are in contact. When we serve others with the fruit of the Holy Spirit, we allow God to have access to others through us.

> *And I will ask the Father, and he will give you another advocate to help you and be with you forever (John 14:16, NIV).*

The Holy Spirit is our ever-present helper. He is here to stay forever in us to help others through us.

June 23

~ Hugging your children in prayers ~

> *I urge you, first of all, to pray for all people. Ask God to help them; intercede on their behalf, and give thanks for them (1 Timothy 2:1, NLT).*

A good mother calls her children regularly to check if they are doing all right. Her children are constantly on her mind and she prays for them all the time. They may no longer be with her in the same house. She may not call their names anymore or wake them up to live their daily schedule but in her heart she freshly wakes them up in prayer. She hugs her children all the time in prayer.

> *Direct your children onto the right path, and when they are older, they will not leave it (Proverbs 22:6, NLT).*

The Holy Spirit is the voice of God that breathes life into the Word, who is Jesus to be fresh, alive and active in our life when we take into us the Word. The Word of God someone spoke into you or you received from hearing it yourself is never wasted. One day, the Word will come to pass, and you will understand how God held you closer in His Word, even though you have gone astray.

> *I have gone astray like a lost sheep; seek your servant, for I do not forget your commandments (Psalm 119:176, ESV).*

> *Every single moment you are thinking of me! How precious and wonderful to consider that you cherish me constantly in your every thought! O God, your desires toward me are more than the grains of sand on every shore! When I awake each morning, you're still with me (Psalm 139:17-18, TPT).*

God thought of you today and woke you up to see and live in this beautiful day He made especially for you.

June 24

~ God's good will for us ~

> *Do not be misled, 'Bad company corrupts good character.' (1 Corinthians 15:33, NIV).*

Mothers know every development phase in their children, whether it be a good or bad habit a child develops, she knows. Her God given instincts mean that she knows her children well. A good mother will always use these bad developments as her working tools to develop a good character in her child.

> *For this very reason, make every effort to add to your faith goodness; and to goodness, knowledge; and to knowledge, self-control; and to self-control, perseverance; and to perseverance, godliness; and to godliness, mutual affection; and to mutual affection, love. (2 Peter 1:5-7, NIV).*

The Holy Spirit inside us is the greatest company that one could ever ask for. He has in store all the good habits of Jesus Christ that He wants to develop in us. We must just surrender our will into the Father's will for His good will to take effect in our lives.

> *Surrender to God! Resist the devil, and he will run from you (James 4:7, CEV).*

Move the wheels of your will only in the direction of God's will and God's will for you in heaven will unfold on earth.

June 25

~ Your story is written by God ~

> *The Spirit gives life; the flesh counts for nothing. The words I have spoken to you—they are full of the Spirit and life (John 6:63, NIV).*

A good mother actions God's love, just as Jesus became the flesh of love to give us access to being God's children. As the first person in her children's life a good mother is the voice of love for her child inspiring them to live a good life. She makes sure 2 Timothy 3:16 is her flesh, so she can be a good inspiration to her children.

> *All Scripture is God-breathed and is useful for teaching, rebuking, correcting and training in righteousness, (2 Timothy 3:16, NIV).*

You have God's Word that has become flesh, which is spirit and life through the Holy Spirit inside you (John 6:63, confirms this). God wrote your story the way He inspired the Bible that wrote the stories of prophets and kings.

> *For prophecy never had its origin in the human will, but prophets, though human, spoke from God as they were carried along by the Holy Spirit (2 Peter 1:21, NIV).*

Your life is inspired by the Holy Spirit; just seek Him and hear His voice, and what He says of you. Look inside you, and seek Him, and discover yourself. The Holy Spirit is God's love in action in spirit, and Jesus is God's love in action in flesh. Your love story is written by them for you to action it.

June 26

~ Sword of the Spirit ~

> *Take the helmet of salvation and the sword of the Spirit, which is the Word of God. And pray in the Spirit on all occasions with all kinds of prayers and requests. With this in mind, be alert and always keep on praying for all the Lord's people (Ephesians 6:17-18, NIV)*

The sword of the Holy Spirit is the teaching of God's Word, and it's the sword that frightens the devil away. It teaches the devil lessons that scare him. A mother's mouth is like a sword, she talks and talks. She can make or break down her household and all that is within. A good mother uses her tongue wisely. She is always in the Word and uses the sword of the Holy Spirit appropriately in all situations. She builds up her home in wisdom. She speaks timely words and that is wisdom. Every situation teaches her a lesson to better herself. She uses the sword of the Holy Spirit and chases the devil away from her household.

The Holy Spirit is the mouthpiece of God, the voice of God that speaks from within to build us up. He is the Spirit of wisdom that makes us become wise.

> *A house is built by wisdom and becomes strong through good sense (Proverbs 24:3, NLT).*

God's Word is wisdom, keep building yourself in the Word every day to become knowledgeable and wiser.

June 27

~Holy Spirit, our helper~

> *As for you, the anointing you received from him remains in you, and you do not need anyone to teach you. But as his anointing teaches you about all things and as that anointing is real, not counterfeit—just as it has taught you, remain in him (1 John 2:27, NIV).*

A good mother is an everyday helper, teaching and reminding her children all the time to do the necessary good things in their life.

She doesn't give up on her children. She keeps going until her child can master the skill. She seeks help from the Holy Spirit, the helper that Jesus gave her.

Because of what Jesus did the Father has given us the Holy Spirit as our helper and teacher to remind us always to do the right things. He wants to see us grow into becoming more like Christ, and He will never give up on us. The Holy Spirit is a gentleman, and He produces the fruit of gentleness. He will only help if we ask him to help us. A gentleman doesn't force himself on someone.

> *But the Helper, the Holy Spirit, whom the Father will send in my name, he will teach you all things and bring to your remembrance all that I have said to you (John 14:26, ESV).*

God will never give up on you so do not give up by giving in to the temptations of the evil one. Angels are all around to rescue you and the Holy Spirit is inside you to help you always.

June 28

~ Seeing through the eyes of faith ~

> *For no matter how many promises God has made, they are 'Yes' in Christ. And so through him the 'Amen' is spoken by us to the glory of God (2 Corinthians 1:20, NIV).*

A good mother has good eyes that look on the promises of God rather than the circumstances of her household. Just as God led Moses to the edge of the Promised Land and told him this:

> *'Send some men to explore the land of Canaan, which I am giving to the Israelites. From each ancestral tribe send one of its leaders' (Numbers 13:2, NIV).*

God is also giving her the land as He promised to His children. God didn't tell Moses to go and conquer and invade the land. No, He said, 'I am giving you the land.' And this is the story of a strong, courageous and good mother, she will not look at circumstances that say, 'No way…stay out…. there are giants in the land!'

> *They gave Moses this account: 'We went into the land to which you sent us, and it does flow with milk and honey! Here is its fruit. But the people who live there are powerful, and the cities are fortified and very large. We even saw descendants of Anak there (Numbers 13:27-28, NIV).*

Rather she will claim and receive God's promise that says 'The land is yours. The victory is yours…take it.'

She has the 'Caleb kind of faith'.

> *Then Caleb silenced the people before Moses and said, 'We should go up and take possession of the land, for we can certainly do it.' (Numbers 13:30, NIV).*

The Holy Spirit is being given to us through the victory of Jesus Christ. All the promises of God are received through Him. Now we inherit the eternal joy and peace from the victory of Jesus Christ. We can now not only be joyful of the victory of Jesus Christ but we are at peace because Jesus won the battle for us.

> *…by setting aside in his flesh the law with its commands and regulations. His purpose was to create in himself one new humanity out of the two, thus making peace, (Ephesians 2:15, NIV).*

Victoriously step into your day with your inner peace, and it will shut out any disturbance that seeks to knock on your door.

June 29

~ The Holy Spirit guides ~

When the Spirit of truth comes, he will guide you into all truth. He will not speak on his own but will tell you what he has heard. He will tell you about the future (John 16:13, NLT).

A good mother is like a professional tour guide, she guides her children and leads them on the right path that leads to the destiny God has planned for her children. She connects herself every day to the Word of God and goes by the voice of the Word.

The Holy Spirit is the guide to our new life in Christ. He leads us on the path of life to become more like Jesus every day. The Word of God that we receive into us is God's guideline that the Holy Spirit breathes upon it to guide our lives.

So I say, let the Holy Spirit guide your lives. Then you won't be doing what your sinful nature craves (Galatians 5:16, NLT).

As long as you house the Holy Spirit, your flesh will be guided to move by the Word that has become flesh.

June 30

~ God is closer to the brokenhearted ~

Praise be to the God and Father of our Lord Jesus Christ, the Father of compassion and the God of all comfort, who comforts us in all our troubles, so that we can comfort those in any trouble with the comfort we ourselves receive from God (2 Corinthians 1:3-4, NIV).

A good mother never abandons her children when they are broken. She is always there comforting them and going through their pain with them until they come out of it. And even when they come out of it, she is still there for them.

The Holy Spirit is our great comforter and is closer to us when we are broken. He is the very breath we breathe. He will never leave nor forsake us. He prays on our behalf to the Father. Break yourself in the Word and He will mend you in His Word.

> *The Lord is close to the brokenhearted and saves those who are crushed in spirit (Psalm 34:18, NIV).*

When you are broken, your friends and families may neglect you, but not God. When you are broken, He gets closer to you to comfort and save you.

JULY

~ A mother's role of feeding her family ~

> *That is why I tell you not to worry about everyday life—whether you have enough food and drink, or enough clothes to wear. Isn't life more than food, and your body more than clothing? (Matthew 6:25, NLT).*

I was feeding my one-year-old son and like all other mothers it worries me a bit when our children do not eat what we offer. As mothers we will give our kids the best we can afford that is good for them. We try as much as possible to give them healthy and good food.

This is what the Holy Spirit taught me: The kingdom of God is like this; God said, do not worry about what you are going to eat or drink because He is going to provide. He is a good Father, and when He provides for our physical food, our health is also provided. The physical food keeps us strong and healthy. This is God's gift to us.

> *And people should eat and drink and enjoy the fruits of their labor, for these are gifts from God. (Ecclesiastes 3:13, NLT).*

God works when we pray, and His Spirit works when we take in His Word. Everything is done in Jesus, the Word of God that has become flesh.

When we take in His Word He sustains us with health and more strength. Getting spiritual food gives access to receiving physical food. Whatever is loose on earth will be loosed in heaven.

> *And I will give you the keys of the kingdom of heaven, and whatever you bind on earth will be bound in heaven, and whatever you loose on earth will be loosed in heaven.'(Matthew 16:19, NKJV).*

For God to provide us with physical food adequately, we must give Him access spiritually by taking in the spiritual food of His Word. We know that fruit is nutritious and good for our physical health, in the same way as the fruit of the Holy Spirit is good for our spiritual and physical health and wellbeing.

> *But the fruit of the Spirit is love, joy, peace, patience, kindness, goodness, faithfulness, gentleness, self-control; against such things there is no law (Galatians 5:22-23, ESV).*

The things of the spirit sustain both our physical and spiritual being. Our spirit is connected to the Holy Spirit and is housed in our physical body. Our physical needs are automatically met when we meet our spiritual needs, because God is the source of everything, and is in control.

Each day of the month of July and EVERY DAY get God to work in your life by praying and get the Holy Spirit to work on your life by listening and hearing the Word of God. The Holy Spirit works upon the Word of God to bring it into the physical realm. God spoke the Word in the beginning to create, and the Holy Spirit carried out the work. When we pray, we get God to work, and when we receive into us the Word of God, the Holy Spirit sets out to work inside us.

> *In the beginning was the Word, and the Word was with God, and the Word was God (John 1:1, NIV).*

In the beginning God created the heavens and the earth. Now the earth was formless and empty, darkness was over the surface of the deep, and the Spirit of God was hovering over the waters (Genesis 1:1-2, NIV).

July 1

~ *The inner strength* ~

So the Lord God caused the man to fall into a deep sleep; and while he was sleeping, he took one of the man's ribs and then closed up the place with flesh (Genesis 2:21, NIV).

God invented sleep when He put Adam into a deep sleep and removed his rib to fashion a woman. The reason we need sleep is to recharge our strength to wake up to another gift of life. The woman was the inner strength of the man taken from within him then given to him when he was awake. The man said, 'Wow, bone of my bone and flesh of my flesh.' He was referring to strength. A good mother is the strength of her household. She is the inner strength to her husband, and she is always strong for her children. She seeks God's strength in His Word to keep getting stronger and stronger.

Then the Lord God made a woman from the rib he had taken out of the man, and he brought her to the man. The man said, 'This is now bone of my bones and flesh of my flesh; she shall be called 'woman,' for she was taken out of man.' (Genesis 2:22-23, NIV).

The Holy Spirit is the strength of Jesus, and this is why Jesus said we can do even greater things than Him because He is going to the Father (John 14:12-14). The Holy Spirit is the Spirit of the Father;

He is the strength from within the Father in which Jesus lives. And because Jesus lives in us, we live in Him too.

> *On that day you will realize that I am in my Father, and you are in me, and I am in you (John 14:20, NIV).*

The glory, power and strength of the kingdom of God is here, and He is the Holy Spirit.

July 2

~ Holy Spirit interceding on our behalf ~

> *In the same way the Spirit also helps our weakness; for we do not know how to pray as we should, but the Spirit Himself intercedes for us with groanings too deep for words; and He who searches the hearts knows what the mind of the Spirit is, because He intercedes for the saints according to the will of God. (Romans 8:26-27, NASB).*

Most often, a child will bring their needs to the mother. A good mother always consults the Holy Spirit to involve Him before she takes her children's needs to their father to be discussed.

A good mother creates the best plans for her children with their father. She intercedes and communicates on behalf of the child to the father in their language of love so that together they can create something that is better for their child.

This is what the Holy Spirit does on our behalf to the Father. He intercedes on our behalf to the Father in moans and groans that only the Father knows in their language of love.

He lives in our heart, and He knows what we want even before we ask in prayer. And so He answers before we even ask.

> *Before they call I will answer; while they are still speaking I will hear (Isaiah 65:24, NIV).*

Appreciate and give thanks to the Holy Spirit for always being there already to our needs even before our needs arise.

July 3

~ Feeling valued ~

> *The living, the living—they praise you, as I am doing today, parents tell their children about your faithfulness (Isaiah 38:19, NIV).*

3 July 2019. I was thinking of those little things my five-year-old would do to try to help me. Most of the time it wasn't in the way I wanted, but she felt important by doing something to help. This is what the Lord taught me in my thinking: A good mother always appreciates everything their children do. When you keep appreciating all the things your child does in obeying you, they feel that they belong and are of value. When they feel they belong, they feel loved and accepted. They will keep obeying you, so that they can see their value to you.

The Holy Spirit is well pleased with us when we walk in obedience to the Father's will. He is God's will in Christ for us to rejoice in always, pray continually, and to give thanks and appreciate every situation in our lives. We must always accept and appreciate both the good and the bad things we receive in life.

Should we accept only good things from the hand of God and never anything bad? So in all this, Job said nothing wrong (Job 2:10, NLT).

Rejoice always, pray continually, give thanks in all circumstances; for this is God's will for you in Christ Jesus (1 Thessalonians 5:16-18, NIV).

This is a new day to rise up and rejoice in the Lord with prayers of thanksgiving.

July 4

~ God made a good woman and a good mother ~

The LORD God said, 'It is not good for the man to be alone. I will make a helper suitable for him.' (Genesis 2:18, NIV).

4 July 2019. While out jogging in the morning, the Holy Spirit spoke to me saying, 'Everything God created was good'. But then, God said it was not good for man to be alone, so He created a woman for the man, and of course she was a good woman because everything God made was good. Sadly, she was deceived and disobeyed God. To bring His Son into the world, God had to create a good mother and this is where He released His Holy Spirit into the womb of the virgin to conceive the birth of His Son.

A mother goes through the journey of NINE MONTHS of pregnancy to bring a life into the world. We too have to produce the NINE FRUIT of the Holy Spirit all the time to give birth to the life of Christ in us. The devil easily deceived the first woman which caused the whole of the human race to fall into sin. The devil could not deceive the virgin woman whose womb God used because the Spirit of truth was inside her.

> *Now the Spirit expressly says that in later times some will depart from the faith by devoting themselves to deceitful spirits and teachings of demons, (1 Timothy 4:1, ESV).*

A good mother fills herself in the Holy Spirit every day so that she cannot be deceived and fooled by the lies of devil.

> *Do not get drunk on wine, which leads to debauchery. Instead, be filled with the Spirit, speaking to one another with psalms, hymns, and songs from the Spirit. Sing and make music from your heart to the LORD, always giving thanks to God the Father for everything, in the name of our LORD Jesus Christ (Ephesians 5:18-20, NIV).*

God made a suitable helper for the man from within Him, and she was deceived by the father of lies and darkness. Be grateful to Jesus that through Him, we now have a suitable helper who is from within the Father of truth and light, and the father of lies and darkness can no longer deceive us.

July 5

~ The strength of a mother ~

> *Your words were found, and I ate them, and your words became to me a joy and the delight of my heart, for I am called by your name, O Lord, God of hosts (Jeremiah 15:16, ESV).*

Every mother is strong because of her children. A good mother activates her strength when she awakes to a new day. She knows that the joy of the Lord is her strength. She fills herself with the joy of the Lord in Word and prayer, and with praise and gratitude in her heart. Once she does that she knows that she is now stronger to carry her children through the day.

> *This day is holy to our Lord. Do not grieve, for the joy of the Lord is your strength.' (Nehemiah 8:10, NIV).*

The Holy Spirit makes Jesus come alive inside of us and produces the joy of God's character. A good mother actions that with gratitude and thanksgiving. It's a joy knowing that Jesus is alive through His Spirit inside us.

> *Satisfy us in the morning with your unfailing love, that we may sing for joy and be glad all our days (Psalm 90:14, NIV).*

A woman is taken out of a man and so she is his inner strength. Children come out of a woman; they are a mother's strength.

July 6

~ Word become flesh ~

> *'For I know the plans I have for you,' declares the Lord, 'plans to prosper you and not to harm you, plans to give you hope and a future' (Jeremiah 29:11, NIV).*

When we come to know God as a friend, as did Abraham, then we will never doubt Him. We will just praise Him for His greatness and His control and power. A good mother has no doubts about her tomorrow. She smiles into the future not because she knows the future of her household but because she knows who God is. God is not only a Father but her close friend who she trusts completely and shares her future with.

Jesus has given us hope and a future through the gift of His Holy Spirit inside us.

He is our close friend, and He knows what we want before we ourselves discover what we want. God knows what is best for us, and we will only come to know what is best for us when we know God. Knowing God is knowing your SELF in the new life of Jesus.

> *Christ is the visible image of the invisible God. He existed before anything was created and is supreme over all creation, (Colossians 1:15, NLT).*

Jesus is the visible body image of the God family. The Word has become flesh so we can action the Word with our body, and make our flesh become the Word of God.

July 7

~ Reflect, recharge and renew in the Word ~

True, God made everything beautiful in itself and in its time (Ecclesiastes 3:11, MSG).

A good mother reflects, recharges and renews herself in the Word every day. She is thankful for every moment all the time. She creates beautiful moments every day because God made everything beautiful in its time.

Every mother is busy and tired but a good mother keeps going because she knows how to recharge herself. She reflects on her plans and schedules and commits them all to God by recharging herself in prayer. She spends time in the Word and renews herself in the mercies of God. She always asks for God's mercy so she can make it through each day.

The Holy Spirit who lives within us is God's Spirit who is plugged in to God ready to charge and connect whoever connects through Him from within. He is new all the time with God's mercy to renew us.

> *The steadfast love of the Lord never ceases; his mercies never come to an end; they are new every morning; great is your faithfulness. 'The Lord is my portion,' says my soul, 'therefore I will hope in him. 'Lord is good to those who wait for him, to the soul who seeks him (Lamentation 3:22-25, ESV).*

Each morning of every day, stay hydrated in the living water of God's Word, and reflect, recharge and renew yourself in God's mercy.

July 8

~ *Walk by the Spirit* ~

> *Devote yourselves to prayer, being watchful and thankful (Colossians 4:2, NIV)*

A good mother carries her life well as she starts her day feeding into the Word of God in prayer before being distracted by her day's schedule. She would rather be distracted by God's plan and schedules than her own.

The Holy Spirit within us is our day's schedule as soon as He awakens our spirit to live another day. We have to feed our spirit with the food of the Spirit to walk in the Spirit and not the flesh in this physical world.

> *So I say, walk by the Spirit and you will not gratify the desires of the flesh. For the flesh desires what is contrary to the Spirit, and the Spirit what is contrary to the flesh. They are in conflict with each other, so that you are not to do whatever you want (Galatians 5:16-17, NIV).*

Each and every day, submit your plans and schedule into God's plans and schedule and your day will go well.

July 9

~ Storing the Word ~

I am the Lord your God, who brought you up out of Egypt. Open wide your mouth and I will fill it (Psalm 81:10, NIV).

7 December 2019. I remember opening a 2 L bottle of Coke to pour into a 250 ml bottle of Coke. The Holy Spirit pointed out to me the size of the mouth of the 2 L and the 250 ml bottle and taught me this: You see, it doesn't matter how big or small the bottle container is. They both have the same mouth size, so the same lid can fit onto both. God's Word is big and great and we receive and store it. The Word can fit into all of our mouths when it is released to us. It's about how available an individual is to keep taking in the Word; the more someone keeps taking in the Word, the bigger their heart grows to receive more of the Word and contain it. Someone who keeps receiving the Word has a bigger storage capacity within them like that of the 2 L Coke. There is enough to refresh themselves and others.

All mothers speak words that have an influencing power. What mothers have inside them is poured out to serve their household. A good mother pours out her heart to God in prayer and refills herself with the Word. She contains the Word, and when she speaks it is with grace and light to give direction to her children.

> *Wise words satisfy like a good meal; the right words bring satisfaction (Proverbs 18:20, NLT).*

Jesus is the Word that gives us light through the Holy Spirit so we can walk in His righteousness to the Father. The Holy Spirit produces His fruit of righteousness within us so we can refill ourselves and burn it out in action as we journey heavenward.

Your word is a lamp for my feet, a light on my path (Psalm 119:105, NIV).

Keep receiving and storing the Word every day. The Word you contain will help in your times of need and others as well.

July 10

~ *God with us* ~

For I am convinced that neither death nor life, neither angels nor demons, neither the present nor the future, nor any powers, neither height nor depth, nor anything else in all creation, will be able to separate us from the love of God that is in Christ Jesus our Lord (Romans 8:38-39, NIV).

Parents love it when their grown up children, who are leading their own lives, are able to live closer to them. A good mother prays and holds her children deep in her heart. Even when they are adults, and have their own lives, there is still a bond that brings them closer to their mother. She connects her children in the love of God in Romans 8:38–39. As long as it's the love of God that connects them, nothing will come between them to separate them.

Nothing can ever separate us from God's love. His love in action, Jesus, is now living inside us through the Holy Spirit that we house. God is not only living closer to us but He lives inside us through His Spirit. He is Emmanuel, God with us.

Behold, a virgin shall be with child, and shall bring forth a son, and they shall call his name Emmanuel, which being interpreted is, God with us (Matthew 1:23, KJV).

He is not the God of the dead, but of the living, for to him all are alive.' (Luke 20:38, NIV).

Flesh has become Word. God breathed into man and He became alive. God is now living with us in His Spirit that Emmanuel gave.

July 11

~ Testing of Faith ~

'Look!' he answered, 'I see four men loose, walking in the midst of the fire; and they are not hurt, and the form of the fourth is like the Son of God.'(Daniel 3:25, NKJV).

A good mother knows she will get burnt out most of the time as she constantly serves her household. The furnace of performing household roles brings her many tests. She makes a daily time where she can refill herself and sit in the council of God's Word, so she can sit comfortably in her test. At the end of the test she always comes out shining more than before.

It's right here in her furnace that the image of Christ comes out of her. Daniel and his friends went through their furnace until the image of Christ appeared among them. Whatever price she has to pay she will go through it with her house until the image of Christ appears.

The Holy Spirit produces His fruit inside us so that we too can produce that fruit to bring out the image of Christ for others to see. To bring out the image of Christ, you have to at least burn out producing the good fruit of the Spirit to someone who betrays you and doesn't deserve your love. The Holy Spirit is right inside you to help do it with you.

> *In this you rejoice, though now for a little while, if necessary, you have been grieved by various trials, so that the tested genuineness of your faith—more precious than gold that perishes though it is tested by fire—may be found to result in praise and glory and honour at the revelation of Jesus Christ (1 Peter 1:6-7, ESV).*

Every day, look forward to sitting your test; some can catch you by surprise. Life is a gift and is full of surprises.

July 12

~ *Giving glory to God* ~

> *Bring my sons from afar and my daughters from the ends of the earth— everyone who is called by my name, whom I created for my glory, whom I formed and made. (Isaiah 43:6-7, NIV).*

A mother is always on call to serve. A good mother never complains, she serves with all her heart because she knows this is an opportunity to give glory to God. She gives all her services cheerfully and this is where she finds new strength to serve more.

> *Each one must give as he has decided in his heart, not reluctantly or under compulsion, for God loves a cheerful giver (2 Corinthians 9:7, ESV).*

The Holy Spirit produces the joy of God all the time, and He is the power and strength of Jesus by which the life of Jesus is produced in us.

To give God glory is to serve in whatever you do as serving the Lord, not man.

When God blesses and surrounds you with favour He is taking you from glory to glory for His glory and from strength to strength. And with this you also step up to a new level to give more glory to God.

> *Praise and glory and wisdom and thanks and honor and power and strength be to our God for ever and ever. Amen! (Revelation 7:12, NIV).*

To give God everything back in all you do is to give God glory in whatever you do with the strength God gives you each day. When God sees the character of Jesus in your characters which the Holy Spirit has produced in you, He is glorified through you.

July 13

~ Jesus, the wisdom of God ~

> *...but to those whom God has called, both Jews and Greeks, Christ the power of God and the wisdom of God (1 Corinthians 1:24, NIV).*

A good wife is given and from that good wife you gain a good mother who builds her house on wisdom. She asks God for wisdom and God, who is Jesus, gives her wisdom. As long as she is connected to Jesus every day she produces the fruit of righteousness in her house. Wisdom is given as a gift (Jesus), and from that you gain knowledge, understanding, power, fear of the Lord and council of the Lord. Love is given as a gift and from it you gain love, joy, peace, goodness, kindness, patience, gentleness, self-control and faithfulness. Jesus is the wisdom given to us by God who gave us the Holy Spirit, the Spirit of wisdom.

> *It is because of him that you are in Christ Jesus, who has become for us wisdom from God—that is, our righteousness, holiness and redemption (1 Corinthians 1:30, NIV).*
>
> *The Spirit of the LORD will rest on him – the Spirit of wisdom and of understanding, the Spirit of counsel and of might, the Spirit of the knowledge and fear of the LORD – (Isaiah 11:2, NIV).*

God gave us His wisdom, Jesus, and Jesus gave us the Spirit of wisdom, the Holy Spirit.

July 14

~ Living waters ~

> *Whoever believes in me, as the Scripture has said, 'Out of his heart will flow rivers of living water'. (John 7:38, ESV).*

Living LIFE each day is hearing and drinking from the fountain of life from within. Any woman can bring a life into this world but a good mother knows how to nourish this life to make it a purposeful life. Every day she drinks from the fountain of life and makes sure that she remains connected, so that fresh living water can flow out from her to all that she serves in all seasons.

> *On that day living waters shall flow out from Jerusalem, half of them to the eastern sea and half of them to the western sea. It shall continue in summer as in winter (Zachariah 14:8, ESV).*

The Holy Spirit is given as a gift from the living water to remain in us. He serves us by producing the fruit of righteousness through all seasons, so we can serve all with whom we come into contact with.

> *Jesus answered her, 'If you knew the gift of God and who it is that asks you for a drink, you would have asked him and he would have given you living water.' (John 4:10, NIV).*

Refresh yourself in the living waters every day and live that life you were called to live.

July 15

~ Be wise ~

> *Therefore everyone who hears these words of mine and puts them into practise is like a wise man who built his house on the rock (Matthew 7:24, NIV).*

A good mother is wise in spending her time on what is wise. She knows that because even God's foolishness is wiser than humans' wisdom. She spends more time in God's wisdom, which is His Word. It's the Word she receives into her that causes the Holy Spirit to breathe life into it to make it flesh.

> *The wise person has his eyes in his head, but the fool walks in darkness (Ecclesiastes 2:14, ESV).*

The Holy Spirit is the Spirit of wisdom to make us wise in how we spend our life every day. When we look carefully into the Word of God we will see how Jesus walks wisely in His Spirit.

> *So be very careful how you live, not being like those with no understanding, but live honorably with true wisdom, for we are living in evil times. Take full advantage of every day as you spend your life for his purposes (Ephesians 5:15-16, TPT).*

Every day spend more time gaining LIFE from God's Word of wisdom rather than on gaining the riches of this world.

July 16

~ Comforted by the Word of God ~

> *As a mother comforts her child, so will I comfort you; and you will be comforted over Jerusalem (Isaiah 66:13, NIV).*

A good mother comforts her children with words from the Word of God. She is that mother who keeps her heart quiet and gently applies the Word of God. So her spirit within her can be quiet and gentle. This is how she makes her heart beautiful and of great worth in God's sight.

> *Rather, it should be that of your inner self, the unfading beauty of a gentle and quiet spirit, which is of great worth in God's sight (1 Peter 3:4, NIV).*

The Holy Spirit is the eternal beauty of God's love that pours out peace and joy into our life giving us hope to live each day. He is a gentleman who comforts us when we give Him a position within our heart.

> *And hope does not put us to shame, because God's love has been poured out into our hearts through the Holy Spirit, who has been given to us (Romans 5:5, NIV).*

Each and every day learn and lean on God's Word to comfort you. You will never look at anything from this world to comfort you if you can find your comfort and rest in God's promises.

July 17

~ Feasting in the fruit of the Holy Spirit).

You prepare a table before me in the presence of my enemies. You anoint my head with oil; my cup overflows (Psalm 23:5, NIV).

She prepares a table for her house to sit and dine and in her mind she smiles. She is reminded of how God prepared a table for her in front of her enemies to feast. As long as she is eating what God has prepared for her, the enemy will never interrupt her when she is eating what God is serving her.

A good mother renews her mind constantly to connect what she does to what God is doing. She fills her mind to the good things of God's Word. If she is resting, she renews her mind to know she is resting also in God's peace.

The Holy Spirit is always preparing the fruit of righteousness for us to feast on. He prepares it for us to feast on in front of our enemies. When we feast on love, joy, peace, goodness, patience, kindness, faithfulness and self-control, the enemy cannot offend us or interrupt our life in any way.

> *For the kingdom of God is not a matter of eating and drinking, but of righteousness, peace and joy in the Holy Spirit, because anyone who serves Christ in this way is pleasing to God and receives human approval (Romans 14:17-18, NIV).*

Celebrate each day by feasting on the fruit of righteousness all the days of your life.

July 18

~ Make the Holy Spirit feel at home ~

Then Jesus called for the children and said to the disciples, 'Let the children come to me. Don't stop them! For the Kingdom of God belongs to those who are like these children (Luke 18:16, NLT).

A good mother loves the treasures of the Word, not the treasure of the world. She shelters and feed herself in the Word. She knows she belongs to the Word, and so she brings all her belongings and surrenders them to the will of God in His Word. She will always be her Father's little child who belongs to His Father's kingdom. She feels belonged and loved. In that condition she can now pour out love to everyone who belongs in her household.

We know and believe God loves us and sent His Son to die for us so the Holy Spirit can come and live inside us. When we house and feed the Holy Spirit in the Word of God He feels at home, and we can literally feel that we belong and are loved by experiencing the goodness of God.

We do not belong to this world; we belong to the kingdom of God. He loved the world so much, because we are in the world, and so He sent His LOVE in the form of flesh to rescue us.

To feel at home with God, let's not lust after the things of this world, but love the things of the Kingdom with a child-like character of Christ-like mind.

> *For everything in the world—the lust of the flesh, the lust of the eyes, and the pride of life—comes not from the Father but from the world (1 John 2:16, NIV).*

Love is a person and He makes you feel belonged with His actions towards you. God is love. Jesus now actions God's love inside us through the fruit of the Holy Spirit.

July 19

~ *The joy of life* ~

This is the day that the Lord has made; let us rejoice and be glad in it (Psalm 118:24, ESV)

A good mother wakes up in the morning and cheerfully strengthens her children with joy to look forward to seeing goodness in their day. She talks to them with much joy and love. Within, her heart beats with delights to God's Word in Psalm 16:11:

You will show me the way of life, granting me the joy of your presence and the pleasures of living with you forever.

Before they go to sleep, she asks them how their day was, and speaks more light from God's Word into them.

She knows that the joy of the Lord is her strength to keep her house functioning well.

The Holy Spirit produces joy inside us all the time to rejoice for the day the Lord has made. He is the eternal Spirit of God given to live inside us in all our days of life. Each and every day we should be renewing our mind in Christ's mind in Psalm 27:4.

I ask only one thing, Lord: Let me live in your house every day of my life to see how wonderful you are and to pray in your temple (Psalm 27:4, CEV).

July 20

~ Love is kindness ~

Watch out! Be on your guard against all kinds of greed; life does not consist in an abundance of possessions. (Luke 12:15, NIV).

One day on 20 July 2019 I remember a vision where I saw myself fighting with empty space or the air. I was throwing my hands as if waving. Then, I heard the Holy Spirit speaking into my heart, saying, it's the dark forces of air that fight with you, not flesh and blood.

> *For our struggle is not against flesh and blood, but against the rulers, against the authorities, against the powers of this dark world and against the spiritual forces of evil in the heavenly realms (Ephesians 6:12, NIV).*

You see, that empty space when your SELF is in greed and envious of something others have, has created an empty space for that spirit of envy to occupy and that gives access for this dark force to attack you. This is how someone feels jealousy towards another person. They want what others have. A good mother is clothed with love and kindness flows out of that love. There is no space for greed or jealousy.

> *When she speaks, her words are wise, and she gives instructions with kindness (Proverbs 31:26, NLT).*

The Holy Spirit is the love of Christ in action and that love produces kindness.

But when the kindness and love of God our Saviour appeared, he saved us, not because of righteous things we had done, but because of his mercy. He saved us through the washing of rebirth and renewal by the Holy Spirit, whom he poured out on us generously through Jesus Christ our Saviour, (Titus 3:4-6, NIV).

Whenever you become jealous of someone because they have what you think you deserve put out that ferocious fire of jealousy with a water bucket of kindness towards that person; surprise them with a gift.

July 21

~ Mustard seed faith that moves mountains ~

Lazy people should learn a lesson from the way ants live. They have no leader, chief, or ruler, but they store up their food during the summer, getting ready for winter (Proverbs 6:6-8, GNT).

The bible tells us to learn from ants. They are tiny yet they work hard to store up food and are never lazy. A good mother always starts small with her small mustard seed of faith, and that's how she can move mountains. Even if it is only a little financial saving she does for her children's future, she applies the fruit of the Holy Spirit by patiently doing it with faith. God is faithful in His patience towards us.

We do not want you to become lazy, but to imitate those who through faith and patience inherit what has been promised (Hebrews 6:12, NIV).

The Holy Spirit is God's action of patience and faithfulness towards us. We are small like an ant to Him yet He is patient in what we do for Him. He is always faithful and remains so even when we fail Him most of the time with our lack of faith.

> *And he was patient with them for 40 years in the desert (Acts 13:18, ERV).*

Just as ants store their food, we too must store the Word of God; it is our mustard seed faith to move our mountains.

July 22

~ *Freshen up someone with Gods Word* ~

Then the Lord God formed a man from the dust of the ground and breathed into his nostrils the breath of life, and the man became a living being (Genesis 2:7, NIV).

This happened on 22 July 2019 and I wrote it down in my journal.

There is a steel water bottle that I have which is rainbow in colour. I thought to myself, 'the water is not only so cool in there but it tastes so fine too when I drink it'. This is what the Holy Spirit taught me: You see, the kingdom of God is like this, you are made out of the Word of God. The Word created you and you need the Word of God inside you so that whatever words come out of you will be refreshing and satisfying to anyone who hears them.

A good mother knows this secret and so she stores within her the Word of God so that every time she speaks, her words are full of kindness and sweet like honey to the soul.

> *How sweet are your words to my taste, sweeter than honey to my mouth! (Psalm 119:103, NIV).*

The Holy Spirit we contain inside us brings into life the Word of God we store inside us. Our flesh is made out of the Word of God that has become flesh (John 1:14). Our spirit is made out of the Spirit of God that God breathed into us and made us a living soul.

> *The Spirit gives life; the flesh counts for nothing. The words I have spoken to you—they are full of the Spirit and life (John 6:63, NIV).*

> *The generous will prosper; those who refresh others will themselves be refreshed (Proverbs 11:25, NLT).*

Every day fill yourself up in the Word and speak it in your life and to your loved ones. It will freshen you as you freshen others. It is done unto you automatically when you do unto others what you would like them to do for you.

July 23

~ A thanksgiving or a complaining tap ~

> *You prepare a table before me in the presence of my enemies. You anoint my head with oil; my cup overflows. Surely your goodness and love will follow me all the days of my life, and I will dwell in the house of the Lord forever (Psalm 23:5-6, NIV).*

You have the OLD ME and the NEW ME. The OLD ME wants only to complain and that is its nature because it has fallen into sin. The NEW Me wants only to give thanks because it has risen with a new life and is grateful. On 23 July 2019, I remember God showing me the hot and cold water taps that I use and He said, 'You fill your cup with either hot or cold water or sometimes both. You have a complaining tap, and a thanksgiving tap inside you. Whichever one you turn on fills your cup and your cup overflows from it'. A good mother turns on the thanksgiving tap only; though she walks through the valley of death, she will defeat evil with her goodness. Her cup overflows with gratitude for she knows that all things from God are for the good of those who love Him.

The good life of Christ is produced by the fruit of His Spirit and that is goodness. Being thankful is being joyful for what you have and joy is the fruit of the Holy Spirit.

> *But the fruit of the Spirit is love, joy, peace, patience, kindness, goodness, faithfulness, gentleness, self-control; against such things there is no law (Galatians 5:22-23, ESV).*

Just as you tap-and-go with your purchased items, tap-and-go in your new day with a grateful heart full of thanksgiving.

July 24

~ Abundance ~

> *So they gathered them and filled twelve baskets with the pieces of the five barley loaves left over by those who had eaten (John 6:13, NIV).*

A good mother can have only two fish and five loaves of bread for her children. But she knows that when she puts it into the palms of the hands that hold the universe, it is multiplied to feed a whole village. She loves the foot of the cross where her new life begins. The cross indicates to her the sign of addition and multiplication from all directions of her life; it's a place of abundance. There is blessing in her hands on everything she touches because she trusts the hands of the source from where her blessings flow, and the blessings overflow.

The Holy Spirit of God is the source of blessing that forever flows from the new life of Jesus from whom comes the abundance of life. That last resource you have, the Holy Spirit, will breathe into it the living life so that it will grow in abundance.

> *The thief comes only to steal and kill and destroy. I came that they may have life and have it abundantly (John 10:10, ESV).*

The enemy cannot destroy the new life Jesus gave us. We are now to use that life to defeat the enemy every time he lies to us. This is the life of truth and will set us free from the lies of the devil.

July 25

~ *You are on God's mind* ~

> *Every single moment you are thinking of me! How precious and wonderful to consider that you cherish me constantly in your every thought! O God, your desires toward me are more than the grains of sand on every shore! When I awake each morning, you're still with me (Psalm 139:17-18, TPT).*

A good mother keeps her grown-up children in her heart and God's heart by praying for them every time she thinks of them. Even though her children are no longer in her presence when they live their own lives, she prays and bring them together to be in the presence of God. She wakes up together with them in prayers and goes to sleep with them in prayers. Keeping her children in prayer brings her joy and peace. There is joy and peace in the presence of God.

The Holy Spirit is the voice of God that breathes life into the Word who is Jesus, to be fresh, alive and active in our life when we take the Word into us. We are on His mind and He prays for us.

> *Then God promises to love me all day, sing songs all through the night! My life is God's prayer. (Psalm 42:8, MSG).*

Each and every day wake up and clothe yourself in the Word for the strength to make it through the day.

July 26

~ *God is good* ~

> *You intended to harm me, but God intended it all for good (Genesis 50:20, NLT).*

A good mother always looks at the good side of life. She prays for those that curse her and her household. She knows that when she prays for them, she puts an end to any negative vibes thrown towards her. Her prayers turn bad intentions into something good. This is why her life is always good. She sits in the goodness of God's teaching and she has tasted and seen that the Lord is good.

> *Taste and see that the Lord is good; blessed is the one who takes refuge in him (Psalm 34:8, NIV).*

The Holy Spirit is the power of God inside us that is always working for good when we pray. All the goodness of the Father that

Jesus actioned and taught is in the Spirit, and He is now right inside us. We cannot escape from His goodness; we need it to use it to overcome all the evil around us.

> *And we know that in all things God works for the good of those who love him, who have been called according to his purpose (Romans 8:28, NIV).*

To taste the goodness of God you have to spend daily time alone with Him in the goodness of His Word. No one can do it for you, you do it yourself.

July 27

~ Image of Christ ~

> *But the fruit of the Spirit is love, joy, peace, patience, kindness, goodness, faithfulness, gentleness, self-control; against such things there is no law (Galatians 5:22-23, ESV).*

All mothers carry their child for nine months and go through body changes as the child develops into a new life. She has to suffer the changes for nine months before a life is finally formed into a complete image. A good mother uses this opportunity to pray for the nine fruit of the Spirit to be developed into the new life formed within her.

> *Not only so, but we also glory in our sufferings, because we know that suffering produces perseverance; perseverance, character; and character, hope. And hope does not put us to shame, because God's love has been poured out into our hearts through the Holy Spirit, who has been given to us (Romans 5:3-5, NIV).*

God carries us in Him through His Spirit with the nine fruit of the characters of Jesus. He allows us to go through the tests He prepares, so we can develop the complete image of Christ.

Be grateful to God for the tests He allows in your life; He is testing that you are growing and developing into a Christ-like character.

July 28

~ Trusting God ~

And my God will supply every need of yours according to his riches in glory in Christ Jesus (Philippians 4:19, ESV).

A good mother always trusts God as the provider. She knows that what she has now is for use in this moment and doesn't worry about the needs of her children's future. She may not know the unknown future but she knows God is the provider and that is enough. When she arrives in the future with her children's needs God will meet that need there. God has given her His Word in Exodus 33:14, and she trusts His Word completely as it's the Word that completes her when she feels empty.

God said, 'My presence will go with you. I'll see the journey to the end.' (Exodus 33:14, MSG).

Jesus is alive in us through the Holy Spirit which gives us the peace to continue to trust God as the provider. The Holy Spirit wants us to experience His fruit that He provides, so our faith in trusting Him can never be shaken.

Those who trust in the Lord are like Mount Zion, which cannot be shaken but endures forever (Psalm 125:1, NIV).

The more we trust God, the more we have peace in trusting that God will always provide on time.

July 29

~ Living your new life in Christ ~

> *Don't compare yourself with others. Just look at your own work to see if you have done anything to be proud of. You must each accept the responsibilities that are yours (Galatians 6:4-5, ERV).*

Focus on who you are in Christ rather than who you are in comparison to others. A good mother doesn't compare herself or her children with other mothers and their children. She focuses on comparing what her life would be if she never had a position in Christ. She focuses on maintaining her position in Christ, and to grow and glow from glory to glory for God's glory. She focuses on growing in the Word of God.

> *But grow in the grace and knowledge of our Lord and Saviour Jesus Christ. To him be glory both now and forever! Amen (2 Peter 3:18, NIV).*

The Word you get in you is how the Holy Spirit grows you from glory to glory to the glory of God. And so everything you do is for God's glory. Do not compare yourself with others. Everyone is different to give God glory in their unique special way.

> *For he is sent by God. He speaks God's words, for God gives him the Spirit without limit (John 3:34, NLT).*

Compare your new life in Christ in the light to what you used to be like in your old life in darkness. Appreciate the great miracle God has done in you and that it is a new meaningful eternal life.

July 30

~ Building others with words of kindness ~

Let your speech always be gracious, seasoned with salt, so that you may know how you ought to answer each person (Colossians 4:6, ESV).

A good mother always thinks and speaks positively and sends good wishes not only into the lives of her household but to all that come into contact with her. When her mouth opens it is to build up someone's life or to speak an act of kindness. Her ears listen and respond kindly to her household. When someone is in darkness, her eyes are the light that gives them the light to help them see the way to becoming a better person. She constantly builds herself up in the Word of God so that she can easily build up others.

> *Therefore encourage one another and build each other up, just as in fact you are doing (1 Thessalonians 5:11, NIV).*

The Holy Spirit is the eyes, ears and mouth of God. He helps us to see ourselves the way God sees us. He hears us when we pray and responds to our needs. When he talks with us, it is a feast of celebration, that joy of hearing the Holy Spirit is indescribable.

> *At that time Jesus, full of joy through the Holy Spirit, said, 'I praise you, Father, Lord of heaven and earth, because you have hidden these things from the wise and learned, and revealed them to little children. Yes, Father, for this is what you were pleased to do. 'All things have been committed to me by my Father. No one knows who the Son is except the Father, and no one knows who the Father is except the Son and those to whom the Son chooses to reveal him.' (Luke 10:21-22, NIV).*

You know you have inherited the kingdom of God when you receive the joy of the Holy Spirit by hearing His voice revealing who Jesus is in your life. The joy you receive brings into your life eternal peace.

July 31

~ Complete your life in the LIFE of the Word ~

For we are his workmanship, created in Christ Jesus for good works, which God prepared beforehand, that we should walk in them (Ephesians 2:10, ESV).

A good mother is always working for her house all the time. It's like putting a puzzle together, bringing the right pieces together so that they match up. That's the story of her life; she brings together only the right things for her house. Sometimes she can't find the right pieces that match, but the peace of God that she has placed in her soul to rest puts her mind at ease and she makes it through her tough day. Her home is at peace because she is forever grateful for everything and that opens the tap of joy to flow from inside her.

And whatever you do, in word or deed, do everything in the name of the Lord Jesus, giving thanks to God the Father through him (Colossians 3:17, ESV).

The Holy Spirit will reveal something to you, and then match that piece of you to what the Word of God says of you. The joy and peace that you experience is priceless; you cannot buy it with any amount of money.

The Lord says, 'Come, everyone who is thirsty— here is water! Come, you that have no money— buy grain and eat! Come! Buy wine and milk— it will cost you nothing! Why spend money on what does not satisfy? Why spend your wages and still be hungry? Listen to me and do what I say, and you will enjoy the best food of all (Isaiah 55:1-2, GNT).

Every new day God gifts you an opportunity to enjoy His company in His Word; it costs no money. The gift of life and time in the 24 hours of your day is to be spent getting LIFE in God's Word to complete the missing pieces of your life.

AUGUST

~ A mother's role of cooking ~

> *Your words are so choice, so tasty; I prefer them to the best home cooking (Psalm 119:103, MSG).*

God reminded me of how I would use the same ingredients again and again for different menus, and it would still taste delicious, and give me the strength needed for when I was hungry. You see, the same Word of God can be used again and again for our hunger in a situation that makes us feel empty or burdened. When we feel empty, only God's Word can fill us up and give us the peace and comfort needed. When we feel burdened we are to action the Word of God in that situation and release the burden. Faith without action is dead and our burdens are released when we exercise our faith. Just as when we eat unhealthy fatty foods and excess fat builds up in our body and needs to be released through exercise.

Our breakthrough also comes from filling our emptiness with the Word of God and releasing the Word when we have burdens. When we release the Word it breaks open and people around us see the breakthrough in our life. Let these words in Psalm 119 be our prayer.

> *Break open your words, let the light shine out, let ordinary people see the meaning (Psalm 119:130, MSG).*

The Holy Spirit inside us is the light and life of Christ. Without Him we feel empty. He is a person in Spirit that needs to complete the body. God designed us such in a way to become complete with Him through His Spirit. God becomes complete in us when we bring ourselves to Him in brokenness and fill that brokenness with His Word.

The Lord is close to the brokenhearted and saves those who are crushed in spirit (Psalm 34:18, NIV).

Then Jesus said, 'Come to me, all of you who are weary and carry heavy burdens, and I will give you rest. Take my yoke upon you. Let me teach you, because I am humble and gentle at heart, and you will find rest for your souls. For my yoke is easy to bear, and the burden I give you is light.' (Matthew 11:28-30, NLT).

Each and EVERY DAY of the month of August show that you are empty and fill your brokenness by filling yourself with the Word. Be hungry and thirsty for God's Word. Keep doing it daily and whenever you feel burdened with world issues, problems and the daily bills of life, release the Word in Isaiah 55:22 to God.

Give your burdens to the Lord, and he will take care of you. He will not permit the godly to slip and fall (Isaiah 55:22, NLT).

August 1

~ *Raise your life in the resurrected life of Christ* ~

Blessed be the God and Father of our Lord Jesus Christ! According to his great mercy, he has caused us to be born again to a living hope through the resurrection of Jesus Christ from the dead, (1 Peter 1:3, ESV).

A good mother knows how to sleep through and be calm and peaceful in her storms like a contented baby sleeping. Whatever storms life throws at her, her children's concerns come first. This little life that God entrusted her with is her focus. She raises up their lives in the new resurrected life of Jesus within her to prepare them for their future. Some days she may not be faithful in sharing the Word of God with her children or pray with them, but she never gives up keeping them in the truth of God's Word. She lets God handle her storms while she invests her time and energy to give the best life to her children.

> *We were buried therefore with him by baptism into death, in order that, just as Christ was raised from the dead by the glory of the Father, we too might walk in newness of life (Romans 6:4, ESV).*

The Holy Spirit is the resurrected life of Jesus inside us. He makes Jesus come alive inside us and live again through us. He strengthens us with His peace in our storms to make us stronger to walk with Him towards eternity.

> *And if the Spirit of him who raised Jesus from the dead is living in you, he who raised Christ from the dead will also give life to your mortal bodies because of his Spirit who lives in you (Romans 8:11, NIV).*

Each and every day receive into you the Word of God so that His Spirit will breathe life and light into you, rising you up to shine like the star you were designed to be.

August 2

~ Slaves to righteousness ~

> *You have been set free from sin and have become slaves to righteousness (Romans 6:18, NIV).*

From slave of sin through Adam's disobedience to slave of righteousness through obedience to Jesus. A good mother is a slave to doing the right things for her household. She chooses to serve. Whenever her children are heading the wrong way she is the light of the house that shines the way into bringing them back to the right path. The source from the light she walks on comes from the Word of God. She ensures that she is always connected to the source of light and remains charged. Her children may go astray but the light of God's Word that she shines on them always lead them back to the right path.

> *Your word is a lamp for my feet, a light on my path. Psalm 119:105, NIV).*

The Holy Spirit is now the Light of Jesus that always leads us on the right path to the destiny that Jesus is preparing for us. Being the slave of righteousness we need the fruit of righteousness of the Holy Spirit to serve everyone in our contacts.

> *The one who is the true light, who gives light to everyone, was coming into the world (John 1:9, NLT).*

Keep searching for the true light in the Word of God every day. This light will get you back on the right path when you go off track.

August 3

~ Sharing the suffering and glory of Jesus ~

> *Now if we are children, then we are heirs—heirs of God and co-heirs with Christ, if indeed we share in his sufferings in order that we may also share in his glory (Romans 8:17, NIV).*

I was thinking about how I face a trouble or pain then another comes up and this is what the Holy Spirit explained in the most lovely way. All the pain and suffering Jesus went through on the day he died is broken down into portions which are manageable for you to deal with. Jesus faced it all in just one day and died. But for you it comes day by day, and you have to go through it until the day you die which this is when you will share His glory. We would all be dead by now if we were to go through what Jesus went through before he died.

Praise God, this pain and suffering is being broken down and given to us in portions where it's just enough for us to manage and get through. This is the gift of life; to be alive and carry our cross to follow Jesus.

Jesus showed that to His disciples before He took the cross. He broke His body and gave it to them. He shared the pain and suffering of His body in small portions with his disciples. His body that was going to be broken in pain and cause Him great suffering before death. As His followers, we too receive it.

> *While they were eating, Jesus took bread, and when he had given thanks, he broke it and gave it to his disciples, saying, 'Take and eat; this is my body.' (Matthew 26:26, NIV).*

As the body of Christ we will go through pain and suffering; as soon as one ends another comes up. This is all part of the normal growth to become like Christ. So don't be surprised if you are experiencing pain after pain. It will stop on the day God takes His Spirit back from us. Jesus said, 'It is finished,' and offered His Spirit to God.

> *Yet what we suffer now is nothing compared to the glory he will reveal to us later (Romans 8:18, NLT)*

> *Instead, be very glad—for these trials make you partners with Christ in his suffering, so that you will have the wonderful joy of seeing his glory when it is revealed to all the world (1 Peter 4:13, NLT).*

What we can do is praise God more in our pain because we are experiencing only a small portion of what Jesus suffered for us, and as long as we house the Holy Spirit we are all in it together. We have a helper who Jesus has given to help us get our comfort and strength to make it through each day. This helper is the Holy Spirit.

August 4

~ Carry our universe in prayer ~

> *...bless those who curse you, pray for those who mistreat you (Luke 6:28, NIV).*

When you pray for others you are also creating a positive atmosphere of God's presence around yourself. You may be praying for others but it will have a strong effect on you, because the positive energy which travels out from you towards them is reflected back at you. So praying for people who hate you as well as your enemies will only make things better for you. A good mother has a heart so big she is able to carry all her household inside of her. She expands her heart more to carry all her children's needs and pray for them. She wants nothing but the best for them and she knows that the more she sits in the Word, the bigger her heart grows to hold more.

> *Enlarge your house; build an addition. Spread out your home, and spare no expense! (Isaiah 54:2, NLT).*

The Holy Spirit is the powerhouse of God. God holds the whole universe in His Spirit. God breathes His Word and everything receives life and comes into existence.

> *The world and all that is in it belong to the Lord; the earth and all who live on it are his (Psalm 24:1, GNT).*

Every day talk to God; pray, pray and pray. If you have nothing to say, just say thank you for everything, He is everything to you.

August 5

~ Feed, clothe and shelter yourself in the Word ~

> *Jesus answered, 'It is written: 'Man shall not live on bread alone, but on every word that comes from the mouth of God' (Matthew 4:4, NIV).*

God is there for us and is fighting on our behalf. Keep fighting the good fight by hearing and hearing the Word of God because that is where faith comes from. Most times people will ask you where you are from, you will tell them which country you come from, where you grew up and how you grew up. All these things affect your way of living. You see, you are from Heaven but you grow up and live in faith on earth.

> *So then faith comes by hearing, and hearing by the Word of God (Romans 10:17, NKJV).*

Where does faith comes from? The Bible says faith comes from hearing and hearing the Word of God. The Word of God is Jesus given to us in flesh. Jesus came from the Father, from Heaven.

A good mother understands this and raises her family in faith. She raises them up in the Word of God. This is how she grows their faith. She is not only concerned with feeding, clothing and sheltering her family physically but spiritually too. As long as they are spiritually fed, clothed and sheltered in the Word of God, they are physically fed, clothed and sheltered in this world.

The Holy Spirit lives in us, and for Him to become the powerhouse of God and grow our faith we have to feed, clothe and shelter Him every day in the Word of God. Without faith it is impossible to please God. We please God when He can see himself in us, that is, He can see His Word.

> *This has been my practise: I obey your precepts (Psalm 119:56, NIV).*

Each and every day, make Jesus alive by practising the Word of God. Faith without action is dead.

August 6

~ *New levels, new demons to fight with* ~

> *Dear friends, don't be surprised at the fiery trials you are going through, as if something strange were happening to you. Instead, be very glad—for these trials make you partners with Christ in his suffering, so that you will have the wonderful joy of seeing his glory when it is revealed to all the world (1 Peter 4:12-13, NLT).*

Higher level, higher devils to attack but always remember, there are more angels fighting for you than your enemy (2 Kings 6:15-17).

A good mother is on a mission to take her household to new levels all the time. Every year she always makes sure there is progress in her house. When she reaches new levels, she settles more in the Word of God because she knows that a higher level attracts higher devils to fight with. The Word of God is her sword which she keeps to hand. This is how she continues to maintain her Christ-like character.

The Holy Spirit's mission within us is to progress us all the time to be Christ-like. He puts us through tests so that we come out in the image of Christ. Daniel and his three friends went through the furnace with Jesus, and there in the furnace the Son of God was with them.

> *He said, 'Look! I see four men walking around in the fire, unbound and unharmed, and the fourth looks like a son of the gods.' (Daniel 3:25, NIV).*

Be knowledgeable of God in His Word so you can successfully pass your tests and reach new levels to be more Christ-like.

August 7

~ Break yourself in the Word ~

> *The Lord is close to the brokenhearted and saves those who are crushed in spirit (Psalm 34:18, NIV).*

You have to be broken so God can draw closer to you and mend you. You have to break yourself in the Word, so God is able to mend you in His Word. A good mother never abandons her children when they are broken, she is always there to comfort them. She goes through their pain with them until they come through it, and even then she is still there for them. She is always broken for God to bring Him closer to her. When she gets closer to God, she is able to touch Him and draw out His power. The power she draws out from God strengthens her for her children.

> *Praise be to the God and Father of our Lord Jesus Christ, the Father of compassion and the God of all comfort, who comforts us in all our troubles, so that we can comfort those in any trouble with the comfort we ourselves receive from God (2 Corinthians 1:3-4, NIV).*

The Holy Spirit is our great comforter and is closer to us; the very breath we breathe. He will never leave or forsake us. He prays on our behalf to the Father. We just have to reach within us to touch Him and draw out strength to comfort us.

Never will I leave you; never will I forsake you (Hebrews 13:5, NIV).

Just like the bleeding woman who reached out and touched Jesus to draw out His power for her healing, we can also now reach out and touch the lives of people with the power of the Word which is Jesus within us.

August 8

~ Life guide of God's Word ~

If we live by the Spirit, let us also walk by the Spirit (Galatians 5:25, ESV).

A good mother is like a life guide. She is there to guide her children's lives so they don't drown in the 'bills' of life but become successful and prosperous to stay on top of the world's current storms. Bills of life such as emotional stress, depression or health issues are what we face in this world. When someone is drowning the life guards don't save them while they are struggling in the water. They wait until the victim stops struggling then save them. If they save them while they are struggling then they will both drown. A good mother saves her children before they start to drown and struggle. She seeks the life guide of God's Words and meditates on it in prayer and this is how she is able to help her children with the guidance of God.

> *Show me your ways, Lord, teach me your paths. Guide me in your truth and teach me, for you are God my Saviour, and my hope is in you all day long (Psalm 25:4-5, NIV).*

Jesus saved and gave us the Holy Spirit and He is our life guide. He safely guides our life towards making the right decisions in life so that we don't drown in the evil waves of this world.

> *For all who are led by the Spirit of God are sons of God (Romans 8:14, ESV).*

Each and every day seek the life guard of the life-giving Word of God to give you life and guide you.

August 9

~ *Relationship is important over material things* ~

> *Be completely humble and gentle; be patient, bearing with one another in love. Make every effort to keep the unity of the Spirit through the bond of peace (Ephesians 4:2-3, NIV).*

A good mother knows that relationships are far more important than material things. She may support her children by financially investing so that she can raise daughters to give them the good life she desires for them. Most importantly, she invests her time in talking to God in prayer about them. Whatever she does for them doesn't give her the right to strike out or verbally abuse them if they go off track and fall in love with a man who doesn't meet her expectations. She knows that her children will have pain and suffering if they don't make the right decision. They are responsible for their own lives and the choices they make. She has to just carry on and do what she has to do, and that is praying for them to make wise decisions along the path they travel.

Be joyful in hope, patient in affliction, faithful in prayer (Romans 12:12, NIV).

For God so loved the world that he gave his one and only Son, that whoever believes in him shall not perish but have eternal life (John 3:16, NIV).

Each and every one of us means so much to God that He has to pay a high price to bring us back to Him. He understands that we have always been off track until the day He came to rescue us. Even after He paid a high price to restore our relationship back to Him, we keep choosing to live the way we used to. This has not made God give up on us, instead He faithfully gives us a new life every day and is patiently waiting for us to go back to Him. The parable of the prodigal son (Luke 15:11-32) paints the kind of father He is. The day we return back to Him, He will receive us with open arms and celebrate a happy feast for the reunion being back with Him.

August 10

~ Sharing in the suffering of Jesus ~

Now if we are children, then we are heirs—heirs of God and co-heirs with Christ, if indeed we share in his sufferings in order that we may also share in his glory (Romans 8:17, NIV).

Every mother has to sail through another storm as soon as each one is over. A good mother is always prepared to walk through any storms. She knows that if Jesus is preparing a place for her, she too has to be prepared to share in the sufferings Jesus faced so she can share the glory of Jesus. It's in her storms that she comes out stronger with a new Christ-like character to reach her destiny. Jesus carried that cross for her with pain, and she must bear her cross with whatever pain comes with it.

> *Instead, be very glad—for these trials make you partners with Christ in his suffering, so that you will have the wonderful joy of seeing his glory when it is revealed to all the world (1 Peter 4:13, NLT).*

The Holy Spirit is inside us, and He prepares us in our storms to become Christ-like so we can meet Jesus on that day. He is the gift from Jesus to celebrate the resurrected life of Jesus.

> *Celebrate God all day, every day. I mean, revel in him! Make it as clear as you can to all you meet that you're on their side, working with them and not against them. Help them see that the Master is about to arrive. He could show up any minute! (Philippians 4:4-5, MSG).*

Appreciate the pain you experience in life as it only makes you stronger than you used to be. The stronger you become the more you can deal with any of life's problems.

August 11

~ God has a great plan for your life ~

> *'For I know the plans I have for you,' declares the Lord, 'plans to prosper you and not to harm you, plans to give you hope and a future.' (Jeremiah 29:11, NIV).*

A good mother is always planning something for her children. She plans how great the future of her child will be. Any mother can mother a child, but a good mother is the one who maintains the

Spirit of God in her life and plans the future of her children in what God says in His Word.

God also has great plans for us in the future when He breathes into us His Spirit of life, while knitting us in our mother's womb. The Holy Spirit is within us and there is no place we can go to hide from Him. He wants to carry out God's great plan in our life. He needs us to receive the Word into us to make that plan become a reality.

> *For you created my inmost being; you knit me together in my mother's womb. I praise you because I am fearfully and wonderfully made; your works are wonderful, I know that full well. My frame was not hidden from you when I was made in the secret place, when I was woven together in the depths of the earth. Your eyes saw my unformed body; all the days ordained for me were written in your book before one of them came to be (Psalm 139:13-16, NIV).*

Just as when you have plans for tomorrow and go to sleep. God has a plan for you too; that's why He will wake you up tomorrow. His plans are to prosper you and give you hope and a future.

August 12

~ Free from fear ~

Now the Lord is the Spirit, and where the Spirit of the Lord is, there is freedom. 2 Corinthians 3:17, (NIV)

Being in the life of God in His holy place is a total joy as there is nothing to fear, you are so full of joy, peace and strength, and free to do anything because you are not afraid. A good mother opens the door of her house to anyone and welcomes them. Everyone feels loved and belonged. They feel free and at home because of the vibes and energy that she releases which they receive. This is the energy from the presence of God that she is connected to every day.

The Holy Spirit makes us feel at home when we give our self to Jesus, and house Him in the right way. Where the Spirit of God is, there is freedom, we feel free and right at home. When we are troubled, the Holy Spirit is there with us with His fruit of peace. He will always be there and will never forsake us.

> *Peace I leave with you; my peace I give you I do not give to you as the world gives. Do not let your hearts be troubled and do not be afraid (John 14:27, NIV).*

Keep receiving the truth from God's Word every day; it will set you free from any troubles that are feeding your fears.

August 13

~ Resting in the Holy Spirit ~

> *But now the Lord my God has given me rest on every side, and there is no adversary or disaster. (1 Kings 5:4, NIV).*

To rest in the Lord is not to allow any issues of the world to bother you. You are resting and so you do not want anything to disturb you. When you lie down to sleep at night and someone or some noise disturbs you outside your house, you have the power of control to choose whether to wake up to that disturbance or continue to sleep and let it not bother you.

A mother is always disturbed by her children; she has no privacy. Her children go to her without permission, which is stressful at times. A good mother knows that the moment she becomes a mother her time and her world become her children's time and world; she has to be available for them anytime, all the time. For her to have a life, she sits in Word and prayer to draw out the strength from the eternal life to sustain her.

> *My people will live in peaceful dwelling places, in secure homes, in undisturbed places of rest (Isaiah 32:18, NIV).*

The Holy Spirit inside us is always available to us as long as we live and breathe. And we can go to Him anytime to get LIFE, the life of Jesus. Because we house Him we can now find our rest from within, and even from the evil disturbances outside. The power of the Holy Spirit inside us controls us. We can use this power to choose not to let anything around us rob us of our joy and peace as we rest in the Holy Spirit.

> *The Lord replied, 'My Presence will go with you, and I will give you rest.' (Exodus 33:14, NIV).*

Each and every day find your rest in the Word of God; nothing around you can disturb your inner joy and peace.

August 14

~ Your life revolves around the Word of God ~

> *Love must be sincere. Hate what is evil; cling to what is good (Romans 12:9, NIV).*

If something good comes to mind and you are able to do it just do it. The good you do will come back to you. A small act of goodness adds kindness which adds more weight to that goodness. Be an agent of a good God and do something good. When you do something good you are kind. A good mother is a good steward with everything in her care; even if she fails, she tries to be good. She knows that she doesn't need to please man because not everyone will like her. She lives to please God, and so her faith in God is her priority. Without faith it is impossible to please God, and faith comes from hearing the Word. Her life and her household revolve around the Word of God. It's the Word of God that gives LIGHT and LIFE to her house.

> *So then faith comes by hearing, and hearing by the Word of God (Romans 10:17, NKJV).*

The Holy Spirit revolves around the Word of God. Where the Word of God is, the Spirit of God is to breathe life into it to make Jesus come alive. In the beginning, God spoke His Word to create and His Spirit was present to breathe life into making the Word of God come to life.

> *Now the earth was formless and empty, darkness was over the surface of the deep, and the Spirit of God was hovering over the waters (Genesis 1:2, NIV).*

Every day speak the Word of God into your life, and the Spirit of God will breathe into it to bring it to your life. Speak life into your dry bones. Revive your flesh with the Word.

August 15

~ Gentleness ~

> *Therefore, as God's chosen people, holy and dearly loved, clothe yourselves with compassion, kindness, humility, gentleness and patience (Colossians 3:12, NIV).*

Everyone dresses according to the weather for the day. A good mother wakes up and dresses up in Word and prayer. She clothes herself with compassion, kindness, humility, gentleness and patience. These are the clothes she needs to wear because of the weather she experiences throughout the seasons all year round in her house. She needs to be gentle with her children to take good care of them.

The Holy Spirit is gentle, slow to anger and full of patience towards us. This is how kind He is towards us; His good love covers us fully.

> *A gentle answer turns away wrath, but a harsh word stirs up anger. Proverbs 15:1, (NIV).*

Gentleness is the fruit of righteousness that the Holy Spirit produces within us. Being gentle is not adding problems onto an existing problem but finding a solution to it.

August 16

~ Learn to be grateful and not to complain ~

> *...rooted and built up in him, strengthened in the faith as you were taught, and overflowing with thankfulness (Colossians 2:7, NIV).*

The life of a good mother is always filled with gratitude. Because the Holy Spirit now possesses the new life she has in Christ, the joy from the fruit of the Holy Spirit flows out from within her constantly. The more she is grateful for this new life, the more her life attracts all the good things to be grateful for.

She is full of praise and thanksgiving to God for she knows what her old life was like before Jesus changed her completely. She was always complaining; she was always unhappy in her old life and complained all the time. The more she complained, the more she attracted many things to complain about. Jesus brought this complaining life of her 'old self' to a complete end when He said, 'It is finished', and gave up His Spirit to the Father.

> *All this is for your benefit, so that the grace that is reaching more and more people may cause thanksgiving to overflow to the glory of God (2 Corinthians 4:15, NIV).*

The old life has ended and finished with Jesus at the cross. In the grave, the Holy Spirit resurrected Jesus and brought him to life. The beginning of a new life for which she will forever be grateful. The Holy Spirit grows us in the new Christ-like life to be more grateful, not to complain anymore about our previous way of living.

August 17

~ Clothed in the righteous Word of God ~

> *She selects wool and flax and works with eager hands (Proverbs 31:13, NIV).*

Any woman or mother can sew beautiful garments. But that good woman and good mother does it with passion as a worship to God. Every thread that she puts into the material makes the pattern, and the stitch that runs through it tells her this story. God did the first stitch when He sewed back the flesh of the first man after He removed from him a rib and fashioned a woman from it. It's her desire that God will fashion her with His hands. God does the cutting and sewing on the flesh when He wants to remove you from where you are not supposed to be. This is why you face all this pain and suffering of living in the flesh. The Word has to become flesh to come down to where you are to remove you from where you are not supposed to be, and that is in this sinful world.

The Holy Spirit inside us wants to sew us back into the original pattern God designed and clothes us in the righteousness of Christ. He can only do this when we keep hearing and hearing and storing the Word of God.

> *I delight greatly in the Lord; my soul rejoices in my God. For he has clothed me with garments of salvation and arrayed me in a robe of his righteousness, as a bridegroom adorns his head like a priest, and as a bride adorns herself with her jewels (Isaiah 61:10, NIV).*

Each and every day clothe yourself in the righteous Word of God and produce the fruit of righteousness in whatever you do.

August 18

~ Your desires with God's desire ~

> *For you have given him his heart's desire; you have withheld nothing he requested (Psalm 21:2, NLT)*

I remember once I was in the kitchen cooking, putting all the ingredients together, and the Holy Spirit started teaching me about how God brings our desires into His desires and mixes them up to give us the best.

This is what the Holy Spirit taught me: A good mother intercedes for her children, seeking God in prayer for every need, and for God to make her children succeed in life. The Holy Spirit also prays for us to God in moans and groans that is according to God's will. What happens is that while we may be praying for something else, the Holy Spirit, being the Spirit of God, knows what God's will is for us, and so He talks to God about our desires and they work out what is best for us. God gives us what we want by bringing His desire into our desires, which is more than 100 times better than what we want. Next, God starts combining His desires and our desires into one, and this is like preparing a recipe where you mix all the ingredients together and put it through intense heat to get the finished product. This is where we do not like it, and most of us leave God's preparation in our life. Very often when the mixture of our desires with God's are stirred together to become one and then put into the intensity of God's degrees, we face storms or walk through fire in life. If we just wait patiently and keep hanging onto the cross, we will receive the desires of our heart. Also, sometimes when God is still working on us, the enemy can distract us, and we come out of God's work. This is where we have unanswered prayers, and we do not get the desires of our heart. But if we are patient and sit through it, holding onto the cross and suffering through it all, we will come out stronger and receive the best God has designed for us with so much joy that will make us forget the pain we went through.

In order to share His glory we have to suffer with Him too.

> *And since we are his children, we are his heirs. In fact, together with Christ we are heirs of God's glory. But if we are to share his glory, we must also share his suffering (Romans 8:17, NLT).*

It's a long process where we have to allow God to work in us to prepare us to be stronger to give birth. When a mother is expecting a baby, her body goes through dramatic changes to prepare her to give birth and bring a life out of her. She feels sick and towards the last trimester she is in much pain. This is the last stage before giving birth. When the time is almost here for us to give birth to the life God has for us, we will go through pain and, like the expectant mother that is told to keep pushing and pushing so she can give birth, you too must keep pushing and pushing to give birth to what God has conceived in you.

August 19

~ *Do not fear* ~

For God has not given us a spirit of fear, but of power and of love and of a sound mind (2 Timothy 1:7, NKJV).

I remember that morning of August 19, 2020. I woke up to this beautiful message God has placed in my heart.

The Holy Spirit showed me a shark and said, this is a wild animal that you fear. What happens is the shark will attack you when it senses your fear towards it. Not only the shark, any wild animals will attack you if they sense fear in you. A snake will always attack humans because God has already put fear in the snake that humans will crush its head.

Then the Holy Spirit said, when you fear, you allow the enemy to take over you and give access to attack you because you become weak and afraid. When you are afraid of something, the enemy uses that to make sure what your fear will happen. You see, if you keep fearing that you will get COVID-19, then you will get it. So what the enemy does is he uses your fear against you. He shows your fear as proof and evidence before God so God can allow him to make your fear come to pass. This is what he did with Job. Job said, 'What I fear has happened,' when he lost his children and everything he owned.

> *For the thing I greatly feared has come upon me,*
> *And what I dreaded has happened to me (Job 3:25, NKJV).*

A good mother doesn't accept any fears to have a strong hold of her. She spends time in Word and prayer and has a daily solid relationship with Jesus Christ, the perfect love of God who drives away fear. When she is afraid she stabilises herself by breathing Psalm 56:3, *When I am afraid, I put my trust in you.*

The Holy Spirit is the perfect love from the Father's love that the Son brought to us and gifted us. The Holy Spirit now lives insides us and He drives away fear.

> *There is no fear in love. But perfect love drives out fear, because fear has to do with punishment. The one who fears is not made perfect in love (1 John 4:18, NIV).*

Each and every day, remind yourself that the perfect love of God, Jesus, has driven away fear when He conquered death with His life. He is living inside of us again in the Holy Spirit to drive away any fear from having a hold on us.

August 20

~ Clothed in the presence of God ~

> *For as he thinketh in his heart, so is he (Proverbs 23:7, KJV).*

The enemy doesn't know what's in your mind but he knows about you from the atmosphere in which you live because the kind of atmosphere you live in is determined by how you think. Your emotions and actions towards situations show what's in your mind. Renew your mind in the right things. It's the right atmosphere that draws God's presence to surround you. To attract the right things, be full of gratitude, thanksgiving and praises. Let everything that has breathe praise the Lord.

> *Let your priests be clothed with righteousness, and let your saints shout for joy (Psalm 132:9, ESV).*

When you are expecting a hot day you dress for that weather. So if you want to expect the presence of God and see Him in your life. You have to clothe yourself with garments of praise and thanksgiving. The presence of God brings abundance of life to your life. A good mother wakes up in the morning and gets dressed in the garments of praise and thanksgiving. She is expecting the 'presence of God weather' in her day all the time. Her house is a safe place to live. A place of love, joy and peace.

> *You will show me the way of life, granting me the joy of your presence and the pleasures of living with you forever (Psalm 16:11, NLT).*

The Holy Spirit brings the presence of God into us, producing love, joy and peace. We are clothed in the righteousness of Christ with His presence.

> *Filled with the fruit of righteousness that comes through Jesus Christ, to the glory and praise of God (Philippians 1:11, ESV).*

You are not fully clothed until you put the garments of praise all over you. There is joy in the presence of God.

August 21

~ *Joy in the Word of God* ~

When anxiety was great within me, your consolation brought me joy (Psalm 94:19, NIV).

A good mother is a best friend to this Word in Psalm 119:143.

Even though troubles came down on me hard, your commands always gave me delight (Psalm 119:143, MSG).

Her delight is always in the Word of God, regardless of what troubles can hit her hard. Her focus is to see the desires of her heart become a reality. She delights in the Lord and the Lord grants her the desires of her heart.

Delight yourself in the Lord, and he will give you the desires of your heart (Psalm 37:4, ESV).

The Holy Spirit is her good company who produces joy for her in the Word of God. Every day she rises up, and says, 'this is the day the Lord has made for me; I will rejoice and be glad in it. Even if there is a storm I will still rejoice and be glad for this day. A day specially made for me with love by LOVE to remain in love with the Lord.' She remains in love with the Lord through her company with the Holy Spirit by abiding in the Word.

Whoever keeps his commandments abides in God, and God in him. And by this we know that he abides in us, by the Spirit whom he has given us (1 John 3:24, ESV).

Every day, receive into you the Word of God, and celebrate the resurrected life of Jesus in the Holy Spirit that resides in you.

August 22

~ Replacing the 'OLD' me life with the 'NEW' me life in Christ ~

> *...to put off your old self, which belongs to your former manner of life and is corrupt through deceitful desires, and to be renewed in the spirit of your minds, and to put on the new self, created after the likeness of God in true righteousness and holiness (Ephesians 4:22-24, ESV).*

Whenever any negative thoughts enter the door of the mind of a good mother, she sees it as an opportunity to renew her mind in the Word of God. She starts creating the new life of Christ over her old life that brings in the thoughts of her fleshly desires.

> *...in which you once walked, following the course of this world, following the prince of the power of the air, the spirit that is now at work in the sons of disobedience among whom we all once lived in the passions of our flesh, carrying out the desires of the body and the mind, and were by nature children of wrath, like the rest of mankind (Ephesians 2:2-3, ESV).*

Every day she makes it her priority to sit calm and peaceful in the Word of God, so she can do all things through Christ and become that creative and inventive person that God designed her to be.

The Holy Spirit breathes new life into our life making it new all the time we take in the Word. Our flesh becomes Word when we walk in obedience to the Word. This is how our flesh is renewed and we see something brand new again in the same Word of God. We see the new Christ-like life. We are no longer blind; we can see now.

> *And those who belong to Christ Jesus have crucified the flesh with its passions and desires (Galatians 5:24, ESV).*

Every new day, renew yourself in the Word of God; keep storing and storing the Word of God. When the lust of fleshly thoughts enter your mind, renew your mind in the Word that has become flesh and show your Christ-like mind.

August 23

~ *Doing things together with your loved ones* ~

> *I am a companion of all who fear You, And of those who keep Your precepts (Psalm 119:63, NKJV)*

A good mother understands that to make her children happy and create that lasting bonding between them, she has to love doing with them what they do. I observe from my children that they never play with their toys but prefer to play around with the things I use. However, they always enjoy when we all sit down and play with the toys together. Their happiness is not from what they have but the very presence of being with the person they love. A good mother knows she is a great companion to not only her children but her husband too. She seeks God daily, in His Word and in prayer, to keep her company so she can be a great companion to her household.

> *But whoever is united with the Lord is one with him in spirit (1 Corinthians 6:17, NIV).*

The Holy Spirit, the Spirit of the Father, will keep us company when we invite Jesus to come live inside our hearts. Jesus Christ, the Son of God, became the Son of man, so He can become man's great companion. He has now given us the most precious gift, the Holy

Spirit, to become our spirit man's great companion and become one in Him. We can now enjoy doing everything together all the time as we journey with the Holy Spirit on the path of eternal life.

> *The Spirit gives life; the flesh counts for nothing. The words I have spoken to you—they are full of the Spirit and life (John 6:63, NIV).*

Each and every day receive into your flesh the fresh Word of God, so the Holy Spirit can bring this Word to life into your spirit man.

August 24

~ Guide and protect your marriage in Prayer and Word ~

> *Marriage should be honored by all, and the marriage bed kept pure, for God will judge the adulterer and all the sexually immoral (Hebrews 13:4, NIV).*

A good mother understands that sex is the most beautiful connection to bring a wife and husband into a lasting bond. Not only to bring their flesh together to become one but to allow God to give them the gift of children. They are trusted by God to raise up children who represent His kingdom on earth with their child-like faith. Every day she is before God in her marriage bed for God to anoint that bed and keep it pure and holy. She makes sure to protect her husband not to be stolen by the enemy when he is outside their home. She is the inner strength of her husband and it's her role to protect him and be strong for him by praying for him. She understands that man can be weak in the presence of woman who are enticing. She makes sure the presence of God surrounds her husband every day, so he doesn't fall victim to the sweet talk of an adulterous woman.

For the lips of the adulterous woman drip honey, and her speech is smoother than oil; but in the end she is bitter as gall, sharp as a double-edged sword. Her feet go down to death; her steps lead straight to the grave (Proverbs 5:3-5, NIV).

God has allowed His Spirit to enter the womb of a woman through the virgin birth. He has now restored everything that the fruit of disobedience destroyed inside a woman. As long as a woman houses the Holy Spirit and keeps connecting deeper with Him, her husband will not be unfaithful to her body which houses the Holy Spirit. The Joy from the fruit of the Holy Spirit will cause him to always enjoy his wife.

Let your wife be a fountain of blessing for you. Rejoice in the wife of your youth. She is a loving deer, a graceful doe. Let her breasts satisfy you always. May you always be captivated by her love (Proverbs 5:18-19, NLT).

Every day speak the blood of Jesus to cover your bed, your wedding certificate, and all your happy moments captured in photos. Lock the enemy completely out to prevent them from getting into your marriage and ruin it.

August 25

~ Favouritism ~

Jacob loved Joseph more than any of his other children because Joseph had been born to him in his old age. So one day Jacob had a special gift made for Joseph—a beautiful robe (Genesis 37:3, NLT).

Sibling rivalry in a family is normal. Sometimes siblings will try to compare themselves to see who the parents' favourite is and start hating that favourite child. God's wisdom is needed to handle such situations. Good parents don't show favouritism. The first murder took place because of jealousy between siblings. A good mother knows that all her children will compete for her attention. She treats them equally and has one on one time with each of them. Her personal relationship with each is to make them feel special, unique and different to each other. She avoids commenting on how one child can be more intelligent, physically attractive or gifted with skills and abilities over another. Everyone gets the same praise for how unique and special they are. God doesn't show favouritism.

For God does not show favouritism (Romans 2:11, NIV).

The Holy Spirit is the Spirit of God, and He loves us all the same. He doesn't show favouritism. He is full of patience to go with our flow of movement. The more we hunger and thirst for the Word, the more we move deeper into the depth of His love.

It's our hunger and thirst for the Word that constantly drives us to God to be fed; that one on one time we personally have with Jesus, the Word that has become flesh.

And Jesus grew in wisdom and stature, and in favour with God and man (Luke 2:52, NIV).

When we grow in the Word which is Jesus, wisdom of God, we find favour with God and man.

August 26

~ Beautiful things ~

Then he went down to Nazareth with them and was obedient to them. But his mother treasured all these things in her heart (Luke 2:51, NIV).

A good mother remembers everything about her children. She stores these beautiful moments in her heart. Every good moment she has with her children and the good things they do together is kept in her heart with prayers. She then reminds her children to always remember the good times in their lives. Her household only focuses on the good parts of life. She silently thanks God for all that He has given to her.

The Holy Spirit lives in our heart and makes us remember the goodness of God in our new life in Christ. He produces His fruit of goodness and makes it available for us. Anything that life throws at us is for us to taste and see that God is good, because for all things God works for the good to those that love Him.

> *But the Helper, the Holy Spirit, whom the Father will send in my name, he will teach you all things and bring to your remembrance all that I have said to you (John 14:26, ESV)*
>
> *And we know that in all things God works for the good of those who love him, who have been called according to his purpose (Romans 8:28, NIV).*

Remember that some of the most beautiful moments of your life are not meant to be displayed for the world to see. The evil and foolish energy from the world can ruin it.

August 27

~ *Words of affirmation* ~

> *I praise you because I am fearfully and wonderfully made; your works are wonderful, I know that full well (Psalm 139:14, NIV).*

Words of affirmation is one of the five love languages. If your love language is *'words of affirmation'* you will feel loved when people say words to make you proud or feel special about yourself.

I have come to understand that my daughter's love language is *'words of affirmation'*. She would constantly ask me what I think of everything she does and if I am proud of what she has done. This is how I know that her primary love language is *words of affirmation*.

Also, if you notice your children talking constantly all the time it means their love language is *words of affirmation*, so you have to keep talking with them to make them feel they are loved and belong. Even if they are asking you 101 questions!

A good mother who knows her children's primary love language as *words of affirmation* will always say words that uplift her children; tell them how they are unique and a masterpiece of God's creation and how creative, intelligent and helpful they are. This is how she fills her children's love tank and they feel loved and valued.

Jesus is the *words of affirmation* of God's love language. The Word that has become flesh. Jesus has now given us the Holy Spirit who brings the words of affirmation from God's love in His Word to become alive in us.

God loves us, and thinks how amazing, wonderful and great we are in the Holy Spirit that we house.

Here are just few of the many *words of affirmation* from God in His Word:

> *You are the city of God's delight and His bride. The Lord delights in you and claims you as His bride (Isaiah 62:4, NLT).*

You are a chosen people, a royal priesthood, a holy nation and God's special possession (1 Peter 2:9, NIV).

God has chosen you to make you like His signet ring (Haggai 2:23, NIV).

God says, He is taking away the ashes on your head, and He will give you a crown. He will take away your sadness and give you the oil of happiness. He will take away your sorrow and give you the celebration clothes. You are named the 'Good Trees' and 'The LORD's Wonderful Plant' (Isaiah 61:3, ERV).

A good mother always uses the Word of God, as *words of affirmation* to fill the love tank of her children.

We are to tell ourselves all the great things God thinks and says of us. Every day tell yourself that you are fearfully and wonderfully created for the Father's glory.

August 28

~ Physical touch ~

Truly I tell you, anyone who will not receive the kingdom of God like a little child will never enter it.' And he took the children in his arms, placed his hands on them and blessed them (Mark 10:15-16, NIV).

Physical touch is one of the five love languages. If your love language is *physical touch* you will always want to hug others and feel loved when you are hugged.

A good mother observes her children carefully and learns what their love language is so that she can fill up their love tank. I know one of the love languages of my one-year-old son is *physical touch*; I can get more than ten hugs from him a day. In order to make him feel loved I have to give him back many hugs too.

If you notice your children always wanting to sit closer to you and touch you when talking or laughing (even some who want to sit on top of you or hug you), their love language is *physical touch*.

A good mother meets the love language of *physical touch* in her children at the right time of their needs. She physically is in touch with the Word every day and actions it. She seeks God for wisdom so she is able to fill the love language of her children when there is the right opportunity. She understands she can't just hug her teenagers with a love language of *physical touch* in front of her child's friends as that can cause embarrassment.

> *One of them, the disciple whom Jesus loved, was reclining next to him. Simon Peter motioned to this disciple and said, 'Ask him which one he means.' Leaning back against Jesus, he asked him, 'Lord, who is it?' (John 13:23-25, NIV).*

We can now touch Jesus physically within us in the Holy Spirit by leaning deeper into the Word of God, who is Jesus in flesh.

Jesus is the *physical touch* of God's love language. He speaks love through *physical touch*. He is the Word that became flesh. The Holy Spirit is the *physical touch* of Jesus in the Spirit form. He is the power of God. He resurrected Jesus and brought Him to life. Jesus has now given us the Holy Spirit to live inside us. He produces His fruit of righteousness inside us to reproduce it physically to whoever we come in touch with. When we give the fruit of goodness, kindness and patience to people who need it, we touch their lives and fill them with love.

August 29

~ Quality time ~

Call to me and I will answer you, and will tell you great and hidden things that you have not known (Jeremiah 33:3, ESV).

Quality time is one of the five love languages. If your love language is *quality time* you will always want your loved ones to spend their time with you. You will also have time for others because you also enjoy good company.

A good mother spends *quality time* with her children. To understand the love language of her children, she rests in the Word of God to seek His Spirit of understanding and knowledge. She knows that her children with the love language of *quality time* will always bother her constantly to get her to listen to them. To fill their love tank, she has to give them both her eyes and ears and show that she is interested in what they are saying even if she is not.

The Holy Spirit is actually the *quality time* of God with which Jesus has gifted us. God loved the world so much and gave us Jesus to have eternal life. The Holy Spirit is the eternal life of Jesus. He lives inside us all the time. We can talk to the Father and Son in the Holy Spirit for as long as we want.

So faith comes from hearing, and hearing through the word of Christ (Romans 10:17, ESV).

The love language of God is *quality time* with Him. We must spend *quality time* with Him by listening and hearing the Word, as that is where faith comes from. Without faith it is impossible to please God.

God will always listen to us when we call out to him.

August 30

~ Acts of service ~

> *Now that I, your Lord and Teacher, have washed your feet, you also should wash one another's feet. I have set you an example that you should do as I have done for you. Very truly I tell you, no servant is greater than his master, nor is a messenger greater than the one who sent him. Now that you know these things, you will be blessed if you do them (John 13:14-17, NIV).*

Acts of service is one of the five love languages. If your love language is *acts of service* you will always want to serve others. It just makes you happy to serve your love ones. You are happy when they are happy.

When it comes to *acts of service*, every mother does it out of pure love. A good mother spends time in Word and prayer for God to give her a servant heart to serve her house as a worship unto Him. She understands that her children with the love language of *acts of service* will always want to help her with any chores that need doing. Whether she is washing dishes, cooking or folding clothes they love to help out. To fill their love tank she allows them to help her and thanks them for a job well done. This is how her children feel loved, appreciated and valued, and their love tank is filled. When they grow up they will find their happiness in serving others.

> *...just as the Son of Man did not come to be served, but to serve, and to give his life as a ransom for many. (Matthew 20:28, NIV).*

Jesus is the love in action of God, His *acts of service*. Jesus said himself that He has come to serve and not to be served. He demonstrated that by washing the feet of his disciples and told them to do the same.

The Holy Spirit is the love in action of Jesus. His *acts of service*. The Holy Spirit serves us all the time by producing His fruit of righteousness to us so that we may serve others.

August 31

~ Gifts ~

> *Thanks be to God for his inexpressible gift! (2 Corinthians 9:15, ESV).*

Gifts is one of the five love languages. If your love language is *gifts* you will always love to give people gifts to see them happy. It makes you happy to see people happy to receive your gifts.

Only the good Lord gives a good wife as a gift. A man is happy when he has a good wife. That good wife becomes a good mother to his children. A good mother understands the priceless value of a gift. I know from the actions of my five-year-old that one of her love languages is *gifts*. She will want to check every day if I have any gifts for her, but most of all she would give me something every day as a gift. To fill her love tank, I would wrap up her old toys or books and surprise her with these gifts. The joy and sparkle of light on her face is priceless.

> *Every good gift and every perfect gift is from above, coming down from the Father of lights, with whom there is no variation or shadow due to change (James 1:17, ESV).*

God's love language is *gifts*. He gave His only Son as a *gift* to us in our likeness and nature, so we can connect easily and abide in Him. Jesus, who is our likeness, gave us the Holy Spirit as a *gift* and the Holy Spirit has given us His fruit of righteousness as a *gift*. His fruit of righteousness is the gift of eternal life, the characters and lifestyle living of Jesus. This is the gift we give back to God and make Him happy. God is so happy with us, His children, when we love each other by serving each other the nine fruit of the Holy Spirit mentioned in Galatians 5:22-23.

SEPTEMBER

~ A mother's scars from bringing a life into existence ~

I remember becoming a mother and getting all those stretch marks. And with a newborn baby around I had less sleep or disturbed sleep for the first three to six months. Seeing all the dark circles under my eyes from lack of sleep, and the stretch marks from pregnancy I prayed and asked Jesus to heal me and remove those marks. And this is what Jesus, himself, said, 'The marks you have are the proof and evidence of bringing a life into this world. You see, I too have marks and scars on my hands and feet. The proof and evidence that I died to give life to the world. My Father loved the world so much and gave me to the world to save life with my LIFE. Those scars of mine are there to show that I have given life to everyone in the world to become a child of God. Your scars are there to show you that you have brought life into this world. You have given a child a life to live in this world.'

A good mother understands that she can bring a life into this world but for that life to have a LIFE and live LIFE she has to be connected and charged to the source and giver of life, JESUS CHRIST. She seeks the Word daily first thing before she begins the activities of the day. She celebrates the birth of a new day and rejoices in the day in the same way that she joyfully receives the birth of her child.

Just as she goes through the pain of childbirth before receiving her bundle of joy, she has pains and sorrows too that may last for the night but joy comes in the morning in the birth of a new day for her to start all over again.

> *Weeping may stay for the night, but rejoicing comes in the morning (Psalm 30:5, NIV).*

The Holy Spirit always produces joy in the new life of Christ. Every time the Holy Spirit reveals Jesus to us, He brings Him out from us and, when Jesus is revealed, that joy is indescribable. The Holy Spirit borne out of Jesus from within us to fill us with joy all the time.

> *Very truly I tell you, you will weep and mourn while the world rejoices. You will grieve, but your grief will turn to joy. A woman giving birth to a child has pain because her time has come; but when her baby is born she forgets the anguish because of her joy that a child is born into the world. So with you: Now is your time of grief, but I will see you again and you will rejoice, and no one will take away your joy (John 16:20-22, NIV).*

Each day of the month of September and EVERY DAY, celebrate the birth of another new day for the life you can live in that day. Rejoice and be glad and celebrate your life in what God says of you in His Word. Prepare yourself in the Word to look forward to meeting your Lord and Saviour, Jesus Christ.

> *Celebrate God all day, every day. I mean, revel in him! Make it as clear as you can to all you meet that you're on their side, working with them and not against them. Help them see that the Master is about to arrive. He could show up any minute! (Philippians 4:4-5, MSG).*

September 1

~ Living in righteousness ~

Whoever pursues righteousness and love finds life, prosperity and honour (Proverbs 21:21, NIV).

A good mother asks God to help her action the fruit of righteousness through His Holy Spirit within Her. She asks God until righteousness blooms in her house and she never stops there. She keeps seeking God until she finds her house living in righteousness. She smiles, holds her head up and walks on the path of life, prosperity and honour. She always walks through the right door where God connects her to the right people with the right resources at the right time.

> *The steps of a man are established by the Lord, when he delights in his way (Psalm 37:23, ESV).*

The Holy Spirit produces the fruit of righteousness for us to action it. This is heaven's wealth and riches that the Holy Spirit has in store.

> *For the kingdom of God is not a matter of eating and drinking but of righteousness and peace and joy in the Holy Spirit. (Romans 14:17, ESV).*

September 2

~ *Follower of Jesus* ~

> *Follow my example, as I follow the example of Christ (1 Corinthians 11:1, NIV).*

Every mother knows that her children follow her actions. But a good mother imitates Christ as her children imitate her. She spends one on one time with her children and speaks like a friend to them revealing the secrets of God's Word and His great plans for their life.

Jesus had followers who followed Him in His ministry. From those followers He chose twelve to be His disciples, and from those twelve only one, John, who followed Him to the cross was chosen to be His friend, and what Jesus revealed to John is written in the book of Revelation. We are known as a friend and follower of Jesus when we live by the fruit of the Holy Spirit inside us. As we continue following Jesus all the days of our life, we grow more closer to the Holy Spirit as a close friend.

> *He replied, 'Because the knowledge of the secrets of the kingdom of heaven has been given to you, but not to them (Matthew 13:11, NIV).*

Continue following Jesus all the days of your life, and He will receive you as a friend to share the secrets and revelation of the kingdom.

September 3

~ Having compassion towards others ~

> *Therefore, as God's chosen people, holy and dearly loved, clothe yourselves with compassion, kindness, humility, gentleness and patience (Colossians 3:12, NIV).*

Parents are their children's first followers. A good mother sets a Christ-like example so that her children can imitate her to be like Christ. Compassion is what she serves all the time. She wants her children to feel compassion for all humanity and nature. And so she uses this Word of God as her prayer,

> *Let your compassion come to me that I may live, for your law is my delight (Psalm 119:77, NIV).*

Where there is compassion, there is love and no judgement. Compassion helps you understand why people are what they are and still love them for it. The Holy Spirit is the love of God in action inside us empowering us to have compassion for all with whom we come into contact.

> *The Lord is gracious and righteous; our God is full of compassion (Psalm 116:5, NIV).*

God chose you to clothe your every day with compassion so you can live and walk in love.

September 4

~ Serving others ~

> *Be devoted to one another in love. Honor one another above yourselves (Romans 12:10, NIV).*

A good mother lays down her life to serve her household. She honours others above herself by serving them. She knows that she is the strength that makes her house functions well and so she spends quality time in the Word of God to draw out strength from God to be strong for her family. This is the Word of prayer that she breathes out to God.

> *I love you, O Lord, my strength. The Lord is my rock and my fortress and my deliverer, my God, my rock, in whom I take refuge, my shield, and the horn of my salvation, my stronghold (Psalm 18:1-2, ESV).*

Jesus came to serve and not to be served. He is now serving us through His Holy Spirit who lives inside us. The Holy Spirit is the strength and powerhouse of God that works mightily with us to keep us strong for God.

> *For the sake of Christ, then, I am content with weaknesses, insults, hardships, persecutions, and calamities. For when I am weak, then I am strong (2 Corinthians 12:10, ESV).*

Each new day from God comes with new strength. Strengthen your day more in Word and prayer to become stronger over your weaknesses which can give access for the enemy to attack.

September 5

~ *Sticking with God in all seasons* ~

Marriage should be honored by all, and the marriage bed kept pure, for God will judge the adulterer and all the sexually immoral. Keep your lives free from the love of money and be content with what you have, because God has said, 'Never will I leave you; never will I forsake you.' (Hebrews 13:4-5, NIV).

A good mother is not only faithful in her marriage to her husband but also in her relationship with God. The vows she mentions in her marriage is grounded in God's Word. She honours God in her marriage. There are many times that a financial crisis can hit her house hard, or a health crisis can break her home but as long as she builds her home on the rock, she will not be moved by anything. Her house will only bend and grow its roots deeper, and she will still stand strong through all seasons. The God she serves specialises in doing things out of season. The Word she is rooted in will cause her to blossom in and out of season through all seasons.

Blessed is the one who does not walk in step with the wicked or stand in the way that sinners take or sit in the company of mockers, but whose delight is in the law of the Lord, and who meditates on his law day and night. That person is like a tree planted by streams of water, which yields its fruit in season and whose leaf does not wither— whatever they do prospers (Psalm 1:1-3, NIV).

The Holy Spirit produces the fruit of righteousness through all seasons. It is in the driest season that we need more fruit to be produced to sustain our life from withering. The moment we receive Jesus into our lives, our days are now to live for Him. Our spirit becomes one with His Spirit for 'better', because Jesus sacrificed Himself for our 'worse'. We become 'rich' for Jesus has become 'poorer' for us; we are healthy as Jesus has removed all the curses of sicknesses and diseases. He loves us so much that even death cannot hold Him back from us. He rose up from the death by the power of the Holy Spirit for us to live His new resurrected life.

> *You know the generous grace of our Lord Jesus Christ. Though he was rich, yet for your sakes he became poor, so that by his poverty he could make you rich (2 Corinthians 8:9, NLT).*

> *'Blessed is the man who trusts in the Lord, whose trust is the Lord. He is like a tree planted by water, that sends out its roots by the stream, and does not fear when heat comes, for its leaves remain green, and is not anxious in the year of drought, for it does not cease to bear fruit.' (Jeremiah 17:7-8, ESV).*

Each and every day through all seasons focus on reproducing the fruit of the Holy Spirit.

September 6

~ Bearing the fruit of the Spirit ~

> *But the fruit of the Spirit is love, joy, peace, patience, kindness, goodness, faithfulness, gentleness, self-control; against such things there is no law (Galatians 5:22-23, ESV).*

A good mother's goal is to make the fruit of the Holy Spirit productive in her house and so her rules and regulations to her children are to be kind, patient and good. She teaches her children to be faithful in doing so, and to have self-control to try not to do anything wrong. She also makes it clear to be careful and be gentle to life. Life is fragile. She teaches her children that no other relationship must steal the love, joy and peace they have found in their relationship with Jesus in the fruit of His Spirit.

> *My life fades like a shadow at the end of day and withers like grass (Psalm 102:11, CEV).*

The Holy Spirit produces His fruit for us to have a fruitful life in our relationship with Christ Jesus.

> *You did not choose me, but I chose you and appointed you that you should go and bear fruit and that your fruit should abide, so that whatever you ask the Father in my name, he may give it to you (John 15:16, ESV).*

God chose a good woman to be your mother and appoint her to go and bear fruit of the Holy Spirit.

September 7

~ Be faithful ~

> *Whoever believes in me, as Scripture has said, rivers of living water will flow from within them. (John 7:38, NIV).*

A good mother will always be faithful in raising her children even if her husband or partner is not faithful to her, or even if things do not turn out the way she hoped. She accepts what God allows into her life. She remains faithful and seeks God to excel where He has placed her. In her desert she needs the spring of living water, Jesus, to be nourished, and to spring forth to bloom in life. To her unfaithful husband or partner she hands him over to God who is the righteous judge.

> *'It is God alone who judges; He decides who will rise and who will fall.' (Psalm 75:7 NLT)*

The Holy Spirit produces the fruit faithfulness, so we can remain faithful in any relationships. It is more important to maintain our faithful relationship with God who never fails us than man who will fail us.

> *But the Lord is faithful, and he will strengthen you and protect you from the evil one (2 Thessalonians 3:3, NIV).*

Be always faithful in your relationship with God and every other relationship will enjoy your company.

September 8

~ Growing in wisdom ~

> *My goal is that they may be encouraged in heart and united in love, so that they may have the full riches of complete understanding, in order that they may know the mystery of God, namely, Christ, in whom are hidden all the treasures of wisdom and knowledge (Colossians 2:2-3, NIV).*

A good mother wants growth and progress in all that is in her care. Knowing her children are physically growing every day she tries to grow spiritually each day to balance it out. She needs the timely wisdom of God to offer to her children in their times of need at their level. She wants to grow her faith so she can progress in life. Not only is Jesus the wisdom of God, our heavenly Father, He is the only way, the truth and the life to the Father as well. She seeks and asks God to give her wisdom to grow and progress in it. God is waiting on us to ask Him, so He can pour out His wisdom through His Holy Spirit inside us.

> *If any of you lacks wisdom, you should ask God, who gives generously to all without finding fault, and it will be given to you (James 1:5, NIV).*

The Holy Spirit, the Spirit of wisdom is inside us in Christ Jesus, who is the wisdom of God. He loves giving wisdom freely to all that ask Him.

> *It is because of him that you are in Christ Jesus, who has become for us wisdom from God—that is, our righteousness, holiness and redemption (1 Corinthians 1:30, NIV).*

Each and every day ask God for His wisdom for the day to grow and progress in life.

September 9

~ *Living gratefully in the house of God* ~

> *But when you pray, go into your room, close the door and pray to your Father, who is unseen. Then your Father, who sees what is done in secret, will reward you (Matthew 6:6, NIV).*

A praying wife and mother brings success to her husband and children. She is that good mother that carries her house into God's house so God can carry them all to enjoy life in His house. She watches in joy as blessings flow right out from God onto her husband as the head. This is what she always tells God.

> *One thing I ask from the Lord, this only do I seek: that I may dwell in the house of the Lord all the days of my life, to gaze on the beauty of the Lord and to seek him in his temple (Psalm 27:4, NIV).*

The Holy Spirit wants our flesh to be His house so the Word can become flesh, and when we carry into our heart the Word, who is Jesus, His Spirit uses our body as His house. We actually live in the house of God, His very presence, when we house the Holy Spirit.

> *I appeal to you therefore, brothers, by the mercies of God, to present your bodies as a living sacrifice, holy and acceptable to God, which is your spiritual worship (Romans 12:1, ESV).*

Be grateful for your body and offer it as a sacrifice of thanksgiving and worship unto God in whatever service your body provides to meet the daily demands of today.

September 10

~ *The womb of a mother* ~

> *Upon you I have leaned from before my birth; you are he who took me from my mother's womb. My praise is continually of you (Psalm 71:6, ESV).*

A good mother understands her children well because she prays and seeks God in His Word to lean on His Spirit of understanding.

> *The unfolding of your words gives light; it gives understanding to the simple (Psalm 119:130, NIV).*

Filled with praises and thanksgiving she leans on the Spirit of understanding to direct her path, to live in the fear of God when she was born again.

Jesus is her only close friend who she trusts and leans on to stop from falling into the temptation of this world. Just as God took her from her mother's womb, God took her children from her womb too. To remain in God's womb she teaches her children to be born again into God's womb, into His Spirit, into His kingdom.

> *Jesus replied, 'Very truly I tell you, no one can see the kingdom of God unless they are born again.' (John 3:3, NIV).*

The Holy Spirit is the womb of God where the Word was conceived to give birth to flesh. The Word became flesh. The womb of a woman and the womb of God became one in Spirit and conceived the Word which has become flesh. We are in one in the Lord in Spirit.

> *Before I was born the LORD called me; from my mother's womb he has spoken my name (Isaiah 49:1, NIV).*

> *But whoever is united with the LORD is one with him in spirit (1 Corinthians 6:17, NIV).*

Every day live your life in the womb of God and feed on the fruit of the Holy Spirit.

September 11

~ Living heaven on earth ~

You became imitators of us and of the Lord, for you welcomed the message in the midst of severe suffering with the joy given by the Holy Spirit (1 Thessalonians 1:6, NIV).

Every home must be a safe haven. A good mother makes her home a safe haven by connecting to heaven and living heaven on earth, where she can serve everyone in her household. Her home is safe for everyone. The perfect love of God fills the house removing fears and every individual's imperfection is loved unconditionally through the perfect love of God. The only way she maintains this environment and energy in her home is by being grateful to God in everything and anything life gives her. Whether pain, sorrow or joy her heart is always full of gratitude.

Rejoice in the Lord always. I will say it again: Rejoice (Philippians 4:4, NIV).

The Holy Spirit brings heaven into our hearts. He is the Spirit of God and operates from the throne of God. The Holy Spirit produces immeasurable joy within us and it overflows when we begin to live a life of gratitude. Joy is one of the fruit of the Holy Spirit on which the devil works hard to steal from us every moment.

And the disciples were filled with joy and with the Holy Spirit (Acts 13:52, NIV).

Splendor and majesty are before him; strength and joy are in his place (1 Chronicles 16:27, ESV).

Just as parents are joyful in seeing their children filled with joy, God feels the same when we are filled with joy.

September 12

~ Quit comparing ~

> *Because of the privilege and authority God has given me, I give each of you this warning: Don't think you are better than you really are. Be honest in your evaluation of yourselves, measuring yourselves by the faith God has given us (Romans 12:3, NLT).*

The devil makes you start comparing and feel as though you are not worthy to be a child of God. This is a lie from the devil. God loves you so much that He wants His Spirit to become productive in you so you can experience His power and become stronger in your faith.

A good mother doesn't compare her children with her other children or with others. She knows that they are unique and designed by God according to their calling and purpose. She lets them know they are loved and accepted the way they are and nothing they do will stop her love. She loves them just the way they are. She makes it clear to them that God loves all of us the way He made us and not to try and be someone we are not. Their uniqueness is worth more than anything they try to pretend to be. She teaches them Romans 12:3.

The Holy Spirit doesn't condemn and compare those that are weak in their faith to other family members of Christ who are strong in their faith. He accepts us just the way we are and loves us so much because of who we are created for.

> *But God demonstrates his own love for us in this: While we were still sinners, Christ died for us (Romans 5:8, NIV).*

When you see others through the lens of compassion, you will never compare how you are better off than them but love them for who they are and help them in whatever way you can.

September 13

~ Build a Christ-centred life ~

> *Unless the Lord builds the house, the builders labor in vain. Unless the Lord watches over the city, the guards stand watch in vain (Psalm 127:1, NIV).*

A good wife makes her marriage Christ-centred and from there she builds up a Christ-centred home. Her aim is to build her children's character to be like Christ. To make good choices and create habits to build Christ-like characters, she pays the price by sacrificing her time in prayer and the Word of God. She needs the light from the Word of God to give her the right direction to making right decisions for her household. She tells God in Psalm 119:130.

> *The unfolding of your words gives light; it gives understanding to the simple (Psalm 119:130, NIV).*

The Holy Spirit is Christ-centred in us. He produces the character of Christ to build us to be like Christ in our character. We have to receive the Word into us and be obedient to the voice of the Holy Spirit on the Word we received. Goodness is one of the fruit of the Holy Spirit, and we need that to have the godly character of Christ.

Not only so, but we also glory in our sufferings, because we know that suffering produces perseverance; perseverance, character; and character, hope. And hope does not put us to shame, because God's love has been poured out into our hearts through the Holy Spirit, who has been given to us (Romans 5:3-5, NIV).

Bury your self-centred lifestyle in the Holy Spirit's Christ-centred life inside you. Nourish yourself from the fruit of life, and not the fruit of the knowledge of good and evil.

September 14

~ God carrying you ~

Even to your old age and gray hairs I am he, I am he who will sustain you.

I have made you and I will carry you; I will sustain you and I will rescue you (Isaiah 46:4, NIV).

Mothers carry their children in their heart no matter how grown up they are. A good mother not only carries her children in her heart, she carries them in the promises of God's Word. Those promises of God keep giving her hope to continue trusting God when her faith starts to fade.

The Holy Spirit you carry inside you will give you hope to keep trusting God, making your faith stronger and firmer. When you keep carrying the Holy Spirit He will go before you and carry you into God's promises.

> *The Lord Himself goes before you and will be with you; he will never leave you nor forsake you. Do not be afraid; do not be discouraged (Deuteronomy 31:8 NIV).*

Be a carrier of God's Word every day and experience the joy of God's strength. When you carry God's Word, He carries you. You draw closer to Him, and He draws closer to you.

September 15

~ Shine for Jesus ~

> *In the same way, let your light shine before others, that they may see your good deeds and glorify your Father in heaven (Matthew 5:16, NIV).*

This woman is not just any ordinary woman; every time she wakes up darkness around her flees. She carries the light inside her. She seeks the SOURCE OF LIGHT to be her source of light. She is a good mother who is always there with that light not only for her household but to help anyone who can't really see where they are going. She is clothed with strength and dignity. She can laugh at the days to come because the light shines through all her days making all that is under her care glow with a brighter future.

> *She is clothed with strength and dignity; she can laugh at the days to come (Proverbs 31:25, NIV).*

Jesus Christ is the light of the world, and His Spirit of light lives in us. He lights up our dark mind so we can see.

> *Satan, who is the god of this world, has blinded the minds of those who Don't believe. They are unable to see the glorious light of the Good News. They don't understand this message about the glory of Christ, who is the exact likeness of God (2 Corinthians 4:4, NLT).*

The Word of God is the light that will remove the darkness that is blinding you from seeing how great God has designed you in the GREAT I AM, who is Jesus.

September 16

~ The joy in the pain ~

> *May your father and mother rejoice; may she who gave you birth be joyful! (Proverbs 23:25, NIV).*

All mothers are strong. That strength was received when they felt the pain of bringing their children into this world. With this strength they are capable of doing anything to raise their child up in this fallen world. A good mother does more than this, she seeks the goodness of God in His Word to give His children a life. They not only live that life but love and live that life in its highest calling. She pays the price today in seeking God and His righteousness, so all her needs for tomorrow are already provided for when the need arises.

This is the reason she smiles through her pain and she is not worried about tomorrow.

> *But seek first His kingdom and his righteousness, and all these things will be given to you as well. Therefore do not worry about tomorrow, for tomorrow will worry about itself. Each day has enough trouble of its own (Matthew 6:33-34, NIV).*

The Holy Spirit, the righteous kingdom of God, is inside us; if we just seek Him from inside then all other things will be given to us in our time of need. Keep feeding on the Word of God because it attracts the breath of the Holy Spirit to bring it to life. When the Word wants to give you the LIFE and become ALIVE in you, you will go through a pain process from which you will come out stronger to be able to maintain that new life. It is the same as a mother who goes through pain to bring a life into this world. Through this pain process, she gains a strength that enables her to look after her children and also be strong for them.

September 17

~ Love God, love people ~

He who finds a wife finds a good thing, and obtains favour from the Lord. (Proverbs 18:22 NKJV).

The man who receives his wife as a favour from God also receives a good mother to his children. She is a good thing from God and has His favour. Like a father taking his daughter and giving her hand in marriage to her husband-to-be, God takes this woman's hand and gives it to the good man with whom He has found favour. She is not just any woman; she is the daughter of the Hand that keeps the universe going.

Then the Lord God made a woman from the rib he had taken out of the man, and he brought her to the man (Genesis 2:22, NIV).

When we produce the fruit of the Holy Spirit, and are good, kind and patient to others, we gain favour not just with God but also with people. The woman was taken from within a man to be a man's gift from God. The Holy Spirit was taken from God through what Jesus sacrificed and given as gift to us. The Holy Spirit's fruit of righteousness within us is to be taken from within us and given as a gift to others. This is how we love God by loving those who God loves so much.

> *No one has ever seen God. But if we love each other, God lives in us. If we love each other, God's love has reached its goal—it is made perfect in us (1 John 4:12, ERV).*

Balance yourself in the love of God. Love God by loving people who God loves so much.

September 18

~ Wisdom from God ~

> *Do not forsake wisdom, and she will protect you; love her, and she will watch over you. The beginning of wisdom is this: Get wisdom. Though it cost all you have, get understanding (Proverbs 4:6-7, NIV).*

A good mother's best friend is wisdom with whom she spends time in the Word of God. Before she does anything she seeks wisdom for the opinions about every situation she is going to go through. Because of this, a good mother always has a timely word for everyone that needs her words of encouragement.

> *She opens her mouth in wisdom, and the teaching of kindness is on her tongue (Proverbs 31:26, NASB).*

> *To one there is given through the Spirit a message of wisdom, to another a message of knowledge by means of the same Spirit, (1 Corinthians 12:8, NIV),*

The Holy Spirit breathes wisdom into our spirit, so we can do the right things at the right time. The more we receive into us the Word of God who is Jesus, the wisdom of God, the Holy Spirit, breathes life into it, and wisdom becomes alive in us.

> ...but to those whom God has called, both Jews and Greeks, Christ the power of God and the wisdom of God (1 Corinthians 1:24, NIV).

Ask God every day to give you the Spirit of wisdom to connect to the right people and do the right things at the right time.

September 19

~ Understanding from God ~

> *But love your enemies, do good to them, and lend to them without expecting to get anything back. Then your reward will be great, and you will be children of the Most High, because he is kind to the ungrateful and wicked (Luke 6:35, NIV).*

A good mother continues to love the wrong people in her life even though they make life hard for her. She understands that they are actually the right people for her to produce the fruit of righteousness that they need and she lets them bother her. She is very understanding because of the light from the Word of God that lights up her mind.

> *The unfolding of your words gives light; it gives understanding to the simple (Psalm 119:130, NIV).*

The Holy Spirit of God breathes understanding into our spirit, so we can discern why people act the way they do so that we can accept them with His love. The more we receive into us the Word of God, the more the Holy Spirit breathes life upon it. His presence of light shines upon the Word of God inside us, giving us understanding.

> *So we have not stopped praying for you since we first heard about you. We ask God to give you complete knowledge of his will and to give you spiritual wisdom and understanding (Colossians 1:9, NLT).*
>
> *Cause me to understand the way of your precepts, that I may meditate on your wonderful deeds (Psalm 119:27, NIV).*

Let Psalm 119:27 always be your prayer every day.

September 20

~ *Path of righteousness* ~

> *You make known to me the path of life; you will fill me with joy in your presence, with eternal pleasures at your right hand (Psalm 16:11, NIV).*

One day while noticing things I don't want lying around the house and trying to put them back in their right place, Blessed, my 11-month-old son, hurt himself. This is what the Holy Spirit taught me: A good mother always directs her household in God's path of righteousness. There is danger on any other path, and she knows Jesus is the only way, the truth and the life to the Father, the source of life and righteousness. She always takes everything that is not right in her and offers it to the righteous one to restore it in its right place.

> *Restore to me the joy of your salvation and grant me a willing spirit, to sustain me (Psalm 51:12, NIV).*

The Holy Spirit is the righteousness and holiness of Christ. He enables us to produce His fruit of righteousness to those that need it. When we receive into us the Word of God, the Holy Spirit brings it to life. Every time our OLD LIFE wants to have its selfish way, the life-giving Word of God directs us back to the path of righteousness

> *I am the LORD, I have called You in righteousness, I will also hold You by the hand and watch over You, And I will appoint You as a covenant to the people, As a light to the nations, (Isaiah 42:6, NASB).*

Remind yourself all the time that you are the righteousness of God in Christ.

September 21

~ The satisfaction of God's love brings joy ~

> *No one has ever seen God. But if we love each other, God lives in us. If we love each other, God's love has reached its goal—it is made perfect in us (1 John 4:12, ERV).*

A good mother aims to fill her home with love. It's her office where she practises love. She is the CEO and it doesn't matter how many times she fails she tries all over again. It is God's goal for His love to become perfect in the household where they live in love, and so every day she empties herself out and fills herself with the love and joy of the Lord. This is where she strengthens her strength.

The joy of the Lord is my strength (Nehemiah 8:10). She prays using the words from Psalm 90:14.

> *Satisfy us in the morning with your unfailing love, that we may sing for joy and be glad all our days (Psalm 90:14, NIV).*

> *…for this day is holy to our Lord. And do not be grieved, for the joy of the Lord is your strength. (Nehemiah 8:10, ESV).*

The Holy Spirit produces the joy of the Lord and He is the strength and power of God. It is through Him that we receive in our heart the joy and strength of God which flow out from the Word of God. The Holy Spirit breathes upon the Word.

September 22

~ *Make God your priority* ~

> *We know that we live in God and God lives in us. We know this because he gave us his Spirit (1 John 4:13, ERV).*

A good mother's priorities are to protect her family's time together and to be successful she invests one-tenth of her time in Word and prayer. She knows her time is in God's hands.

> *My times are in your hands; (Psalm 31:15, NIV).*

For her house to be successful, God must be Number One in her priorities. She sets her priorities in the righteousness of God. She is seeking the righteousness of God so that all the other things she needs are added into her life. It's God first, then family.

> *No one has ever seen God. But if we love each other, God lives in us. If we love each other, God's love has reached its goal—it is made perfect in us. (1 John 4:12, ERV)*

The Holy Spirit produces the fruit of righteousness and it is God's first priority for His Holy Spirit to produce the fruit of righteousness within us. The Holy Spirit produces the characters of the love of God who is Jesus in the form of His nine fruit. God's priority and goal is for us to live and walk in His love.

> *But seek first his kingdom and his righteousness, and all these things will be given to you as well (Matthew 6:33, NIV).*

Make it your priority to delight in God's righteous Word every day and action the fruit of righteousness. Then all your dreams and desires will be given.

September 23

~ Preparation ~

> *And if I go and prepare a place for you, I will come again and will take you to myself, that where I am you may be also (John 14:3, ESV).*

A good mother prepares the day for her household by waking up early in the morning while it is still dark. She prepares herself to get fed in the Word before she prepares food for her family for the day.

> *She gets up while it is still night; she provides food for her family and portions for her female servants (Proverbs 31:15, NIV).*

> *...being confident of this, that he who began a good work in you will carry it onto completion until the day of Jesus Christ (Philippians 1:6, NIV).*

Jesus has prepared each day for us to live in His Spirit. It is the Holy Spirit who is preparing us to meet Jesus on the day He comes.

> *It was the Lord's Day, and I was worshiping in the Spirit (Revelation 1:10, NLT).*

Every new day is the Lord's day to rejoice and be glad in it because the saviour is coming soon to meet you.

September 24

~ Ask the Holy Spirit to teach you ~

> *Teach me, Lord, the way of your decrees, that I may follow it to the end. (Psalm 119:33, NIV).*

A good mother asks God to teach her His Word so she can teach her children. Whatever God teaches is timely. She knows God does things in His perfect timing, that He made a time for everything and made everything beautiful in its time. The timely Word that God teaches her to teach her children is all they need to make their life beautiful.

> *True, God made everything beautiful in itself and in its time—but he's left us in the dark, so we can never know what God is up to, whether he's coming or going (Ecclesiastes 3:11, MSG).*

The Holy Spirit is the right time of God. He produces the fruit of righteousness according to our need at that moment in time. If we become impatient, patience is produced for us to use and it's up to us to choose to use it or not.

> *'Today I have given you the choice between life and death, between blessings and curses. Now I call on heaven and earth to witness the choice you make. Oh, that you would choose life, so that you and your descendants might live! You can make this choice by loving the Lord your God, obeying him, and committing yourself firmly to him. This is the key to your life. And if you love and obey the Lord, you will live long in the land the Lord swore to give your ancestors Abraham, Isaac, and Jacob.' (Deuteronomy 30:19-20, NLT).*

Jesus is a good teacher through the Holy Spirit who is our helper. If we ask the Holy Spirit to help us and teach us how to produce His fruit, He will.

September 25

~ Perfect love of God drives out fear ~

> *Do not be misled: 'Bad company corrupts good character.' (1 Corinthians 15:33, NIV).*

A good mother teaches her children to stay away from negative people as they drain out the positive energy in them. She knows that whatever evil happens has happened already and there is nothing new under the sun. She has no fear of troubles and problems of the world or any diseases striking the universe. She operates from the perfect love of God and it drives away fear.

The Holy Spirit is the goodness of God and teaches us about the good things in life that God loves to see in us. The Holy Spirit within us is the perfect love of God and perfect love drives out fear.

> *There is no fear in love. But perfect love drives out fear, because fear has to do with punishment. The one who fears is not made perfect in love (1 John 4:18, NIV).*

The perfect love of God from the Holy Spirit inside us drives out fear.

September 26

~ Be full of appreciation ~

Be thankful in all circumstances, for this is God's will for you who belong to Christ Jesus (1 Thessalonians 5:18, NLT).

A good mother appreciates every little effort her child makes. Even if the child is not doing it right, she still appreciates it as she knows her child is trying. She is full of appreciation because she is doing what she would like others to do for her. So whenever she cleans or cooks for her children, they appreciate her. Because she appreciates her children's effort, they appreciate her effort too.

The Holy Spirit produces the fruit of righteousness for us. For that is what He would like us to produce for Him in our relationship with Him. We must always appreciate the Holy Spirit for the love, joy and peace He produces for us in our relationship with Him. This is produced from within us and the devil cannot steal it. We too must produce that love, joy and peace in our relationship with the Holy Spirit.

> *But we request of you, brethren, that you appreciate those who diligently labor among you, and have charge over you in the Lord and give you instruction (1 Thessalonians 5:12, NASB).*

September 27

~ Praise and worship God in spirit and in truth with your new life ~

Let everything that has breath praise the Lord. Praise the Lord (Psalm 150:6, NIV).

A good mother teaches her children that being alive and living is the definition of God blessing you with life. She teaches her children to faithfully appreciate every breath of air that they breathe as that is God being faithful in giving and blessing them with life.

> *Those who live to bless others will have blessings heaped upon them, and the one who pours out his life to pour out blessings will be saturated with favor (Proverbs 11:25, TPT).*

The Holy Spirit faithfully gives us eternal life. We are able to wake up to a new day every day because of the faithful love of God.

> *The living, the living—they praise you, as I am doing today; parents tell their children about your faithfulness (Isaiah 38:19, NIV).*

Each and every morning when you first wake up, let God take your first breath away as you breathe out praises for being alive in Him for the day. Let everything in your house that has breath praise the Lord.

September 28

~ *Approaching God's throne room from where you are* ~

> *He is before all things, and in him all things hold together (Colossians 1:17, NIV).*

God places you right where you are, and He is right where He is, and He will always be where He is, on His throne. It doesn't matter where you are, as long as you are connected to Him your source of abundance will flow out from the river of life where the throne of God is. A good mother knows that she is where God has placed her; it doesn't matter what is placed in her hands, as long as she places her hands into God's hands, she is connected to the source of abundance. God will always be at His throne. Wherever she is, she can access God's throne room anytime, all the time, for her needs.

> *Let us then approach God's throne of grace with confidence, so that we may receive mercy and find grace to help us in our time of need (Hebrews 4:16, NIV).*

The Holy Spirit is always with us and He is connected to the source of abundance. We can seek Him from within us anytime all the time to receive the abundance of life. All we have to do is simply receive into us the Word of God that will connect us from where we are to God's throne room.

> *For through him we both have access to the Father by one Spirit (Ephesians 2:18, NIV).*

Connect yourself to the Word of God every day to get easy access to the throne room of God through His Holy Spirit.

September 29

~ A strong heart to love ~

My flesh and my heart may fail, but God is the strength of my heart and my portion forever (Psalm 73:26, NIV).

Every mother falls apart at times. No one knows those hidden tears behind those strong smiles. A good mother keeps her heart strong when she falls apart by falling in love with the source of LOVE AND LIGHT. It's the power of the perfect love of God that comforts all the imperfections around her. A perfect love that drives out all her fears of attacks from this world. And this is how strong her heart becomes as she serves more love in her house.

There is no fear in love. But perfect love drives out fear, because fear has to do with punishment. The one who fears is not made perfect in love (1 John 4:18, NIV).

The Holy Spirit always produces the love of God from inside us. When we don't feel loved, He sends someone to us to show us we are loved. He reminds us we are loved through people we love.

And so we know and rely on the love God has for us. God is love. Whoever lives in love lives in God, and God in them (1 John 4:16, NIV).

God loves us so much He sent His only Son into the world to demonstrate His love. We now have the love of God to give to our world.

September 30

~ *God is working for good only* ~

...if we endure, we will also reign with him (2 Timothy 2:12, NIV).

Every mother forgets the pain of bringing a child into this world after the baby is born. A good mother knows that every pain she goes through brings something good. Instead of complaining about the pains, she has a grateful attitude, only seeing the best coming out. With God by her side she will be rewarded for her faithfulness.

Let love and faithfulness never leave you; bind them around your neck, write them on the tablet of your heart. Then you will win favour and a good name in the sight of God and man (Proverbs 3:3-4, NIV).

The Holy Spirit goes through our pains with us and comforts us, and we come out with the abundance of Christ-like life. He produces joy and peace from His love towards us which comforts our pain. In all things God works for the good of those who love Him.

Blessed be the God and Father of our Lord Jesus Christ, the Father of mercies and God of all comfort, who comforts us in all our affliction, so that we may be able to comfort those who are in any affliction, with the comfort with which we ourselves are comforted by God (2 Corinthians 1-3-4, ESV).

Each and every day learn to comfort and cheer yourself in the Word of God, so you can help others who need comfort.

OCTOBER

~ A mother's role of cleaning ~

A mother cleans daily.

As mothers we clean out any dirty areas in the house that come to our attention. In the same way, whenever dirty thoughts rush into our mind to leave a stain we have to renew our mind right away.

4 May 2020. I remember I was walking past a real estate agent building and on their big TV screens they were showing 'before and after' amazing photos of some of the properties that had been renovated and were now in their 'for sale' listings. This is what the Holy Spirit taught me: You see, to be renewed in the Word and be that new creation in Christ all the time is like the 'after' of what you used to be 'before'.

Every time you renew your mind you become a better, newer and fresher person. Like those 'before and after' images on the screen. When you renew your mind, the images in your mind take on a new way of thinking.

Think about what you are thinking because as a man thinketh so is he (Proverbs 23:7). To have the mind of Christ (1 Corinthians 2:16) and become Christ-like you have to align your thoughts to what God says of you. You have to be knowledgeable of God's Word and what He says of you so that when others say something against you to put you off from what God designed you for, you can renew your thoughts back to what God thinks and says of you.

> *And I will give you a new heart, and a new spirit I will put within you. And I will remove the heart of stone from your flesh and give you a heart of flesh (Ezekiel 36:26, ESV).*

Jesus is the heart of flesh that God has given us. The Word that has become flesh. We have the mind of Christ by renewing our mind in the Word.

> *For, 'Who has known the mind of the Lord so as to instruct him?' But we have the mind of Christ (1 Corinthians 2:16, NIV).*

When you wake up to a new day you are blessed with a new life. You have a new clean heart and new spirit, and you have the mind of Christ. Therefore, let the first breath of your lungs praise the Lord with hymns and thanksgiving. Let the first beat of your heart sing a new song to the Lord as a worship in Spirit and truth. Let the first thought in your mind be renewed and transformed to think what God says of you.

Each day of the month of October and EVERY DAY, declare Psalm 51:10.

> *Create in me a clean heart, O God; and renew a right spirit within me (Psalm 51:10, KJV).*

October 1

~ *Exposing the lies of the devil* ~

> *For the word of the Lord is right and true; he is faithful in all he does (Psalm 33:4, NIV).*

The devil is the father of lies. A good mother will never be deceived by his lies because she spends time in the store house of God's truth, His Word. She can always free herself from the clever lies of the devil because she knows the truth.

> *And you shall know the truth, and the truth shall make you free. (John 8:32, NKJV).*

She stays fully charged all the time to her good Father of truth. She is so full of light and truth that the kingdom of darkness is threatened by what her next move will be.

The Holy Spirit is the Spirit of life, truth and light. As long as we regularly receive into us the Word of God He breathes His life into us and the truth from the light of God's Word exposes the lies of the devil in the dark that lead to death.

> *Jesus answered, 'I am the way and the truth and the life. No one comes to the Father except through me (John 14:6, NIV).*

> *The prayer of a righteous person is powerful and effective, (James 5:16, NIV).*

When we produce the fruit of righteousness we action the true kingdom lifestyle and our prayers become so effective that the kingdom of darkness is threatened.

October 2

~ *Worship God in Spirit and in truth* ~

> *For though we live in the world, we do not wage war as the world does. The weapons we fight with are not the weapons of the world. On the contrary, they have divine power to demolish strongholds (2 Corinthians 10:3-4, NIV).*

It's in the tone of every mother. Their voices are like the sounds of gunshots trying to bring calm and peace to the house. A good mother is already calm and at peace so she doesn't need the voice of a firing gun. She keeps 2 Corinthians 10:3-4 handy with her all the time. Her weapons for warfare are not carnal but mighty in God for pulling down strongholds. Her weapons are prayer, worship and scriptures. She worships God in Spirit and truth with prayers of scripture and praises. Her worship puts God right on the throne to rule in her favour. Satan will not linger long where God is praised and prayers are offered.

> *But the king will rejoice in God. All who swear to tell the truth will praise him, while liars will be silenced (Psalm 63:11, NLT).*

We worship God through the Holy Spirit within us when we worship Him in Spirit and truth. This is right where God feels complete in us through His Holy Spirit.

> *God is spirit, and his worshipers must worship in the Spirit and in truth.' (John 4:24, NIV).*

> *I was in the Spirit on the Lord's day, and I heard behind me a loud voice like a trumpet (Revelation 1:10, ESV).*

Every day is the Lord's day to be in the Spirit to worship God in Spirit and in truth. Whatever you plan to do for the day, ask the Holy Spirit to do it with you.

October 3

~ Watch and pray ~

> *Look to the Lord and his strength; seek his face always (1 Chronicles 16:11, NIV).*

A good mother doesn't talk about her problems and battles to people, she takes them to God. She doesn't need sympathy from people, she wants solutions and so she seeks God's face. Prayer is not her last resort but her first resort where she seeks God to get strength and if she is desperate for a solution she adds fasting to her prayer. She is that woman who wants God's intervention so quickly that she is willing to sacrifice whatever path she needs to take to make it work.

> *Before they call I will answer; while they are still speaking I will hear (Isaiah 65:24, NIV).*

The Holy Spirit connects more strongly to our spirit being when we combine fasting and praying. The flesh becomes weaker and our spirit becomes strong and receives clearly from the Holy Spirit.

> *Watch and pray so that you will not fall into temptation. The spirit is willing, but the flesh is weak. (Matthew 26:41, NIV).*

Just as we watch our diet and eat the right foods for our weight, when we pray and fast we are watching the focus of our prayer.

October 4

~ The will and plan of God in our lives ~

> *Commit to the Lord whatever you do, and he will establish your plans (Proverbs 16:3, NIV).*

A good mother makes many good plans for her house and submits them to God. All her plans are along the will of God and they all stand on God's promises. She makes her plans and brings God into them so he can direct her to step into in the right direction.

'A man's heart plans his way, but the LORD directs his steps' (Proverbs 16:9, NKJV).

The Holy Spirit is the Spirit of God, and He knows what will and plan God has for our life. He then conceives this will and plan into our spirit as the desires of our heart. When we delight in Him God gives us the desires of our heart, which are His will and plan for us, by producing the joy of the Holy Spirit in all circumstances and situations.

Take delight in the Lord, and he will give you the desires of your heart (Psalm 37:4, NIV).

Plan each day to delight in the Lord and He will give you the desires of your heart.

October 5

~ You do not have because you do not ask ~

Yet God has made everything beautiful for its own time. He has planted eternity in the human heart, but even so, people cannot see the whole scope of God's work from beginning to end (Ecclesiastes 3:11, NLT).

Right where she is, with what she has in her house, with what she faces, is where God allowed her to be planted on earth. She is a good mother and she doesn't complain when darkness hits her hard and she is unable to see well to do what she needs to do. Instead, she uses that position of nothingness to stand on God's promises to make something beautiful out of it. She knows that she doesn't have because she didn't ask.

> *You do not have because you do not ask God (James 4:2, NIV).*

Out of nothing God makes amazing wonderful things that no eyes have seen or heard. The Holy Spirit inside us is what God sends to us. No eyes have seen or ears have heard and no mind can perceive how the Holy Spirit works in and through us.

> *However, as it is written: 'What no eye has seen, what no ear has heard and what no human mind has conceived' the things God has prepared for those who love him— (1 Corinthians 2:9, NIV).*

Each and every day ask God to give you what He has prepared for you that no eyes have seen, no ears have heard and no mind has conceived. This is what God is willing to give you.

October 6

~ *Inheriting spiritual blessings* ~

> *Now I commit you to God and to the word of his grace, which can build you up and give you an inheritance among all those who are sanctified (Acts 20:32, NIV).*

While she is taking care of her earthly family, she knows she has legal rights to the family business and fortune of heaven. The will has been executed. The courts have been satisfied. Her spiritual account has been funded. She has been blessed by the Father with spiritual blessings in heavenly places. She is a good mother and she connects her earthly family to her heavenly family. She is inheriting more patience, more joy and more wisdom to fuel her up to use with her earthly family.

and giving joyful thanks to the Father, who has qualified you to share in the inheritance of his holy people in the kingdom of light (Colossians 1:12, NIV).

The Holy Spirit being alive in us through Christ Jesus connects us to receiving all the spiritual blessings available for us. Through what Jesus' acts we have the access to be part of His heavenly family.

All praise to God, the Father of our Lord Jesus Christ, who has blessed us with every spiritual blessing in the heavenly realms because we are united with Christ. Even before he made the world, God loved us and chose us in Christ to be holy and without fault in his eyes. God decided in advance to adopt us into his own family by bringing us to himself through Jesus Christ. This is what he wanted to do, and it gave him great pleasure (Ephesians 1:3-5, NLT).

God has so many great plans lined up to do with you that He wants to adopt you into His own family. Accept His offer and live a life of abundance in Him.

October 7

~ *Plant yourself in the Word* ~

Truly he is my rock and my salvation; he is my fortress, I will not be shaken (Psalm 62:6, NIV).

Like a great tree with roots that extend right down into the earth that cannot be shaken in a great storm, so is a good mother. She is so rooted in the Word to build her home that when people offend, discourage or upset her it doesn't move her. She stays right in the

Word of God where she is planted and nourishes herself in a prayer of declaration of who God created her to be.

> *You can't find firm footing in a swamp, but life rooted in God stands firm (Proverbs 12:3, MSG).*
>
> *God blesses those people who refuse evil advice and won't follow sinners or join in sneering at God. Instead, the Law of the Lord makes them happy, and they think about it day and night. They are like trees growing beside a stream, trees that produce fruit in season and always have leaves. Those people succeed in everything they do (Psalm 1:1-3, CEV).*

The Holy Spirit inside us gives us peace so that nothing can ever offend us. He brings to life the Word we receive that our faith can never be shaken in any storms that we must face in life.

> *Great peace have those who love your law, and nothing can make them stumble (Psalm 119:165, NIV).*

Each and every day step and walk into the Word of God before you step into starting your day. Plant all your days in the Word and nothing of this world will shake you.

October 8

~ *Feeling loved and belonged* ~

> *Then Jesus called for the children and said to the disciples, 'Let the children come to me. Don't stop them! For the Kingdom of God belongs to those who are like these children'. (Luke 18:16, NLT).*

God gave every mother the instinct that enables her to read her children's needs when they are at a younger age before talking. A good mother relies heavily on the Holy Spirit to interpret the love language of God, so that she can action the love of God to her children, so they feel that they belong. When you are loved, you feel that you belong. The kingdom of God belongs to children and a good mother actions God's love so her children feel they belong.

> *All your children will be taught by the Lord, and great will be their peace (Isaiah 54:13, NIV).*

The Holy Spirit is the love of Jesus in action that makes us feel we belong without being judged or condemned. He convinces us when we go off the right track to come back. The more we receive the Word of God into us, the more we attract God and grow in His Spirit. God breathes on the Word and makes it alive in us so that we feel we belong and are loved by Him.

> *And when he comes, he will convict the world of its sin, and of God's righteousness, and of the coming judgment (John 16:8, NLT).*

When you own something, it belongs to you. Look into God's Word every day and own it. God's promises are for His children and you are always your Father's little child. The kingdom of God belongs to little children.

October 9

~ You are the apple of God's eye ~

> *...for he who touches you touches the apple of his eye... (Zechariah 2:8, ESV).*

A good mother keeps sight of her children in her prayers every day. She keeps them as the apple of her eye in her prayers and she thanks God for keeping them all as the apple of His eye.

> *'Keep me as the apple of your eye; hide me in the shadow of your wings' (Psalm 17:8 NIV).*

This precious breath of God's Word is her prayer, which keeps her children safe in this evil world. She is comforted knowing that whatever vessels evil travels through to touch her and her house will touch God's eyes. It hurts God's eyes to see her loved ones touched by evil. You hurt someone when you touch a person's eye and that is also how God feels.

The Holy Spirit inside us produces goodness, and it is only good that can overcome evil. We are the apple of God's eye that when evil touches us it touches the eye of God. The eye of God is good, and He changes the perspective of that evil into something good. He works only for good to those who love Him.

> *And we know that in all things God works for the good of those who love him, who have been called according to his purpose (Romans 8:28, NIV).*

Your eyes are the lamp of your body in which the Holy Spirit lives. When your eyes are good, your mind and heart are good as well. The Holy Spirit inside you lights up the Word of God which you receive into you with life and your whole body is filled with light (Matthew 6:22).

October 10

~ *To become one with the Holy Spirit* ~

But the Helper, the Holy Spirit, whom the Father will send in My name, He will teach you all things, and bring to your remembrance all things that I said to you (John 14:26, NKJV).

She is designed to be a helper to her husband. Taken from the rib of her husband, she is always by his side to help Him through good and bad. She is a good mother and she knows she can't be a strong helper in her own strength. She needs the power that comes from God's Spirit to be a powerful and effective helper to her husband who is one with her in flesh. For that to happen she becomes one in spirit with the Holy Spirit.

But whoever is united with the Lord is one with him in spirit.(1 Corinthians 6:17, NIV).

A glove on its own is limp and powerless. But once a hand fills that glove it becomes useful and effective. The body that clothes us on earth is limp and powerless but once the Holy Spirit fills our body we become useful and powerful.

'But you shall receive power when the Holy Spirit has come upon you.' (Acts 1:8 NKJV).

We have to fill our spirit with the Holy Spirit every day by receiving into us the Word of God, so we can become effective and powerful in serving others with the fruit of the Holy Spirit.

October 11

~ Worrying about the unknown future ~

Fear not, for I have redeemed you; I have called you by your name; You are Mine (Isaiah 43:1, NKJV).

It is a typical human response to look ahead into the future and see problems and begin to panic and fear. A good mother goes through this all the time but she uses that fear to motivate her to get closer to God. She doesn't get discouraged, give up, get angry and start asking, 'Why me Lord?' Instead of filling herself with fear and anxiety for her household's unknown future, she stands on God's promise in Isaiah 41:10 and walks like the queen she was designed to be. She is a king's daughter and her Father will always be there for her on time.

Fear not, for I am with you; be not dismayed, for I am your God. I will strengthen you, yes, I will help you, I will uphold you with My righteous right hand.'(Isaiah 41:10 NKJV)

The Holy Spirit is the perfect love of God inside us that drives out fear and strengthens and comforts us with God's promises to lead us through the path of abundance. He knows our future and has made great plans for us to enjoy it with Him. We just need to know Him better by receiving into us the Word of God so we can know what our great future is in Him.

There is no fear in love. But perfect love drives out fear, because fear has to do with punishment. The one who fears is not made perfect in love (1 John 4:18, NIV).

The 'GREAT I AM', Jesus Christ, planned out a great future for you to give you hope and prosperity. He must become greater and greater, and you become less and less (John 3:30).

October 12

~ God's will is done according to your faith ~

> *So then, just as you received Christ Jesus as Lord, continue to live your lives in him, rooted and built up in him, strengthened in the faith as you were taught, and overflowing with thankfulness (Colossians 2:6-7, NIV).*

A good mother's priority is to build up her faith account first because this is the account that will determine the success of everything she does for her house. She spends and invest her time listening and hearing the Word of God as this is how she builds her faith muscles. She then exercises her faith muscles by being a 'doer' of that faith. This is the reason that healing, blessings and deliverance of all her needs follow her, in all the days of her life. It is her faith level that determines how effective the power of God flows through her to meet all her needs. God doesn't respond to your need. He responds to your faith in relation to that need.

> *Then he touched their eyes and said, 'According to your faith let it be done to you' (Matthew 9:29, NIV).*

> *So then faith comes by hearing, and hearing by the Word of God (Romans 10:17, NKJV).*

The Holy Spirit is the faith in action of God's righteous Word by breathing into it to make it become alive. He produces the fruit of righteousness so that we can also become faith in action of God's righteous Word by producing it. We are empowered by the Holy Spirit to produce the fruit of His righteousness inside us.

Each and every day walk in love by actioning a fruit of the Holy Spirit to someone who needs it. Say a kind Word, be patient with someone you are teaching and just be good to everyone that comes your way. God is good, only goodness can overcome evil.

October 13

~ Trusting God's Word ~

> *Agree with God, and be at peace; thereby good will come to you. Receive instruction from his mouth, and lay up his words in your heart (Job 22:21-22, ESV).*

She looks into the promises of God and trusts God just as her children look upon her with trust. A good mother trusts God completely; she knows that the more you spend time with someone, the more you know about their nature or character. As she spends more time in Word and prayer with God, she has come to know how trustworthy God is. She can depend entirely on Him without giving up because the times spent with God have built her faith muscles to be strong and renew her faith to place her hopes in God.

The more she has seen the hand of God move on time to meet her needs, the higher her level of trust in God. Her trust, faith, hope and love for God is rooted like a mountain.

> *Those who trust in the Lord are like Mount Zion, which cannot be shaken but endures forever (Psalm 125:1, NIV).*

No problems and worries can shake away her faith. Her mind is regularly renewed in the peace of God.

> *You will keep in perfect peace those whose minds are steadfast, because they trust in you. Trust in the LORD forever, for the LORD, the LORD himself, is the Rock eternal' (Isaiah 26:3-4, NIV).*

God keeps us in perfect peace through His perfect love, the Holy Spirit. The more we put our trust in God the more we perfectly feel at peace with the peace from the Holy Spirit.

October 14

~ *Your tears are God's collections* ~

> *This poor man cried out, and the LORD heard him, And saved him out of all his troubles (Psalm 34:6, NKJV).*

You can see that she is stronger than her circumstances and situations but you can't see how her eyes have burned with tears and God has collected those tears from her. This is the story of a good mother; she knows that only God can hold water in his palms. And this is why she only goes to God in tears of pain and suffering. She tells God, in the words of Psalm 61:1-2 and Psalm 56:8,

> 'Hear my cry, O God; listen to my prayer. From the ends of the earth I call to you, I call as my heart grows faint; lead me to the rock that is higher than I.' (Psalm 61:1-2 NIV).

> 'You keep track of all my sorrows, You have collected all my tears in your bottle. You have recorded each one in your book' (Psalm 56:8 NLT).

Only God can collect your tears and count them. Jesus Christ, the rock of our faith, has given us the Holy Spirit who lives in us to lead us to higher places, and it's the cry from our hearts that moves God in His Spirit to answer our prayers.

> *They cried out to God during the battle, and he answered their prayer because they trusted in him. So the Hagrites and all their allies were defeated (1 Chronicles 5:20, NLT).*

God treasures every tear that rolls down your face and records every drop in His book. He returns those tears back to you in the form of joy.

October 15

~ Rejoice in what you do ~

> *Do everything without complaining and arguing. (Philippians 2:14, NLT)*

A good mother doesn't complain, instead she tries to fix or improve the problem. She does what needs to be done within her ability and if it's not within her power to control she just accepts whatever it is. She focuses on loving and delighting in God who is in control of working for the good of those Who love Him.

> *Rejoice always, pray continually, give thanks in all circumstances; for this is God's will for you in Christ Jesus (1 Thessalonians 5:16-18 NIV)*

The Holy Spirit carries out the will of God within us by producing joy all the time in all seasons of our lives. We are to celebrate that joy from the Lord in the Holy Spirit and rejoice every day in that gift of life which is today. This is God's will for us in Christ.

This is the day that the Lord has made; let us rejoice and be glad in it (Psalm 118:24, ESV).

October 16

~ *Holy Ghost-like mind is a good mother-like character* ~

The Spirit of the Lord will rest upon him, the Spirit of wisdom and understanding, the Spirit of counsel and power, the Spirit of knowledge and fear of the Lord. (Isaiah 11:2, ISV).

Your body is the temple of the Holy Spirit; make sure to have a balanced life. A good mother does not stress out the house of God by overworking her body. She has a house to run and everyone looks to her all the time so she has no privacy to herself. She uses her body to feed and fuel her spirit and soul by doing everything from her heart as a worship unto God. She worships God in Spirit and truth by giving cheerfully from her heart what her hands offer to do for her house. She connects her spirit to God's wisdom, knowledge, understanding, power, fear of the Lord and council of the Lord in His Holy Spirit. The Holy Ghost-like mind is a good mother-like character through the actions of being fruitful in the righteous fruit of the Spirit.

To maintain a healthy balanced relationship spiritually, mentally and physically she produces the fruit of the Holy Spirit in her relationship with God, others and herself.

Her relationship with God spiritually is a priority and so she is fully connected daily with God in Word and prayer. She guides and makes sure the enemy will never steal the love, joy and peace found in her relationship with God.

She speaks and actions kindness, goodness and patience in her relationship with her family, as well as whoever she comes in contact with to build them up. She fills herself and practises self-control, faithfulness and gentleness in her relationship with herself so that her relationships with God and others are productive and fruitful. She controls her SELF, to be FAITHFUL with a GENTLE heart to maintain LOVE, JOY and PEACE in her relationship with God, so that no other relationship in her life will steal that love, joy and peace if she is betrayed. She also controls her SELF to be FAITHFUL with a GENTLE heart to produce KINDNESS, GOODNESS and PATIENCE in her relationships with her family, friends and whoever she comes in touch with that needs it.

She is focused on living the nine fruit of the Holy Spirit, the characters of Christ. This is living the heaven lifestyle.

The Holy Spirit is the Spirit of truth and He is inside you so you can worship God through Him by producing His fruit of righteousness.

> *But the fruit of the Spirit is love, joy, peace, patience, kindness, goodness, faithfulness, gentleness, self-control; against such things there is no law (Galatians 5:22-23, ESV).*
>
> *God is spirit, and his worshipers must worship in the Spirit and in truth.' (John 4:24, NIV).*

October 17

~ The peace of God gives you inner strength ~

The Lord gives strength to his people; the Lord blesses his people with peace (Psalm 29:11, NIV).

It's so tiring for a working mom to rush home to little hungry humans who look up to her to satisfy their hunger. A good mother knows where to draw out strength to continue her role at home so there is peace around her. She walks right into the throne of God and receives the grace of Psalm 29:11.

The Holy Spirit inside us gives us strength to be at peace with our surrounding chaos. The peace Jesus gave us is the Holy Spirit and He is the very strength and power of God.

Peace I leave with you; my peace I give you. I do not give to you as the world gives. Do not let your hearts be troubled and do not be afraid (John 14:27, NIV).

Strong people make the first move to make peace even when they are the victims. The peace and joy of the Lord is your strength to overcome this evil world.

October 18

~ Renewed and refreshed like a youth ~

He fills my life with good things. My youth is renewed like the eagle's! (Psalm 103:5, NLT).

The app of the Holy Spirit is to make you as fresh and renewed as ever in the Word of God you receive into you. And this is the app a good mother uses. She is often worn out from all the weariness of worrying about what the world throws at her. All that she aches for is to recharge herself in Word and prayer, so the Holy Spirit can renew and freshen her flesh to be like a youth.

> *I will refresh the weary and satisfy the faint (Jeremiah 31:25, NIV).*

The Holy Spirit inside you breathes life into the Word of God making it new, fresh and alive the moment you take it into you. You are growing newer in His mercy and grace.

> *…he saved us, not because of righteous things we had done, but because of his mercy. He saved us through the washing of rebirth and renewal by the Holy Spirit (Titus 3:5, NIV).*

Keep downloading the app of the Holy Spirit and stay fully charged and connected to get new, fresh and timely messages from the throne room of God.

October 19

~ Everything you need is in Jesus ~

> *And my God will meet all your needs according to the riches of his glory in Christ Jesus (Philippians 4:19, NIV).*

A good mother takes care of her household needs by alerting God about it before the need appears. She rises up with full strength like a sunrise at the break of dawn and spends her time in Word and prayer. This is how she enters God's throne of grace in the time of her needs.

> *Let us then approach God's throne of grace with confidence, so that we may receive mercy and find grace to help us in our time of need (Hebrews 4:16, NIV).*

The Holy Spirit knows our needs already before they arise. He is the power of God working inside us to meet our needs at the time of our needs. He already answers us before we even call for Him.

> *'Before they call I will answer; while they are still speaking I will hear' (Isaiah 65:24 NIV).*

Your needs are met on the path God is taking you through; listen to His voice through the Holy Spirit and walk on the path of righteousness.

October 20

~ The fear of the Lord ~

> *For you created my inmost being; you knit me together in my mother's womb.*
>
> *I praise you because I am fearfully and wonderfully made; your works are wonderful, I know that full well (Psalm 139:13-14, NIV)*

A good mother praises God all the time for breathing His Spirit of fear to make her a wonderful being; she is praised by her children and husband and all who know her because she fears the Lord.

> *Charm is deceptive, and beauty is fleeting; but a woman who fears the Lord is to be praised (Proverbs 31:30, NIV).*

She knows well that the Spirit of the fear of the Lord made her and therefore she walks, moves and lives in the fear of the Lord.

She passes these genes down to her children so that they grow up living in the Spirit of the fear of the Lord. She works harder to beautify her inner beauty by being kind. The Holy Spirit not only breathes into our spirit the fear of the Lord which makes us live in God's fear, but He also produces His righteous fruit of kindness, so we can use it to serve others. The fear of the Lord that made us is the beginning of wisdom. We are wonderfully and fearfully created to live in the fear of God.

October 21

~ *Delight in the Lord with gratitude, thanksgiving and praises* ~

> *Delight yourself in the Lord, and he will give you the desires of your heart (Psalm 37:4, ESV).*

A good mother is aware that God has great plans for her and her house and He provides according to the desires of their heart. She has experienced and tasted the goodness of God of how He gives her more than she has ever asked for or imagined. To receive more from God she empties out her heart and fills it with gratitude, thanksgiving and praises to God. This is her tradition of delighting in the Lord, as she prays the Word of God in Psalm 43:3-4.

> *Send out your light and your truth; let them guide me. Let them lead me to your holy mountain, to the place where you live. There I will go to the altar of God, to God—the source of all my joy. I will praise you with my harp, O God, my God! (Psalm 43:3-4, NLT).*

God has given us Jesus who gave us the Holy Spirit, the Spirit of life, light and truth to guide us to walk in truth.

> *But when he, the Spirit of truth, comes, he will guide you into all the truth. He will not speak on his own; he will speak only what he hears, and he will tell you what is yet to come.(John 16:13, NIV).*

We give God the desire of His heart when we produce the fruit of joy from His Holy Spirit in our daily life and make it our lifestyle.

> *I have no greater joy than to hear that my children are walking in the truth (3 John 1:4, ESV)*

October 22

~ *Fighting the good fight of faith* ~

> *For we are God's handiwork, created in Christ Jesus to do good works, which God prepared in advance for us to do (Ephesians 2:10, NIV).*

God orders TIME to put in order all your spiritual blessings that you going to receive. But you have to go through what He allows into your life for you to receive what He has prepared in advance for you in Christ.

A good mother loves meeting her battles as she is always ready for the good fight as it is the way to clear the path for her spiritual blessings to come to her in the physical realm. Because she is always in Word and prayer, she always wins the battle.

> *Fight the good fight of the faith. Take hold of the eternal life to which you were called and about which you made the good confession in the presence of many witnesses (1 Timothy 6:12, ESV).*

The Holy Spirit is our blessing from what Jesus did. He removed the curses and restored us with blessings by giving us the Holy Spirit so we can remain blessed. The Holy Spirit is the only way to direct us to remain on the path of righteousness, so we can meet up with Jesus when He arrives on the clouds.

> *Praise be to the God and Father of our Lord Jesus Christ, who has blessed us in the heavenly realms with every spiritual blessing in Christ. For he chose us in him before the creation of the world to be holy and blameless in his sight (Ephesians 1:3-4, NIV).*

Fight the good fight of faith with hope and perseverance and never quit until you receive all your spiritual blessings that God has stored for you before the creation of the world.

October 23

~ Kindness in action is true beauty ~

> *Because Your loving kindness is better than life, My lips shall praise You (Psalm 63:3, NKJV).*

A good mother is made beautiful by her acts of kindness. She not only opens her mouth in kindness but extends her hands out to the needy. Her acts of kindness are delivered with her smile and the person receiving the kindness knows it's God meeting their needs.

> *Strength and dignity are her clothing, and she laughs at the time to come. She opens her mouth with wisdom, and the teaching of kindness is on her tongue (Proverbs 31:25-26, ESV).*

Kindness is one of the fruit of righteousness that the Holy Spirit produces within us to extend to those who need it. God showed His loving kindness by sending Jesus to us. Jesus gave us the Holy Spirit who constantly produces kindness inside us to give to the needy and the unkind heart.

> *But when the kindness and love of God our Saviour appeared, he saved us, not because of righteous things we had done, but because of his mercy. He saved us through the washing of rebirth and renewal by the Holy Spirit, whom he poured out on us generously through Jesus Christ our Saviour, (Titus 3:4-6, NIV).*

Kindness in action is love. Be kind to someone today not just in words but actions too.

October 24

~ The joy of being born again ~

> *Consider it pure joy, my brothers and sisters, whenever you face trials of many kinds, because you know that the testing of your faith produces perseverance. Let perseverance finish its work so that you may be mature and complete, not lacking anything. (James 1:2-4, NIV).*

She faces trial after trial of many kinds. These trials are her birthing table. She considers it pure joy because this is how she gives birth to strength to make her stronger so as to give birth to great success. It's her constant prayers and bible reading that hold her in place when she is exposed to pain and pressure. Otherwise, she would have given up and stepped out of God's will. She always speaks Romans 12:12 into her life.

> *Rejoice in hope, be patient in tribulation, be constant in prayer (Romans 12:12, ESV).*

The Holy Spirit inside us holds us in place when we want to go off track from God's will. He is the powerhouse of God that strengthens our body which houses Him so we don't give up.

He wants us to give birth to the Christ-like life from Him.

> *But rejoice insofar as you share Christ's sufferings, that you may also rejoice and be glad when his glory is revealed (1 Peter 4:13, ESV).*

It's easy to do a sinner's prayer and accept Jesus into your life, but the moment you are born again Christ comes from inside you to live outside you. You will experience that joy the kingdom of heaven felt when you accept Jesus into your life. We are born again in Christ by the Holy Spirit and resurrect Him from within us by producing the produced fruit of the Holy Spirit in our lives. The devil works so hard to stop us from being in touch with the Word of God, because this will defeat him and give us the power of being born again in Christ Jesus.

October 25

~ *God seeing Himself in you* ~

> *Your hands made me and formed me; give me understanding to learn your commands (Psalm 119:73, NIV).*

A good mother's aim is to restore herself to the original image of who God created her to be. She wants to get into that image and the original design so her children will see and know her from that image. And so this is what she does, she has fellowship with God through His Word and prayer and seeks to reflect His character to glorify Him. God gets true glory when He sees himself in her.

> *But you are a chosen generation, a royal priesthood, a holy nation, His own special people, that you may proclaim the praises of Him who called you out of darkness into His marvelous light; (1 Peter 2:9, NKJV).*

Jesus is the perfect image of God in everything, He is now made alive in the Holy Spirit who lives inside us. The Holy Spirit produces the character of Jesus within us to make us in the image of God.

> *You, however, are not in the realm of the flesh but are in the realm of the Spirit, if indeed the Spirit of God lives in you. And if anyone does not have the Spirit of Christ, they do not belong to Christ (Romans 8:9, NIV).*

Each and every day, reflect Christ's character in everything you do to give God glory.

October 26

~ Love through God's love ~

> *Praise be to the God and Father of our Lord Jesus Christ, the Father of compassion and the God of all comfort, who comforts us in all our troubles, so that we can comfort those in any trouble with the comfort we ourselves receive from God (2 Corinthians 1:3-4, NIV).*

She is a good mother and a good carer to the lives of the little humans with which God has entrusted her.

She has the passion of compassion towards them that flows right out from the love of God. She knows her human love towards them will fail and so she wants to love them through the love of God that He has poured into her from the Holy Spirit. She rejoices with her children when they rejoice and she weeps with them when they weep. She hurts with them when they are hurting and she is happy for them when they are happy. She teaches her children 1 Peter 3:8 so they can follow her example.

> *Finally, all of you be of one mind, having compassion for one another; love as brothers, be tenderhearted, be courteous (1 Peter 3:8 NKJV).*

The Holy Spirit is inside us, and He feels everything we feel. Whatever we feel He feels it with us and He comforts us. He is the love of our Father who is so full of compassion. The love that understands and keeps loving us because we are blind and do not know what we are doing.

> *Rejoice with those who rejoice, and weep with those who weep.(Romans 12:15 NKJV).*

Fill each day with compassion and mercy so you can easily walk in love and forgiveness to serve whoever needs it from you.

October 27

~ *The Holy Spirit anointing* ~

> *But you will receive power when the Holy Spirit comes on you; and you will be my witnesses in Jerusalem, and in all Judea and Samaria, and to the ends of the earth.' (Acts 1:8, NIV).*

A good mother looks and feels good because she does good things. She actions goodness at a practical level, by listening patiently to someone who needs a friend to talk to or by bringing meals and eating with a grieving person. The love she has is full of compassion and out of it flows goodness. She also sacrifices her own agenda, schedule, desires and dreams to meet the needs of her household.

> *Indeed we count them blessed who endure. You have heard of the perseverance of Job and seen the end intended by the Lord—that the Lord is very compassionate and merciful. (James 5:11 NKJV).*

Jesus was full of compassion. He responded to the sick with healing, to the hungry with food, and to those who were lost with the good news of the gospel. His Holy Spirit is now inside us to continue the ministry of Jesus.

> *..how God anointed Jesus of Nazareth with the Holy Spirit and with power, who went about doing good and healing all who were oppressed by the devil, for God was with Him. (Acts 10:38 NKJV).*

God anoints Jesus with His Spirit. The same Spirit is now inside you. Ask Him to anoint you, so you can be a healing of light, life and love to everyone around you.

October 28

~ *The purity of God's Word* ~

> *I have hidden your word in my heart, that I might not sin against you (Psalm 119:11, NLT).*

A good mother is aware that the way God's kingdom was established and works is similar to how social media operates. To see the face of God, she has to look constantly into God's book, the Bible, and hide His pure Word in her heart.

> *Blessed are the pure in heart, for they will see God (Matthew 5:8, NIV).*

'What's on her mind'? She has the mind of Christ (1 Corinthians 2:16). She renews her mind and uploads it with the image of Christ in His Word. Just as a friend 'likes' someone's post. She is a friend to the heroes of faith that the book of Hebrews describes and 'likes' their great life of faith.

Just as social media wants you to publish your story for your friends to view it, a good mother rewrites her story and her house from what God has written and they live that story. The way they live their stories shows who Jesus is in their lives.

> *How can a young person stay on the path of purity? By living according to your word (Psalm 119:9, NIV).*

The pure Word of God is the pure living water that will not only quench your thirst but keep you pure when you live and abide by it.

> *The fear of the Lord is pure, enduring forever. The decrees of the Lord are firm, and all of them are righteous (Psalm 19:9, NIV)*

The Holy Spirit we receive is the Spirit of the fear of the Lord. He puts us on the path of purity when we house Him. He inbuilt the fear within us to be afraid and flee from any nature of sin, so we remain in the righteousness of Christ and produce His fruit of righteousness. The Holy Spirit makes the Word come alive inside us to live and walk in obedience.

October 29

~ *Jesus is all you need to meet your needs* ~

> *Do nothing out of selfish ambition or vain conceit. Rather, in humility value others above yourselves, not looking to your own interests but each of you to the interests of the others. (Philippians 2:3-4, NIV).*

A good mother is God's love in action and Philippians 2:3-4 is her nature which she does naturally.

This Word of God in Psalm 5:3 is her prayer every morning.

> *In the morning, Lord, you hear my voice; in the morning I lay my requests before you and wait expectantly (Psalm 5:3, NIV).*

Her children and husband's needs come first over her own. She does everything for her husband and children first. She is glued in the Word and prayer with her needs which God always meets through His amazing love in Jesus.

> *And my God will meet all your needs according to the riches of his glory in Christ Jesus (Philippians 4:19, NIV).*

The Holy Spirit is God's love in action in Christ. All the other fruit that the Holy Spirit produces comes from God's love and He is love.

> *But you, dear friends, by building yourselves up in your most holy faith and praying in the Holy Spirit, keep yourselves in God's love as you wait for the mercy of our Lord Jesus Christ to bring you to eternal life (Jude 1:20-21, NIV).*

The Holy Spirit is access to all the riches of Christ. Fill yourself with the Holy Spirit every day and enjoy the riches of God's glory in Christ.

October 30

~ Quit the blame game ~

> *Be glad you can do the things you should be doing. Do all things without arguing and talking about how you wish you did not have to do them. In that way, you can prove yourselves to be without blame. You are God's children and no one can talk against you, even in a sin-loving and sin-sick world. You are to shine as lights among the sinful people of this world. Take a strong hold on the Word of Life. Then when Christ comes again, I will be happy that I did not work with you for nothing. (Philippians 2:14-16, NLV).*

Live a blameless life and do what the Word of God says to do. Quit playing the blame game and be kind, good and patient to those who attack you.

A good mother says NO to the blame game in her house. Instead, everyone must take responsibility by being forgiving, kind and good to each other. It is her aim to bring to life and make the words of Psalm 119: 1 become flesh.

Blessed are those whose ways are blameless, who walk according to the law of the Lord (Psalm 119:1, NIV).

The first man blamed God for giving him the woman who made him eat from the forbidden fruit. Instead of taking responsibility and asking God for His forgiveness, the woman blamed the serpent.

Jesus took upon Him the blame of our sins. God loves us so much He took His responsibility as a loving Father. Jesus, who is the Father's love in action, took upon Him the blame, so that we can become blameless. We now remain blameless in Christ through the Holy Spirit who lives inside us. The Holy Spirit doesn't condemn or blame us when we sin, He understands that we are born sinners. He convinces us to do the right things (John 16:8).

Surely I was sinful at birth, sinful from the time my mother conceived me (Psalm 51:5, NIV).

All the mess and problems of life will be solved instantly if we take responsibility and don't blame each other.

October 31

~ The power of God's touch ~

This day is holy to our Lord. Do not grieve, for the joy of the Lord is your strength. (Nehemiah 8:10, NIV).

Everything we go through each day is to strengthen us for the journey ahead. A good mother sees that the loss of her loved ones to death is a gain. It's painful for her but without pain there is no gain. The strength and courage she gains from that loss builds her up to be that strong person and prepare her for her journey to face her many battles ahead. God's touch is so powerful that when He touches a broken heart He not only mends that broken heart, He strengthens it to the next level and prepares it for victory in the next battle.

> *He heals the brokenhearted and binds up their wounds (Psalm 147:3, NIV).*
>
> *The Lord is my strength and my song; he has given me victory (Exodus 15:2, NLT).*

The Holy Spirit is a gain from the life Jesus lost, and the pain and suffering He tasted. He is the strength and power of God from the life Jesus laid down for us. Jesus died so He can live again forever through His Holy Spirit inside us.

> *And if the Spirit of him who raised Jesus from the dead is living in you, he who raised Christ from the dead will also give life to your mortal bodies because of his Spirit who lives in you (Romans 8:11, NIV).*

Each and every day seek God in His Word. Stay in touch and in tune with Him to receive the latest Word for the season to come right out of His mouth.

NOVEMBER

~ A mother's love ~

> *If I could speak all the languages of earth and of angels, but didn't love others, I would only be a noisy gong or a clanging cymbal. If I had the gift of prophecy, and if I understood all of God's secret plans and possessed all knowledge, and if I had such faith that I could move mountains, but didn't love others, I would be nothing. If I gave everything I have to the poor and even sacrificed my body, I could boast about it; but if I didn't love others, I would have gained nothing (I Corinthians 13:1-3, NLT).*

As a mother with children, you know everything about what they love. You even know about all the food, cartoons and activities they enjoy, what they like to wear and how they want to be treated. When you give them or do something they love, you make them so happy.

It's the same with Jesus when we have Him in our life. When He is literally living and alive in us, we will know everything about LOVE because that is Him. He is LOVE and love is a person. So when we know LOVE who is Jesus, we know God's love. We will know everything LOVE loves. The Holy Spirit flows out the life of LOVE from His fruit. Flowing out from LOVE is: Love, joy, peace, patience, kindness, goodness, faithfulness, gentleness and self-control. We make Jesus happy when we are giving, doing and living in LOVE.

> *But the fruit of the Spirit is love, joy, peace, patience, kindness, goodness, faithfulness, gentleness, self-control; against such things there is no law (Galatians 5:22-23, ESV).*

Each day of the month of November and EVERY DAY let us do what LOVE loves to do to our families, friends, enemies and strangers. Sit and rest daily in Word and in prayer to energize the power of the Holy Spirit so He can bring to life His fruit inside us, so we can produce it to everyone with whom we come in contact.

> *Love is patient and kind. Love is not jealous or boastful or proud or rude. It does not demand its own way. It is not irritable, and it keeps no record of being wronged. It does not rejoice about injustice but rejoices whenever the truth wins out. Love never gives up, never loses faith, is always hopeful, and endures through every circumstance. Prophecy and speaking in unknown languages and special knowledge will become useless. But love will last forever! (1 Corinthians 13:4-8, NLT).*

November 1

~ *Answered prayers* ~

> *But seek first his kingdom and his righteousness, and all these things will be given to you as well (Matthew 6:33, NIV).*

The will of God is to go after His Word and obey it. A good mother seeks first the kingdom of God and His righteousness by producing the fruit of righteousness from the Holy Spirit to her household and whoever she comes in contact with. This is how she gains confidence that all these things she asked God for will be given to her.

> *This is the confidence we have in approaching God: that if we ask anything according to His will, He hears us. And if we know that He hears us—whatever we ask—we know that we have what we asked of Him. (1 John 5:14–15 NIV)*

She is confident in God's Word that she will receive whatever she has prayed for.

> *Therefore I tell you, whatever you ask for in prayer, believe that you have received it, and it will be yours (Mark 11:24 NIV).*

The Holy Spirit inside us is the righteousness of the kingdom of God. We are to seek Him and produce His fruit of righteousness so that whatever we ask of God will be given to us. We are the righteousness of God in Christ, and in Christ we have received everything.

> *For no matter how many promises God has made, they are 'Yes' in Christ. And so through him the 'Amen' is spoken by us to the glory of God (2 Corinthians 1:20, NIV).*

Each and every day look into the promises of God and receive them into your heart and action them with your hands.

November 2

~ Activate that seed of greatness within you ~

> *If you are walking in darkness, without a ray of light, trust in the LORD and rely on your God...'(Isaiah 50:10, NLT)*

As she plants a seed into the dark soil she is reminded of her dark days where there was no light and she couldn't see where she was heading. Everything around her seemed lifeless. She is a good mother, and she uses the light of God's Word to keep her going. She trusts and relies on God. She is in the 'great I am' and it's only in the darkness that the greatness of her seed in the 'great I am' will come out. Just like the seed that must be planted in the soil, in a dark place, so that its potential inside can come to life, so is the Holy Spirit. Jesus has to go into the darkest womb of death so the Holy Spirit can raise Him to life and we all can have that greatness of the new life in the Holy Spirit living inside us. Keep receiving into you the Word of God, who is Jesus, the seed of greatness. Faith comes by hearing and hearing the Word. Even with a mustard seed of faith, you are able to move mountains.

> *Jesus replied, 'The hour has come for the Son of Man to be glorified. Very truly I tell you, unless a kernel of wheat falls to the ground and dies, it remains only a single seed. But if it dies, it produces many seeds.' (John 12:23-24, NIV)*

Jesus can show His light and His greatness only in your darkness. It's here in the dark places that the seeds of greatness in you will come to life.

November 3

~ Watchfully and prayerfully be on guide ~

> *For God gave us a spirit not of fear but of power and love and self-control (2 Timothy 1:7, ESV).*

Mothers are not only under their children's control or schedule but also other issues in their surroundings can take control. This is the reason mothers need to be watchful and prayerful in everything that is of concern to them.

A good mother's best close friend is the Holy Spirit because she needs Him to pour out from His understanding so she can learn to control her SELF with the fruit 'self-control'. With self-control, she can manage what's going on within her even when she cannot control what's going on around her.

> *A man without self-control is like a city broken into and left without walls (Proverbs 25:28, ESV).*

We need self-control, one of the fruit of the Holy Spirit to be able to manage what's going on within us when we cannot control what's going on around us. This is so that we are able to remain in God's schedule with the understanding that He is in control and has allowed the situations that are in our way.

> *Better a patient person than a warrior, one with self-control than one who takes a city (Proverbs 16:32, NIV).*

Things can be kept under control with patience. You become a patient person with self-control; these are two of the nine fruit from the Holy Spirit.

November 4

~ Overflowing abundance of life ~

He must become greater; I must become less. (John 3:30, NIV).

A good mother wakes up in the morning and with a smile full of love and a heart full of thanksgiving she declares who she is with the phrase, 'Great I am!' She says, 'I am blessed. I am strong. I am talented. I am wise. I am disciplined. I am focused. I am prosperous. I am loved and I am great in the "GREAT I AM".' Him alone must become greater and I become less, so His greatness can be shown in me and through me for others to see and come to know Him.

The Holy Spirit within us aims to overflow our cup with His fruit of righteousness from inside out, that we become more of Jesus, and less of our SELF righteousness. Only then we will live the abundance of life that is in Jesus.

> *You prepare a table before me in the presence of my enemies. You anoint my head with oil; my cup overflows. Surely your goodness and love will follow me all the days of my life, and I will dwell in the house of the Lord forever (Psalm 23:5,6, NIV).*

You will enjoy life in abundance in the presence of your enemies who want to steal, kill and destroy you when you abide in the Word.

November 5

~ *Made by LOVE to remain in LOVE* ~

> *And the Lord has declared today that you are people for his treasured possession, as he has promised you, and that you are to keep all his commandments, and that he will set you in praise and in fame and in honour high above all nations that he has made, and that you shall be a people holy to the Lord your God, as he promised.'(Deuteronomy 26:18-19, ESV).*

Each and every day a good mother gets up and invites all the good things into her household. Knowing she is the Creator's treasured possession, she lives as one by walking and living in the love of

God. And so God has set her in praise, and in fame and in honour high above all the nations that He has made. This is how she is loved because she simply moves and has her being in love.

> *No one has ever seen God; but if we love one another, God lives in us and his love is made complete in us. This is how we know that we live in him and he in us: He has given us of his Spirit (1 John 4:12-13, NIV).*

The Holy Spirit living actively inside us is proof that our very being lives and moves in love. We are made by LOVE with love to live, move and have our being in LOVE. We are to remain in LOVE. LOVE is a person. He is God.

> *For in him we live and move and have our being (Acts 17:28, NIV).*

We can't love with our imperfect love but with the perfect love of God we can love all the time in any way.

November 6

~Respect Mother Earth~

> *The Word became flesh and made his dwelling among us. We have seen his glory, the glory of the one and only Son, who came from the Father, full of grace and truth (John 1:14, NIV).*

Mother Earth releases energy that sustains life; when we release bad energy we give it to Mother Earth and this is what she stores for us, yet she is still faithful in nurturing us for we came out from her through the Creator. She serves God faithfully in serving us.

> *While the earth remains, seed time and harvest, cold and heat, summer and winter, day and night, shall not cease. (Genesis 8:22, ESV).*

This is what a good mother does too; she continues to nurture her child regardless of how bad they can be at times. She loves them unconditionally; she has the connection and bonding with her children. They came from inside of her to be with her outside.

The Holy Spirit lives inside us and wants to come out from us. But to make Him come out from us, we have to live His characters by producing the fruit of the Spirit. He lives outside of us when we make the Word become flesh by our actions. When we have a connection and bonding with the Holy Spirit, we produce His love unconditionally to everyone we come in contact with.

> *Dear friends, let us love one another, for love comes from God. Everyone who loves has been born of God and knows God. (1 John 4:7, NIV).*

God's love is shown through His faithfulness in giving birth to a new day and also giving us the breath of life to live in that new day. So live and walk in love with LOVE. God is love.

November 7

~ *Practise obeying God's Word* ~

Be obedient to God, and do not allow your lives to be shaped by those desires you had when you were still ignorant (1 Peter 1:14, GNT).

A good mother trains her mind to be renewed in the Word of God, she trains her heart to love by reaching out her hand to give. She tames her tongue to speak words that can cheer and build someone. She may fail at times but quitting is never an option. She knows practice makes perfect, and so she is committed to Psalm 119:56.

> *This has been my practise: I obey your precepts (Psalm 119:56, NIV).*

The Holy Spirit blazes its light and renews our mind when we get into God's Word. He is there to breathe life upon the Word within us, so we are able to be obedient to the Word.

> *Whoever keeps his commandments abides in God, and God in him. And by this we know that he abides in us, by the Spirit whom he has given us (1 John 3:24, ESV).*

Be obedient to the voice of the Holy Spirit every day, it is LIFE from inside you to give you a life of abundance to live your new life in Christ.

November 8

~ *Strength of a woman* ~

> *I can do all things through Christ who strengthens me (Philippians 4:13, NKJV).*

The strength of a woman is from inside. The power of all her strength is connected to many areas of her life. You touch one area and you affect everything. That's how God designed her complexity. You see, it's just the same as how your internal organs function; when one is affected everything within feels the pain. For example, if your teeth are aching, your ears ache and your head too. Your inner being feels hurt. A good mother understands all this, and so, she is connected to the Holy Spirit to gain the strength and power of the Word of God. Her voice is graced with kindness, her hands become like smooth stone full of strength from her inner strength, and she uses her power from within to provide light and direction for her children to travel in the path of success.

When she is harmed by objects of hurtful things being thrown upon her, she fists out her hand in prayers and reacts by bearing the fruit of the Holy Spirit towards her situation. It's hard but she does it well when she waits for God to renew her strength to be able to do all things through Christ, by the power and strength of the Holy Spirit.

> *He gives strength to the weary and increases the power of the weak. Even youths grow tired and weary, and young men stumble and fall; but those who hope in the Lord will renew their strength. They will soar on wings like eagles, they will run and not grow weary, they will walk and not be faint (Isaiah 40:29-31, NIV).*

The Holy Spirit is the inner power and strength of God that lives inside you to keep you going when you feel you can't go on. At those times when you felt like not going on anymore in life, the strength of the Holy Spirit fuelled you with strength and increased your power to continue having hope to live. You can do all things through Christ who strengthens you.

November 9

~ Strengthen yourself in God's Word ~

But David strengthened himself in the Lord his God. (1 Samuel 30:6 NKJV).

A good mother is stronger than all those problems; like David, she knows how to strengthen herself in God. Instead of looking at her problems she looks to how big and great God is. God has the final say in everything that affects her. Her victory is acknowledging how powerless and weak she is, so God can take over with His power which is made for her weakness.

> *But he said to me, 'My grace is sufficient for you, for my power is made perfect in weakness.' Therefore I will boast all the more gladly about my weaknesses, so that Christ's power may rest on me.(2 Corinthians 12:9, NIV).*

God wants to be part of your problem; He cares about all the happenings in your life. The Holy Spirit produces His fruit all the time to use for our weaknesses. He is the power and strength that has brought Jesus back to Life. Jesus healed everyone and gave them life, and the Holy Spirit healed Jesus and resurrected Him back to life. He now lives right inside us. This is why Jesus said we can do even greater things, more than He has done. God's trinity all working together for our good.

> *Very truly I tell you, whoever believes in me will do the works I have been doing, and they will do even greater things than these, because I am going to the Father (John 14:12, NIV).*

Each and every day strengthen yourself in the Word to do the great things you were born to do.

November 10

~ The peace of God keeps you from stumbling ~

Do not be overcome by evil, but overcome evil with good (Romans 12:21, ESV).

This is how a good mother actions her faith in overcoming evil with good whenever she hears or is aware of something that offends her or that is not right towards her. Thoughts of revenge quickly enter her mind to do something that will punish those that harm her but, because she is a good mother, she overcomes that evil plan from her old self by renewing her mind in this truth from Psalm 119:165:

Great peace have those who love your law, and nothing can make them stumble (Psalm 119:165, NIV).

Her love is to live in the Word of God and whatever she does she must not destroy her relationship with God. The more we feed our spirit with the Word of God, the more the Spirit of God begins to work His perfect love over us and His love overflows, which causes us to desire and love His Word more. And so we do not get offended by the things of this world.

And may the Lord make your love for one another and for all people grow and overflow, just as our love for you overflows (1 Thessalonians 3:12, NLT).

Each and every day walk in peace. When you walk in peace, you walk in love. Peace is a fruit of love from the Holy Spirit. When you are at peace with yourself, you can be at peace with others as well.

November 11

~ *Your decisions must come from your new life in Christ* ~

I have been crucified with Christ. It is no longer I who live, but Christ who lives in me. And the life I now live in the flesh I live by faith in the Son of God, who loved me and gave himself for me (Galatians 2:20, ESV).

A good mother knows that because she matters to God, everything she does also matters to Him. And so she consults God about every matter concerning her house before making any decisions. Even when she is in anger she doesn't react; she waits on God to renew her strength to focus on His goodness. She understands that she is a new being in Christ, a brand new mother. Every day, she has to make her old selfish life die out in the new self-image of the knowledge of Christ, and the new life of Christ has to come out and make the decisions.

Do not lie to each other, since you have taken off your old self with its practises and have put on the new self, which is being renewed in knowledge in the image of its Creator (Colossians 3:9-10, NIV).

The Holy Spirit is the new resurrected life of Christ. Because Christ lives we too are now living in Christ through the Holy Spirit. Christ is living again in us through His Spirit inside us.

Before long, the world will not see me anymore, but you will see me. Because I live, you also will live. On that day you will realize that I am in my Father, and you are in me, and I am in you (John 14:19-20, NIV).

Jesus is in His Father and when we receive Him we are in Him, and He is in us through the Holy Spirit who is in us. We are a new creation.

> *Therefore, if anyone is in Christ, the new creation has come: The old has gone, the new is here! (2 Corinthians 5:17, NIV).*

God gives us every new day to remind us that anyone who is in Christ is a new creation.

November 12

~ Defeat evilness with goodness ~

> *Let us not become weary in doing good, for at the proper time we will reap a harvest if we do not give up (Galatians 6:9, NIV).*

She is a good mother and focuses her mind on not tiring of doing good for her household.

Family is blood and life and serving them is her life on-the-job training for eternity. When she feels like giving in to the attacks of the enemy, she stands up on the promise of Galatians 6:9, holds her head up and walks on.

> *'If we endure, we will also reign with him' (2 Timothy 2:12, NIV).*

The Holy Spirit is not only the power and strength of God, He is also the goodness of God that we house. He has a still, calm, gentle voice that is so powerful it will strengthen us not to give up the good work we are doing in the Lord. Goodness is a fruit of the Holy Spirit that He produces inside us all the time for us to produce outside.

> *But you, friends, must not become tired of doing good (2 Thessalonians 3:13, GNT).*

A good God made a good day for us, but our day is in a fallen evil world. We just have to be good to our day and this is how we can overcome evil in our day.

November 13

~ Be still and let God fight for you ~

> *But thanks be to God, who gives us the victory through our Lord Jesus Christ (1 Corinthians 15:57, ESV).*

A good mother is a great fighter. She knows how to fight her battles by simply being still and letting God fight for her, in her and through her. She is always in the midst of different unexpected storms. Her victory is through her inner peace that she breathes out from the Word of God contained within her. It's easy to live in frustration when no one wants to do what she wants in the house. But she can choose to live in peace or in madness and she always chooses peace. Her victory is from the peace she chooses to live with.

> *The Lord will fight for you; you need only to be still.' (Exodus 14:14, NIV).*

> *Be still, and know that I am God!...' (Psalm 46:10, NLT)*

The Holy Spirit has it all under control, He lives inside us. When we produce His fruit of self-control and control our SELF to be still and allow the Holy Spirit to use His power of control, He will let His peace reign victory in us, and through us over our situations. The Holy Spirit produces the power of victory inside us. He releases it when we claim that victory in Him.

When we are trying to be God and fix things over which we have no control, we become frustrated. We should do only what we can and let God do the rest as we rest in Him. Our job is to use the fruit of self-control and control our SELF to remain at peace, knowing God is in control.

> *For the Lord your God is he who goes with you to fight for you against your enemies, to give you the victory.' (Deuteronomy 20:4, ESV).*

God is for us and is with us fighting on our behalf. Keep fighting the good fight of faith by hearing and hearing the Word of God as that is where faith comes from.

November 14

~ You are righteousness of God in Christ ~

> *Unless the Lord builds the house, the builders labor in vain. Unless the Lord watches over the city, the guards stand watch in vain (Psalm 127:1, NIV).*

A good mother knows that she will fail if she tries to do something without depending on God. As a homemaker and builder of her house she wants only the best for her house and so, she connects her weary flesh to the Word that becomes flesh to be the builder of her house. She whispers the light of Psalm 16:8 to shine forth from her.

> *I keep my eyes always on the Lord. With him at my right hand, I will not be shaken (Psalm 16:8, NIV).*

> *That is why we never give up. Though our bodies are dying, our spirits are being renewed every day (2 Corinthians 4:16, NLT).*

Every day she prays, learns and leans more on the Word of God to be the builder of what she is building. The Holy Spirit is focused on building us to be the righteousness of God in Christ. His work in building us is shown through, and in us from the fruit He produces from inside. It's an inside job. His job is shown on our outer character when we action His fruit of righteousness.

> *God made him who had no sin to be sin for us, so that in him we might become the righteousness of God (2 Corinthians 5:21, NIV).*

Each and every day make sure to serve someone the fruit of righteousness. You are God's righteousness in Christ.

November 15

~ Building God's Holy City ~

> *And he carried me away in the Spirit to a mountain great and high, and showed me the Holy City, Jerusalem, coming down out of heaven from God. It shone with the glory of God, and its brilliance was like that of a very precious jewel, like a jasper, clear as crystal. (Revelation 21:10-11, NIV).*

A good mother collects and uses whatever is thrown at her like those beautiful precious stones on which the new heaven was built to build herself with splendour and live heaven on earth. She builds herself upon Jesus who is the living stone. To maintain and house the Spirit of God, she eliminates all kinds of deceit, hypocrisy, envy and slander of every kind, and she hungers and thirsts for God's spiritual milk.

> *Therefore, rid yourselves of all malice and all deceit, hypocrisy, envy, and slander of every kind. Like newborn babies, crave pure spiritual milk, so that by it you may grow up in your salvation, (1 Peter 2:1-2, NIV).*

Jesus, the living stone, is now living through His Holy Spirit, so we can be built into a spiritual house to be holy and offer spiritual sacrifices acceptable to God.

> *As you come to him, the living Stone—rejected by humans but chosen by God and precious to him— you also, like living stones, are being built into a spiritual house to be a holy priesthood, offering spiritual sacrifices acceptable to God through Jesus Christ (1 Peter 2:4-5, NIV).*

We are the Holy City of God in the Holy Spirit when we live in His fruit of righteousness and reproduce it. We are the righteousness of God in Christ and the holiness of God in the Holy Spirit.

You can build whatever unholiness is thrown at you as long as you live and have your being in the Holy Spirit. Every day keep receiving into you the holy, pure and clean Word of God into your life. It has the power to purify and cleanse any unholy dirt that lands on you.

November 16

~ *Faith without action is dead* ~

I was naked and you clothed me, I was sick and you visited me, I was in prison and you came to me. (Matthew 25:36, ESV).

A good mother lives a life that touches people. She is a doer of her kind words. She doesn't just send a get well card, she visits the sick and sits with them feeling the pain they feel. She paints the pain of others onto herself as well to show how much she cares. Knowing God cares for her so much, she is trying to show the God inside of her to the needy through her actions. She allows her movement to serve others the fruit of the Holy Spirit because that is what her life is founded upon.

So also faith by itself, if it does not have works, is dead (James 2:17, ESV).

She has the power of kindness which she derives from her internal relationship with the Holy Spirit. The Holy Spirit is inside us and He feels the pain we feel. It's the touch of His comfort through the Word of God or through an act from our loved ones that gives us the strength to make it through our healing process. We become stronger and better to live through our days. Whatever pain you go through, remember the pain Jesus had to go through.

So the church throughout all Judea and Galilee and Samaria had peace and was being built up. And walking in the fear of the Lord and in the comfort of the Holy Spirit, it multiplied (Acts 9:31, ESV).

Faith without action is dead. God believes and has faith in His Son, and He actions His faith and love through Jesus.

November 17

~ Eat with your Master, Jesus ~

and the face cloth, which had been on Jesus' head, not lying with the linen cloths but folded up in a place by itself (John 20:7, ESV).

It's the little things she does for her household that reminds her of the great things Jesus has done for her. When she folds the clothes of her household she is reminded of Jesus folding the cloth when He rose from the dead. It's a Jewish custom that the master is coming back to the table to eat if he folds his table napkin after eating.

She prepares herself and opens the door of her heart for her Master, Jesus, to come in and eat with her.

Here I am! I stand at the door and knock. If anyone hears my voice and opens the door, I will come in and eat with that person, and they with me (Revelation 3:20, NIV).

The Holy Spirit is the voice of Jesus leading us on the path of life to be victorious in everything. The more we allow the Word, which has become flesh who is Jesus, into us and feast with Him, the more the Holy Spirit breathes into the Word and makes it alive in our flesh.

Your Words were found, and I ate them, and your Words became to me a joy and the delight of my heart for I am called by your name, O Lord, God of hosts (Jeremiah 15:16, ESV).

Each and every day open the door of your heart and receive into you the Word of God and eat with Jesus. The joy that comes from this is an amazing delight to your heart.

November 18

~ The power to build or break a home ~

For we are God's fellow workers. You are God's field, God's building. According to the grace of God given to me, like a skilled master builder I laid a foundation, and someone else is building upon it. Let each one take care how he builds upon it. For no one can lay a foundation other than that which is laid, which is Jesus Christ. Now if anyone builds on the foundation with gold, silver, precious stones, wood, hay, straw— each one's work will become manifest, for the Day will disclose it, because it will be revealed by fire, and the fire will test what sort of work each one has done (1 Corinthians 3:9-13 ESV).

A mother builds or breaks a home. A good mother knows that even if her husband fails her, God will never fail her. Instead of walking out on her family and breaking her home she stands on the Word of God because she knows that Jesus is the key that she has. He is greater and bigger than all her problems, and He lives right inside her through the Holy Spirit. All these things – pain, suffering, misfortune and sorrows are outside her door and she has the key to allow them to come in and steal her joy or she can use the situation to build her home closer to God. She is a good mother, and she chooses to build her home closer to God.

The Holy Spirit is not only close to us, He is the very life that we live, move and have our being. He builds us up with His fruit of righteousness by allowing us to be kind to the unkind, patient with the impatient and good to those who cause us evil.

> *For in him we live and move and have our being (Acts 17:28, NIV).*

Your every new day given by God is like a home for you to live for God. Build your everyday life by speaking life into your today.

November 19

~ Healthy eye, healthy body ~

> *The eye is the lamp of the body. If your eyes are healthy, your whole body will be full of light. (Matthew 6:22, NIV).*

A good mother sees the bigger picture of things through the lens of the Word of God. She uses the Word of God as the lamp to her path. Because she constantly looks into the Word of God, her eyes are nourished with light and truth. She worships God in Spirit and in truth as she serves her house. Her house receives that full light from her and they are always in the light.

> *The city does not need the sun or the moon to shine on it, for the glory of God gives it light, and the Lamb is its lamp (Revelation 21:23, NIV).*

The Holy Spirit's home is us, and when we are full of His truth, His Word, Jesus will reveal himself to us. He is the Word that has become flesh. We see the glory of God through the revelation of Christ.

> *But he, full of the Holy Spirit, gazed into heaven and saw the glory of God, and Jesus standing at the right hand of God (Acts 7:55 ESV).*

Each and every day look into the Word of God to give light to your eyes to see the truth so that you do not get deceived by the father of lies.

November 20

~ Become one with the Lord ~

Don't you believe that I am in the Father and the Father is in me? The words I speak are not my own, but my Father who lives in me does his work through me (John 14:10, NLT).

A good mother understands that there is power to life when she becomes one with the Creator of life, who is the source of power. She unites with God and where there is unity, there is strength. And it's strength that gives power. She has extraordinary strength as she connects with the Holy Spirit from inside. She is powered by the Spirit of power who she houses and so her household becomes powerful in whatever path of life they desire.

Eager to maintain the unity of the Spirit in the bond of peace (Ephesians 4:3, ESV).

The Holy Spirit who is the power and strength of God becomes one with us when we unite with Him as one with our spirit. The Word of God we receive into us attracts the Holy Spirit to come upon and breathe life into it so the Word can become alive in us.

But whoever is united with the Lord is one with him in spirit (1 Corinthians 6:17, NIV).

Just like the human love in a marriage makes two become one, the love of God in Christ makes us become one with His Spirit.

November 21

~ Arise and shine ~

The path of the righteous is like the morning sun, shining ever brighter till the full light of day (Proverbs 4:18, NIV).

She wants to show the path on which her household will walk; a path of righteousness. A good mother connects her path of life to the Holy Spirit so she can reproduce the fruit of righteousness that the Holy Spirit produces inside her life. She wakes up early with the rising sun and connects to the tree of righteousness so she can direct her house on the right path. This is why a good mother shines ever brighter until the full light of day even on a gloomy and dark day.

Men and women who have lived wisely and well will shine brilliantly, like the cloudless, star-strewn night skies. And those who put others on the right path to life will glow like stars forever (Daniel 12:3, MSG).

The Holy Spirit is the shining glory of Jesus that lives in us. He produces the fruit of righteousness for us to produce to make Jesus shine out from inside us.

For God, who said, 'Let there be light in the darkness,' has made this light shine in our hearts so we could know the glory of God that is seen in the face of Jesus Christ (2 Corinthians 4:6, NLT).

Each and every day arise and shine the light of your spirit that is connected to the Holy Spirit, the shiny glory of Jesus.

November 22

~ Emmanuel – God is with us ~

Behold, a virgin shall be with child, and shall bring forth a son, and they shall call his name Emmanuel, which being interpreted is, God with us (Matthew 1:23, KJV).

A good mother acknowledges the presence of God in her household just like a family member. She understands that she has a family member known as Emmanuel living with her. Emmanuel is not just an imaginary person, He is the righteous one, the healer and provider who provides for her household. She doesn't even need a doctor because the healer of life lives with her.

The Holy Spirit is the Spirit of Emmanuel that lives inside us. The characters of Emmanuel are produced by the Holy Spirit. The fruit of righteousness produced by the Holy Spirit is the character of Jesus, Emmanuel, God with us.

But the fruit of the Spirit is love, joy, peace, forbearance, kindness, goodness, faithfulness, gentleness and self-control. Against such things there is no law (Galatians 5:22-23, NIV).

Each and every day acknowledge the presence of Emmanuel in your household. God is part of your family and He has a name by whom you can approach, talk and appreciate His company.

November 23

~ Praising and thanking God in advance for victory ~

For everyone who has been born of God overcomes the world. And this is the victory that has overcome the world—our faith (1 John 5:4, ESV).

Like Jehoshaphat who praised God in advance for victory and God gave Him victory in his battle, a good mother thanks God in advance for her forthcoming battles. There is always a constant battle taking place in her home. A good mother knows that God will make His access through her praises and defeat her enemies and so she puts on her garments of praise and praises God in advance. She delights in the Lord and the Lord always gives her the desires of her heart (Psalm 37:4)

> *After consulting the people, Jehoshaphat appointed men to sing to the Lord and to praise him for the splendor of his holiness as they went out at the head of the army, saying: 'Give thanks to the Lord, for his love endures forever. As they began to sing and praise, the LORD set ambushes against the men of Ammon and Moab and Mount Seir who were invading Judah, and they were defeated (2 Chronicles 20:21-22, NIV).*

The Holy Spirit resurrected Jesus from life and gave Him victory over sin and death and that same Spirit is inside us: all victory is ours. We just have to produce His fruit of joy and thank God in delightful praise and sing songs for our victory in advance.

> *But thanks be to God, who gives us the victory through our Lord Jesus Christ (1 Corinthians 15:57, ESV).*

Wake up every morning with the garments of praise and start praising and thanking God for giving you a glorious and victorious day.

November 24

~ *Negative bad characters* ~

A good tree cannot bear bad fruit, and a bad tree cannot bear good fruit (Matthew 7:18, NIV).

24 November 2019. I remember one morning after boiling noodles I broke open a raw egg and poured it straight into the boiling noodles only to realize that the egg was rotten. This is what the Holy Spirit taught me: A mother is like these good cooked noodles; she is good but the moment she opens herself and allows negative issues or other people's bad energy into her, she makes her good inner qualities rotten. A good mother has good qualities and stores good vibes for her household so that she doesn't allow any negative situations to get hold of her. Whenever she is around negative people, she instantly feels uncomfortable, and wants to depart from their presence.

Jesus gave us the Holy Spirit to comfort us and keep us in the goodness of God. The moment we associate with bad company, we make Him uncomfortable in us. He brings the presence of God into us, and that presence can depart from us when we constantly make the Holy Spirit uncomfortable by associating with bad company.

Do not be misled: 'Bad company corrupts good character.' (1 Corinthians 15:33, NIV).

Every day be mindful of who you associate with and walk out on any relationship with family members or friends who have negative bad energy towards you.

November 25

~ Release the Word of God and build a life now ~

So shall my word be that goes out from my mouth; it shall not return to me empty, but it shall accomplish that which I purpose, and shall succeed in the thing for which I sent it (Isaiah 55:11, ESV).

25 November 2019. I gave Blessed corn chips while he was holding a little tea biscuit in his hand. As soon as I gave him the corn chip, he threw away that tea biscuit to get the corn chip.

This is what the Holy Spirit taught me: You see, if you want to receive something new, get rid of what you have to make space to receive something new.

A good mother doesn't store riches of this world for her household. She invests her time in Word and prayer. She stores the Word and releases it on whoever in her contacts needs it. She prays with the words in Psalm 119:11: *I have stored up your word in my heart, that I might not sin against you.*

To make space to receive more from God she becomes a channel and vessel for God to use.

The Holy Spirit is the vessel from where the life of Jesus flows abundantly for us to be like Christ. The Holy Spirit uses us according to how much of the Word we have stored within us. The more we receive into us and store the Word of God and then release it to build people, the more the Holy Spirit releases to us new Word.

> *Now in a great house there are not only vessels of gold and silver but also of wood and clay, some for honorable use, some for dishonorable. Therefore, if anyone cleanses himself from what is dishonorable, he will be a vessel for honorable use, set apart as holy, useful to the master of the house, ready for every good work (2 Timothy 2:20-21, ESV).*

Every day is a new day to receive something new from God's Word, and release out new words to build or encourage someone in need. Every Word of God has a purpose to build a life.

November 26

~ Cleansed and covered in the blood of Jesus ~

> *Then I acknowledged my sin to you and did not cover up my iniquity. I said, 'I will confess my transgressions to the Lord.' And you forgave the guilt of my sin (Psalm 32:5, NIV).*

A good mother accepts and takes responsibility; she doesn't play the blame game. If her house has a hidden addiction like lies, failures or disturbing behaviour, she doesn't cover it up, she acknowledges that sin and confronts it. She not only asks for the forgiveness of the blood of Jesus to remove that sin but also to cover all her brokenness with His precious blood. She desires truth to prevail in her house because where there is truth and righteousness the presence of God is attracted.

> *Stand firm then, with the belt of truth buckled around your waist, with the breastplate of righteousness in place, and with your feet fitted with the readiness that comes from the gospel of peace (Ephesians 6:14-15, NIV).*

The Holy Spirit is the gift of Jesus to confirm that Jesus has cleansed and purified us from His precious blood, and we are set free from sin and curses. He was blamed for our sin, and He took the responsibility upon Him and buried it in death. Our sin is dead in Christ on the cross and our righteousness is alive in Christ through the Holy Spirit inside us. There is no law against the fruit of righteousness that the Holy Spirit produces within us (Galatians 5:22-23). We are now blessed and redeemed. Where the Spirit of the Lord is, there is freedom.

> *Now the Lord is the Spirit, and where the Spirit of the Lord is, there is freedom (2 Corinthians 3:17, NIV).*

The blood of Jesus not only cleanses and washes away our sin, it also covers and protects us from any evil that comes near us.

November 27

~ *Tame your tongue in the Word of God* ~

> *Likewise, the tongue is a small part of the body, but it makes great boasts. Consider what a great forest is set on fire by a small spark. The tongue also is a fire, a world of evil among the parts of the body. It corrupts the whole body, sets the whole course of one's life on fire, and is itself set on fire by hell (James 3:5-6, NIV).*

She knows what her tongue does; just as a tongue tastes food, it can bring healing or illness to someone when they taste her words. A good mother has taste and has seen that the Lord is good. And so she keeps tasting God's Word so she can tame her tongue to be good and overcome its world of evil.

> *Taste and see that the Lord is good; blessed is the one who takes refuge in him (Psalm 34:8, NIV)*

When she speaks it's full of kindness, honey to the soul and healing to a heart. The Holy Spirit is the good Spirit of God, He lives within us and produces self-control and goodness so we can control our tongue to overcome evil and declare goodness everywhere.

> *Rather, he must be hospitable, one who loves what is good, who is self-controlled, upright, holy and disciplined (Titus 1:8, NIV).*

Each and every day control your tongue to be good when it is talking. Let it only deliver kind words that will build up lives.

November 28

~ Building up your faith ~

> *In him and through faith in him we may approach God with freedom and confidence (Ephesians 3:12, NIV).*

A good mother builds up her child's self-esteem and confidence so they can become independent in life. She builds herself firstly in God's righteous Word and in prayer. And once her faith muscle is firmer and stronger she actions it on her house.

> *The fruit of that righteousness will be peace; its effect will be quietness and confidence forever (Isaiah 32:17, NIV).*

The Holy Spirit lives in us and bring into life the Word of God to live in us. God wants us to fully depend on His Word so we can live our newfound life in Christ. The more we depend on the living

Word of God, the more we are able to discern and understand what life is meant to be.

> *I am your servant; give me discernment that I may understand your statute (Psalm 119:125, NIV).*

Every day build your faith muscles in the Word to become strong to walk by faith and not sight.

November 29

~ *The lifestyle in the kingdom of God* ~

> *For the kingdom of God is not a matter of eating and drinking, but of righteousness, peace and joy in the Holy Spirit, because anyone who serves Christ in this way is pleasing to God and receives human approval (Romans 14:17-18, NIV).*

A good mother teaches her children all the good things that they are allowed to do. Her children know the 'YES' and the 'NO' given by their mother. She accesses herself daily into the Word of God to seek His guidance, light and love to give direction to her children. She makes rules according to what the regulations of the Word says. All the promises of God are 'Yes' in Christ, and she has the strength to do all things with her house through Christ and what He promised. She teaches her house to walk by faith in the life of the Holy Spirit and not to walk by sight in the life of the flesh. She teaches her children about what Galatians 5 says about 'YES' and 'NO' to enter and live in the kingdom of God.

Not allowed to enter the kingdom of God:

> *The acts of the flesh are obvious: sexual immorality, impurity and debauchery; idolatry and witchcraft; hatred, discord, jealousy, fits of rage, selfish ambition, dissensions, factions and envy; drunkenness, orgies, and the like. I warn you, as I did before, that those who live like this will not inherit the kingdom of God (Galatians 5:19-21, NIV).*

Allowed to enter and live in the kingdom of God:

> *But the fruit of the Spirit is love, joy, peace, forbearance, kindness, goodness, faithfulness, gentleness and self-control. Against such things there is no law (Galatians 5:22-23, NIV).*

The Holy Spirit is the kingdom of God that Jesus has given to us. He is the King of kings and Lord of lords over all kingdoms. We enter the kingdom of God because of God's love, mercy and grace, not our righteous deeds. To live and experience the good life in the kingdom of God, we are to live and walk in love, serving each other with love.

> *For it is by grace you have been saved, through faith— and this is not from yourselves, it is the gift of God— (Ephesians 2:8, NIV).*

> *You, my brothers and sisters, were called to be free. But do not use your freedom to indulge the flesh; rather, serve one another humbly in love. For the entire law is fulfilled in keeping this one command:'Love your neighbor as yourself.' (Galatians 5:13-14, NIV).*

Enjoy the freedom to live and love everyone. You can even love your enemies; you are free to love in the kingdom of God. You can't live in the kingdom of God if you have hate.

November 30

~ Making time for God ~

Therefore, let all the godly pray to you while there is still time (Psalm 32:6, NLT).

A good mother is very productive with her 168 hours each week. She gives a tenth to God every week. She knows that God has everything and doesn't need anything; all He wants is to spend time with Her. Time is the most precious gift. For God to get closer to her and her house, she has to make the first move and get closer to God.

This is the prayer of a good mother.

Teach us to use wisely all the time we have (Psalm 90:12, CEV).

The Holy Spirit inside us is just a breath away. We just have to declare the Word of God and He is there breathing upon the spoken Word of God. He is always with us. He is the love of God through Jesus defeating death. Nothing can ever separate us from God's love, not even death. The Holy Spirit is our every day time given to us as the precious gift from Jesus. He lives inside us and our life is in Him.

My times are in your hands (Psalms 31:15, NIV).

Each and every day, give one-tenth of your time back to the Master.

DECEMBER

~ The gift package from God is wrapped in that storm you are facing ~

> *For by grace you have been saved through faith. And this is not your own doing; it is the gift of God, (Ephesians 2:8, ESV).*

29 November 2019. I was wrapping a birthday present for Angelilly's friend whose party she was attending. I wrapped it so nicely and beautifully. This is what the Holy Spirit taught me:

There is a beautiful gift you have wrapped in there; as the sender, you have wrapped it so nicely. The receiver will have to destroy the neat work you did to get to what is inside.

You see, God also sends you a beautiful gift and as you receive it and want to unwrap it, you start going through a storm when you try to destroy the wrapping. The wrapping is like your old life, your fleshy desires. You are doing away with it to get the new life that's inside your old life. The Christ-like life.

> *For the wages of sin is death, but the free gift of God is eternal life in Christ Jesus our Lord (Romans 6:23, ESV).*

Like that receiver of the gift destroying the wrap, you are also opening up your gift and destroying the wrap, and you feel the effects. Continue to unwrap and peel off your old life and open the gift of your new life in Christ and live that life.

A good mother is a gift to her household every day. For the best of her house to come out, they have to go through the strict rules of her principles. She may be hard but she wants to see the best in them.

She may fail, but she is trying and as long as she surrenders to God in Word and prayer, her house keeps standing through the bad storms.

The Holy Spirit convicts us again and again every time we go off the path of righteousness. He will also put us through a hard situation to teach us a lesson to get us back on the right path, so that we can enjoy the abundance of life God has in store for us. The Holy Spirit is God's gift to us to enjoy the abundant life of Jesus. When we unwrap the beautiful gift of the fruit of the Holy Spirit to respond to people who have hurt us and been unkind to us, we feel that pain and suffering in unwrapping the gift of God's love and wrapping that love around someone who has hurt us.

> *And Peter said to them, 'Repent and be baptized every one of you in the name of Jesus Christ for the forgiveness of your sins, and you will receive the gift of the Holy Spirit (Acts 2:38, ESV).*

Sometimes, God wraps His beautiful gifts to us in a package of storms. When the storm is over we receive that beautiful gift.

Each day and EVERY DAY of the month of December, wrap yourself in the love of God in His Word. Show everyone with whom you come in contact, the gift of love you have in your house where the Holy Spirit lives. Offer that gift of love and wrap it on anyone that needs it.

December 1

~ Remain clean ~

Remove my sin, and I will be clean; wash me, and I will be whiter than snow (Psalm 51:7, GNT).

A good mother does everything as a worship unto God. She connects her daily physical chores to what God's Word says. When she is cleaning the house, she reminds herself that the Word from Psalm 51:10 is her flesh.

> *Create in me a clean heart, O God; and renew a right spirit within me (Psalm 51:10, ESV).*

The Holy Spirit is the power that resurrects Jesus from life and keeps us clean in the righteousness of Christ all the time. We become His clean nature when we produce His fruit of righteousness in this unrighteous world.

> *Wash yourselves and be clean! Get your sins out of my sight. Give up your evil ways (Isaiah 1:16, NLT).*

Each and every day keep yourself clean by producing the fruit of righteousness to all unrighteous attacks towards you.

December 2

~ The strength of God ~

> *Because our gospel came to you not simply with words but also with power, with the Holy Spirit and deep conviction. You know how we lived among you for your sake (1 Thessalonians 1:5, NIV).*

A wife is the inner strength of her husband as she was taken from within him. The mother of all living beings was deceived by the devil and that was how the human race was cursed. A good mother understands this and strengthens herself in Word and prayer. The Word is the truth that flashes its light on any dark lies the devil puts into her.

The Holy Spirit is the strength and power of God that was given by what Jesus did for us, so we will never be deceived by the devil. He is the Spirit of truth that gives the POWER OF LIFE to make the Word of God light up within us. We have to contain the Word of God in order for Him to perform this role.

> *But I will send you the Advocate—the Spirit of truth. He will come to you from the Father and will testify all about me (John 15:26, NLT).*

The Holy Spirit, the strength and power of God, now lives inside us because of Jesus and is our inner strength. The Word, who is Jesus, has become flesh and it is upon the Word that we received into us that the Holy Spirit will testify Jesus to us. We can do all things through Christ who strengthens us.

December 3

~ Nursed by God's Word ~

> *The Lord nurses them when they are sick and restores them to health (Psalm 41:3, NLT).*

When God allows her to be a mother, He also qualifies her to be a nurse to nurse that life.

A good mother seeks God's prescription that He prescribed in His Word to heal her sick children. As long as she has fellowship with God she ensures her family takes in the blood of Jesus as their blood and His flesh as their flesh every day. This prescription has the power to heal, and also to give strength to carry her and her house in their time of sickness.

> *Whoever eats my flesh and drinks my blood has eternal life, and I will raise them up at the last day. For my flesh is real food and my blood is real drink (John 6:54-55, NIV).*

The Holy Spirit nurses us with His fruit of righteousness to keep us in good health. Regardless of what kind of sicknesses the world tries to give us, He stabilizes us in peace that we can wake up with joy to face the challenges and nothing will offend us.

> *You give peace of mind to all who love your Law. Nothing can make them fall (Psalm 119:165, CEV).*

Download the app of God's Word into you and subscribe to receiving every Word that comes out of His mouth. When He speaks His Word, it brings healing.

December 4

~ Knowing God ~

> *My people are destroyed for lack of knowledge; (Hosea 4:6, ESV).*

4 December 2019. Angelilly was almost 5 years' old and I was watching ABC Kids with her, a kids program. We were guessing what programme was coming up next. I guessed it right. I told her that I knew it already so I got it right. Instantly the Lord spoke to my heart through the Holy Spirit, 'When you know something

already, you have knowledge of it, and so you will get it right. It's like sitting a test, and when you have knowledge of the test given to you, you get it right. So is having the knowledge of God; when you know God you will want to walk in His righteousness, wanting to do the right thing.

> *So whoever knows the right thing to do and fails to do it, for him it is sin (James 4:17, ESV).*

A good mother spends time more in Word and prayer and is filled with the Spirit of knowledge and so she always knows what the right thing is to do to build her house upright.

> *So as to walk in a manner worthy of the Lord, fully pleasing to him, bearing fruit in every good work and increasing in the knowledge of God (Colossians 1:10, ESV).*

The Holy Spirit within us is the Spirit of knowledge that makes us know God so we can make God known. He is God's Spirit and He produces the fruit of righteousness through us to do the right things.

> *For the kingdom of God is not a matter of eating and drinking, but of righteousness, peace and joy in the Holy Spirit, because anyone who serves Christ in this way is pleasing to God and receives human approval (Romans 14:17-18, NIV).*

Wisdom is given but knowledge is gain. Anyone can ask God for wisdom and He can give it to them, but to gain knowledge one has to seek God's Word to become knowledgeable of Him.

December 5

~ Glorify God in what you do ~

Today is holy to our Lord, so don't be sad. The joy that the Lord gives you will make you strong (Nehemiah 8:10, GNT).

A good mother always shows love no matter how she has been treated. She may not be appreciated for the daily service she performs. She can also be overlooked for being the pillar of strength on which her house is founded. Yet it's the joy from the love she has for her family that gives her the strength to keep going. She draws out God's love from His Word and this is how her strength is built.

The Holy Spirit faithfully produces His fruit of love inside us all the time, regardless of how unfaithful we are. Many times we may fail to walk and live in the love of God but He still produces the fruit of love. Love is faithful.

It's the same as how the sun shines. We may not appreciate the role that God has appointed to it, yet it still performs what God purposed it to be.

> *For the word of the Lord is right and true; he is faithful in all he does (Psalm 33:4, NIV).*

God made you special and unique from everyone to give Him glory in your own special and unique way in which you were designed.

> *So whether you eat or drink or whatever you do, do it all for the glory of God (1 Corinthians 10:31, NIV).*

It doesn't matter if you are not appreciated for what you do, as long as God is glorified in what you do. When God appreciates you, you will win everyone's favour.

December 6

~ Good Mothers are angels without wings ~

> *For even the Son of Man did not come to be served, but to serve, and to give his life as a ransom for many.' (Mark 10:45, NIV).*

A good mother's service is available 24/7. She really is an angel without wings that came from heaven to serve and not to be served. Even with pain, sorrow or worry she continues serving.

No matter how old she is growing she never grows weary of doing good for her children.

> *And let us not grow weary of doing good, for in due season we will reap, if we do not give up (Galatians 6:9, ESV).*

The Holy Spirit is available 24/7 to produce His fruit of righteousness so we can continue to live in the righteousness of Christ.

He never grows weary of showering us with mercy and goodness to bring us back on track when we go off track. That's how He is faithful with His goodness 24/7.

> *You prepare a table before me in the presence of my enemies; you anoint my head with oil; my cup overflows. Surely goodness and mercy shall follow me all the days of my life, and I shall dwell in the house of the Lord forever. (Psalm 23:5-6, ESV).*

As long as you walk in the spirit with the Holy Spirit, the goodness and mercy of the Lord will follow you wherever you go.

December 7

~ Jesus is the only way ~

But those who trust in the Lord will find new strength. They will soar high on wings like eagles. They will run and not grow weary. They will walk and not faint (Isaiah 40:31, NLT).

7 December 2019. I remember fixing my daughter's hair and she told me she doesn't like it when her hair is loose and the curls get in her way.

The Holy Spirit joined in the conversation and taught me this. Many things will get in your way when you go your own way in life. Jesus is the only way to LIFE. HE IS THE LIFE AND IT'S ONLY THROUGH HIM. You see, a good mother keeps going, even when many obstacles come her way or get in her way. She is strong for her children.

She knows that not only is she the only way her children were born into this world, but she is the only way that will help her children to find their way in LIFE. And so she surrenders all her ways into that ONE WAY of Jesus Christ. She submits her many ways, plans and thoughts into God's plan.

The only way to walk in the path of life is to follow Jesus back to the Father and that is through His life by the Holy Spirit within us. Jesus is the only Son of God and the only way back to the Father. He has given us the Holy Spirit to live inside us to help us walk towards eternity.

Jesus answered, 'I am the way and the truth and the life. No one comes to the Father except through me' (John 14:6, NIV).

Each and every day nourish yourself in the life-giving Word of God, as you continue your journey towards eternal life with the Holy Spirit.

December 8

~ Engaged to Jesus ~

Here I am! I stand at the door and knock. If anyone hears my voice and opens the door, I will come in and eat with that person, and they with me (Revelation 3:20, NIV).

8 December 2019. I was on the train and wanted to go and use the toilet. The sign said 'Engaged' because someone was using it. This is what the Holy Spirit taught me: You see, when you are engaged to Jesus, you are closed and shut so the devil cannot have access to use you. The toilet entry read engaged, because it is in use, and so the door is also closed.

Jesus said, 'He is standing at the door and knocking, if we hear his voice, and open the door he will come in and eat with us, and we will eat with Him.' When He comes in and eats with us the enemy looks at us and sees an 'engaged sign'. The enemy cannot have access and use us because the Holy Spirit is using us to bring alive the Word of God in us.

A good mother is engaged to Jesus in His Word. Her schedule revolves around her children. Her decisions are made according to what the good principal of God's Word says. The Holy Spirit brings alive the Word of God when Jesus comes in and eats with her.

The Holy Spirit is engaged to us through Jesus. He knows what God's best plans are for us. When we open the door and invite Jesus in to eat with us, we move and have our being in Him and Him alone.

> *For in him we live and move and have our being (Acts 17:28, NIV).*

Engage each and every day using the Word of God in all areas of your life, and the devil won't be able to find access to get into your life.

December 9

~ Be fruitful and multiply ~

> *We who are strong ought to bear with the failings of the weak and not to please ourselves (Romans 15:1, NIV).*

A good mother always shows her children that she believes in their strength to achieve anything by giving them her full support. She turns her children's cloudy day with her sunshine strength to bring a brighter future for them. For that to happen, she burns her energy and uses her strength in prayers to God and spends time in His Word. She sharpens her children in the Word of God like a friend sharpens a friend.

> *As iron sharpens iron, so a friend sharpens a friend (Proverbs 27:17, NLT).*

The Holy Spirit believes that we can do all things in Christ who strengthens us. He lives right in the most secret place in our body which is our heart. He gives us that support we need right where God placed us. The Father believes in the Son and gave Him over to us in order to receive us back to Him. Jesus believes in the Holy

Spirit and has given Him to us in order for Him to live again in us. The Holy Spirit, the Spirit of the Father, believes in us and has given His fruit of righteousness for us to be fruitful and multiply.

Then God blessed them and said, 'Be fruitful and multiply (Genesis 1:28, NLT).

The Holy Spirit is the true close friend who sharpens us in the Word of God that we receive. He makes us look sharp and shiny regardless of how gloomy life can get at times.

December 10

~ *Giving* ~

Since he did not spare even his own Son but gave him up for us all, won't he also give us everything else? (Romans 8:32, NLT).

A good mother gives all the best she can to her child according to what she is able to. She can go way out of her comfort zone just so her child's needs are met. She understands that God knows that she can meet the needs of her children because He trusts her capabilities and potential. She trusts God completely to meet her needs. She builds her trust in the Word of God daily. She can move mountains with her mustard seed faith and nothing can doubt her.

Those who trust in the LORD are like Mount Zion, which cannot be moved, but abides forever (Psalm 125:1, NKJV).

And my God will meet all your needs according to the riches of his glory in Christ Jesus (Philippians 4:19, NIV).

The Holy Spirit gives the best of what we could ever imagine or ask of according to the power that is at work within us. He knows our needs and how to meet them even before we know.

> *Now to him who is able to do far more abundantly than all that we ask or think, according to the power at work within us, (Ephesians 3:20, ESV).*

The provision of God in Christ through the Holy Spirit has already met our daily needs. We just have to enjoy our every day and thank God for the strength that we made it through the day.

December 11

~ *The favour of God* ~

> *Surely, Lord, you bless the righteous; you surround them with your favour as with a shield (Psalm 5:12, NIV).*

A good mother still carries out her roles as a good mother even though things are not always in her favour. The needs of her children come first over her own needs and she accepts whatever is being thrown at her on that day. Even if she is not treated right she still cares for her children. She would rather have the favour of God upon her life than what is not being done in her favour. She seeks God's face in His Word and prayer to surround herself with the favour of the Lord.

> *May the favour of the Lord our God rest on us; establish the work of our hands for us—yes, establish the work of our hands (Psalm 90:17, NIV).*

The Holy Spirit is full of God's goodness inside us. Most times we may not produce the goodness of God around those that are unkind to us, yet the Holy Spirit keeps going with our flow. He is still faithful and gives us another opportunity to be good by allowing difficult people into our lives.

> *For the Lord is good and his love endures forever; his faithfulness continues through all generations. (Psalm 100:5, NIV).*

The favour of God in our lives attracts difficult people towards us so that we can give them the love of God they need.

December 12

~ *The fear of the Lord* ~

> *The fear of the Lord is the beginning of wisdom, and knowledge of the Holy One is understanding (Proverbs 9:10, NIV).*

The Spirit of wisdom, understanding, knowledge and the Spirit of the fear of the Lord was at work in the beginning when God created the universe with His wisdom, knowledge and understanding (Isaiah 11:2-3).

A good mother knows that since God's wisdom will never end, her goal is to get her children to grow up in the fear of the Lord so that God's wisdom can begin in their life. She demonstrates this by walking and living in the fear of God so her children do the same.

> *The fear of the Lord is the beginning of wisdom; all who follow his precepts have good understanding. To him belongs eternal praise (Psalm 111:10, NIV).*

The Holy Spirit is the Spirit of the Lord, He is the Spirit of wisdom, knowledge, understanding and fear of the Lord. He produces the fruit of righteousness inside us so we can do the right things to please God.

> *The Spirit of the Lord will rest on him – the Spirit of wisdom and of understanding, the Spirit of counsel and of might, the Spirit of the knowledge and fear of the Lord – and he will delight in the fear of the Lord (Isaiah 11:2-3, NIV).*

The beginning of the life of wisdom starts with the fear of the Lord. To have fear of the Lord is to be afraid of doing anything that God sees as unrighteous. Because you fear and respect the Lord, you will want to stay away from sin.

December 13

~ *The voice of a mother* ~

> *I am Wisdom, and I have insight; I have knowledge and sound judgment (Proverbs 8:12, GNT).*

Every child knows their mother's voice so clearly. She keeps calling her children's names non-stop. She repeats the same thing over and over again because her kids don't do it right. Even when she is not around her children, they can still hear her voice in their head if they try to do something wrong.

A good mother is that voice of wisdom that is loud and clear calling out in her children's head to do the right thing.

> *Wisdom cries aloud in the street, in the markets she raises her voice; at the head of the noisy streets she cries out; at the entrance of the city gates she speaks: (Proverbs 1:20-21, ESV).*

> *Listen to my excellent words; all I tell you is right (Proverbs 8:6, GNT).*

The Holy Spirit is the voice of God inside us to lead us on the right path. The Word of God is the same and will never change; it is repeated over and over by the voice of the Holy Spirit for us to obey. And when we are about to go astray we will hear that voice of the Holy Spirit convincing us to go the right way.

> *Whether you turn to the right or to the left, your ears will hear a voice behind you, saying, 'This is the way; walk in it.' (Isaiah 30:21, NIV).*

It's the voice of God that wakes us up to arise and live to a new day EVERY DAY.

December 14

~ *The Holy Spirit as a gift* ~

> *Thanks be to God for his indescribable gift! (2 Corinthians 9:15, NIV).*

Mothers love receiving gifts from their loved ones. When they receive one, they show it off with joy and pride. A good mother shares her gift cheerfully and enjoys it with those who are with her. She loves sharing her blessings as that makes way for more to come through.

> *Now he who supplies seed to the sower and bread for food will also supply and increase your store of seed and will enlarge the harvest of your righteousness. You will be enriched in every way so that you can be generous on every occasion, and through us your generosity will result in thanksgiving to God (2 Corinthians 9:10-11, NIV).*

The Holy Spirit is the gift to us from Jesus. The Holy Spirit loves it when we give Him as a gift to anyone we come in contact with by sharing His fruit of righteousness with them.

> *...if you then, though you are evil, know how to give good gifts to your children, how much more will your Father in heaven give the Holy Spirit to those who ask him!' (Luke 11:13, NIV).*

> *But the fruit of the Spirit is love, joy, peace, patience, kindness, goodness, faithfulness, gentleness, self-control; against such things there is no law (Galatians 5:22-23, ESV).*

Give a fruit of the Holy Spirit as a gift to whoever needs it. It is free. Every good and perfect gift is from above and is free.

December 15

~ Nine months of pregnancy and nine fruit of the Holy Spirit ~

> *So then, just as you received Christ Jesus as Lord, continue to live your lives in him, rooted and built up in him, strengthened in the faith as you were taught, and overflowing with thankfulness (Colossians 2:6-7, NIV).*

When a woman conceives her body goes through many changes to cater for the growing baby. There are also many developments in her body that build up her strength to be able to give birth, and mother and nurse her baby. A good mother speaks life from the NINE fruit of righteousness of the Holy Spirit into the NINE MONTHS of the baby's life in the womb.

> *So we fix our eyes not on what is seen, but on what is unseen, since what is seen is temporary, but what is unseen is eternal (2 Corinthians 4:18, NIV).*

The Holy Spirit develops and builds you in His NINE FRUIT of righteousness before He gives you what you requested. You are the house He lives in, and He has to build you up in the way that you will be strong enough to give birth to your spiritual blessings which are found in Him.

> *For we are God's fellow workers. You are God's field, God's building (1 Corinthians 3:9, ESV).*

The more you conceive the Word, the more the Holy Spirit will work in your life to make you stronger to give birth to your spiritual blessings.

December 16

~ The joy after the pain ~

> *Even though I walk through the valley of the shadow of death, I will fear no evil, for you are with me; your rod and your staff, they comfort me (Psalm 23:4, ESV).*

Though Mothers go through suffering they always give their children that smile of encouragement and confidence that everything is alright. A good mother understands that she has to go through the shadow of death in order to see the light of life and enjoy it. She connects deeper into the source of light from God's Word to provide light on her path when she is walking in the valley of darkness.

> *But the fruit of the Spirit is love, joy, peace, long-suffering, gentleness, goodness, faith, meekness, temperance: against such there is no law (Galatians 5:22-23, KJV).*

The Holy Spirit produces long-suffering within us to endure the pains or suffering we encounter. He gives us joy in every new day to strengthen us to continue to serve God faithfully regardless of the storms we face. He is the light of the new life in Christ that enables us to see even in our darkest days.

> *This is the day that the Lord has made; let us rejoice and be glad in it.(Psalm 118:24, ESV).*

A new day God gives is a birth of new life to enjoy, just as mothers rejoice in giving birth to their newborn baby.

December 17

~ Build your strength in the Holy Spirit ~

> *'The virgin will conceive and give birth to a son, and they will call him Immanuel' (which means 'God with us') (Matthew 1:23, NIV).*

The devil knows that a woman has been inbuilt with the characters of the Holy Spirit, and so he is after mothers and daughters. When God removed the rib of the man and fashioned a woman, He removed the inner strength of a man and this is why men are weak around women. A good woman and a mother will use that strength to build her home and not wreck another woman's home.

> *But a woman will be saved through having children, if she perseveres in faith and love and holiness, with modesty (1 Timothy 2:15, GNT).*

The Holy Spirit is the inner strength and power of God. The power of God was put back into a woman's inner being through the virgin birth. The Holy Spirit, the power and strength of God entered the woman for the virgin birth.

> *But after he had considered this, an angel of the Lord appeared to him in a dream and said, 'Joseph son of David, do not be afraid to take Mary home as your wife, because what is conceived in her is from the Holy Spirit. She will give birth to a son, and you are to give him the name Jesus, because he will save his people from their sins.' (Matthew 1:20-21, NIV).*

Every new day is a new opportunity to build our inner strength in the Word of God to be able to do everything through Christ who strengthens us.

December 18

~ Appreciate the gift of life ~

> *Though you have not seen him, you love him; and even though you do not see him now, you believe in him and are filled with an inexpressible and glorious joy, for you are receiving the end result of your faith, the salvation of your souls (1 Peter 1:8-9, NIV).*

A good mother appreciates more the gift of life and feels complete when she sees that her children are full of joy and in good health. She wears an attitude of gratefulness in every situation and she understands that God will always bring His will and purpose in every situation. She makes 1 Thessalonians 5:16-18 come alive in her.

> *Rejoice always, pray continually, give thanks in all circumstances; for this is God's will for you in Christ Jesus (1 Thessalonians 5:16-18, NIV).*

The Holy Spirit is the gift of life from the life Jesus laid down for us. He produces joy and that joy is complete when He lives inside us and we reproduce that joy of Him.

> *If you keep my commands, you will remain in my love, just as I have kept my Father's commands and remain in his love. I have told you this so that my joy may be in you and that your joy may be complete (John 15:10-11, NIV).*

Every new day is made with love and joy for us to live in peace with each other and be happy and grateful for the life God gave us.

December 19

~ Laying down your life for someone ~

Whoever has the Son has life; whoever does not have the Son of God does not have life (1 John 5:12, NIV).

A good mother lays down her life to serve her children. The moment she brings a life into this world she sees her own life in her child's life. She gives the best of all that she can to her child. She sees how God loved the world so much he gave His life through His Son. She can now understand how she loves her child so much that she gives her life to her child. She lives the life Jesus laid down for her by spending daily time in Word and prayer so she can serve her children in the way God designed them.

> *For God so loved the world that he gave his one and only Son, that whoever believe in him shall not perish but have eternal life (John 3:16, NIV).*

Jesus is not only our saviour and redeemer but a friend. A friend always lays down his life for a friend. He laid down His life to come and live inside us through the Holy Spirit. The Holy Spirit now gives us life in His fruit of righteousness so we can live that life of righteousness and not the old life from the fruit of the knowledge of good and evil.

> *Greater love has no one than this: to lay down one's life for one's friends (John 15:13, NIV).*

Each day if you can lay down your life to serve someone the fruit of righteousness, do it so they can glorify God. You not only give glory to God but your receiver also glorifies God.

December 20

~ Talking confidently with God ~

> *This is the confidence we have in approaching God: that if we ask anything according to his will, he hears us. And if we know that he hears us—whatever we ask— we know that we have what we asked of him (1 John 5:14-15, NIV).*

She walks on her path in the path of God's Word in 1 John 5:14-15; she walks confidently as if she has everything that she has asked of God. A good mother chooses to live her life as if she already has everything she has been asking God for. She is filled with thanksgiving, praise and appreciation to God for giving Jesus who is His glorious riches. She knows that she will not only get what she is after but much more than what she is asking for. A perfect Father she is dealing with, and in its perfect time she will have it.

> *If you, then, though you are evil, know how to give good gifts to your children, how much more will your Father in heaven give good gifts to those who ask him! (Matthew 7:11, NIV).*

> *Now to Him who is able to do exceedingly abundantly above all that we ask or think, according to the power that works in us, (Ephesians 3:20, NKJV).*

The Holy Spirit is confident that we have Jesus who is the glorious riches of God. When we house the Holy Spirit within us, we have housed all the spiritual blessings that God promised to give us even before creation. No eyes have seen, no ears have heard, and no mind can perceive what God has in store for those that love Him (1 Corinthians 2:9).

The Holy Spirit is the power of God that works upon the Word of God we received into us to give us more than we could ever dream of.

December 21

~ Right lane ~

> *For 'you were like sheep going astray,' but now you have returned to the Shepherd and Overseer of your souls (1 Peter 2:25, NIV).*

21 December 2019. One morning while I was driving, I saw a lady indicating where she was trying to go. Something I normally see, but this morning the Lord taught me this:

You see, whether she turns to the right or left she will stay in her right lane, because this is the law of driving on the road. The law in God's Word also tells us to stay in our right lane. If she doesn't stay in her right lane she will meet accidents that could even lead to death. Jesus Christ is the only way for you to walk to stay in your right lane. You will meet accidents and even death if you go the wrong way.

> *Whether you turn to the right or to the left, your ears will hear a voice behind you, saying, 'This is the way; walk in it.' (Isaiah 30:21, NIV).*

A good mother is always guiding her children in the right path every time they go astray. Her strength flows through her from the quality time she spends in Word and prayer.

Even when her children go astray, they will always get back to the right path and this is because they have been trained in the Word of God from early childhood.

> *Before I was afflicted I went astray, but now I obey your word (Psalm 119:67, NIV).*

The Holy Spirit is the voice of Jesus that always puts us back on the path of righteousness and guides us. He is the voice that says, 'This is the way, walk in it when we go astray.' Jesus is the only way to the way of right living, and the Holy Spirit is the only voice of Jesus that leads us on.

December 22

~ *Unconditional love of God* ~

We love because he first loved us (1 John 4:19, NIV).

The love of a good mother is developed unconditionally towards the baby she has not yet met during the NINE months of pregnancy. Though she may fail at times, she never quits trying to reproduce the NINE fruit of the Holy Spirit she contains in the Word of God that she receives into her.

The unconditional love of God is shown through His Holy Spirit who the world cannot see because He lives within you. You know Him because He lives inside the Word who is Jesus and you live in Him.

The Holy Spirit produces His NINE fruit within us to develop us in the image of Christ.

> *'If you love me, obey my commandments. And I will ask the Father, and he will give you another Advocate, who will never leave you. He is the Holy Spirit, who leads into all truth. The world cannot receive him, because it isn't looking for him and doesn't recognize him. But you know him, because he lives with you now and later will be in you (John 14:15-17, NLT).*

God's unconditional love is given to us every day in the new day. He faithfully put our life into the new day He made so we can live in it. Because Jesus lives, we will also live (John 14:19).

December 23

~ Grow in the wisdom of God ~

Like newborn babies, crave pure spiritual milk, so that by it you may grow up in your salvation, now that you have tasted that the Lord is good (1 Peter 2:2-3, NIV).

A mother longs to receive her baby when the nine months of pregnancy come to pass. A good mother receives her baby and nourishes that life in the life she found in Jesus. Like her newborn baby, she too is hungry and thirsty for spiritual milk. She craves to grow in wisdom so her child can live and grow in an environment that is filled with wisdom. The Word that has become flesh not only increases our wisdom but also surrounds us with the favour of God.

And Jesus grew in wisdom and stature, and in favor with God and man (Luke 2:52, NIV).

The Holy Spirit longs for you to receive His nine fruit from within you and use it so you can give birth to the life of Christ. When you birth the life of Christ, you give birth to wisdom as well. You begin to live and grow in wisdom. The Holy Spirit is God's Spirit of wisdom (Isaiah 11:2).

The life of Christ you gave birth to can serve you and others that hunger and thirst for a life of righteousness.

Blessed are those who hunger and thirst for righteousness, for they will be filled (Matthew 5:6, NIV).

Each new day surround yourself with God's favour by speaking life from God's Word into your life. The favour of God around you attracts the favour of man.

December 24

~ Let God run our body that houses His Spirit ~

I run in the path of your commands, for you have broadened my understanding (Psalm 119:32, NIV).

It is always in a mother's character that she wants to get things done her way for her family. Running the household she knows what is best to keep her family going. A good mother knows this is a big responsibility and for her to prosper, she needs to sit under the council of God's Word for the insights to help her see through all seasons of time.

Oh, the joys of those who do not follow the advice of the wicked, or stand around with sinners, or join in with mockers.

But they delight in the law of the Lord, meditating on it day and night. They are like trees planted along the riverbank, bearing fruit each season. Their leaves never wither, and they prosper in all they do (Psalm 1:1-3, NLT).

Jesus is resurrected in our life through His Holy Spirit and our body is His house. He wants to run His house, which is our body, in the way God wants it to be run, when we receive Jesus into our life.

Jesus will baptize us from inside with the Holy Spirit when we make Him come alive in us and take complete control over our body, soul and spirit.

I baptize you with water, but he will baptize you with the Holy Spirit.'(Mark 1:8, NIV).

Each new day, rise up and shine up in the Word of God. Let the Word of God run your thoughts.

December 25

~ Every day is Christmas for Jesus to be born in us ~

So in everything, do to others what you would have them do to you, for this sums up the Law and the Prophets (Matthew 7:12, NIV).

I was wrapping up my household's present on Christmas Eve. While I was doing that, this is what the Holy Spirit taught me: You see, you can wrap up your own gift which is the gift of today in the way you want and gift it to everyone with whom you come in contact. You are doing to others what you would like them to do for you. A good mother wakes up early in the morning to prepare herself to reach out to those in her household and to be reachable. She reminds herself every day that she has the nine fruit from the Holy Spirit as a gift that needs to be given to anyone that needs it. If she meets an impatient person, she needs to give them the fruit of patience. She gives goodness to bad people, kindness to the unkind. And so it is with the rest of the other fruit of righteousness.

But the fruit of the Spirit is love, joy, peace, patience, kindness, goodness, faithfulness, gentleness, self-control; against such things there is no law (Galatians 5:22-23, ESV.).

The Holy Spirit is just within reach, all we have to do is wake up in our spirit and reach out to Him. He wraps us around His gift package of LOVE that contains His fruit of righteousness. We are to unwrap and reproduce His nine fruit of righteousness, and gift it to the needy. Our enemies are in more need of it because of their unloving character towards us.

'For this reason it says, 'Awake, sleeper, And arise from the dead, And Christ will shine on you.' (Ephesians 5:14, NASB).

Every day is the birth of a brand new life, let every day be Christmas, and let Jesus be born within you. Give a Christmas gift of the nine characters of Jesus to anyone with whom you come into contact today and every day. Stored inside the gift package of LOVE is the Holy Spirit's nine fruit which are the characters of Christ.

December 26

~ Fruit package of the Holy Spirit ~

Jesus answered, 'It is written: 'Man shall not live on bread alone, but on every word that comes from the mouth of God.'(Matthew 4:4, NIV).

A good mother always plans meals and has them available when her children are hungry. She doesn't want to see her house live in a state of hunger. She wakes up while it is still dark as she needs to satisfy her hunger in God's Word before she satisfies the hunger in her house. The food for her spiritual house comes first, then the food for her physical home. Man can't live by bread alone but on every Word that comes from the mouth of God. Psalm 119:148 is her breathe.

My eyes are awake before the watches of the night, that I may meditate on your promise (Psalm 119:148, ESV).

She gets up while it is still night; she provides food for her family and portions for her female servants (Proverbs 31:15, NIV).

God has great plans and hopes for our future when we seek the righteousness of His kingdom, His Word, the meal to give us strength to be successful. God's Holy Spirit constantly produces this meal, and it comes in a fruit package. His fruit of righteousness is available all the time inside us to sustain us.

> *But the fruit of the Spirit is love, joy, peace, patience, kindness, goodness, faithfulness, gentleness, self-control; against such things there is no law (Galatians 5:22-23, ESV).*

The righteousness of joy and peace in the Holy Spirit that you will receive from seeking God's kingdom of righteousness first is the gift from this new life of Jesus in the Holy Spirit.

December 27

~ Feasting in the Word of God ~

> *Therefore I tell you, do not worry about your life, what you will eat or drink; or about your body, what you will wear. Is not life more than food, and the body more than clothes? Look at the birds of the air; they do not sow or reap or store away in barns, and yet your heavenly Father feeds them. Are you not much more valuable than they? (Matthew 6:25-26, NIV).*

It is always her joy to see that her children are well fed and clothed. A good mother will do anything with her strength to bring food to the table for her children. It breaks her heart when she doesn't know where her next meal will come from or how to get it. But as long as she brings her brokenness to God in Word and prayer, He fills her with peace and removes her worries. There is always provision.

> *Blessed are those who hunger and thirst for righteousness, for they will be filled (Matthew 5:6, NIV).*

The Holy Spirit living in us wants us to be filled with His spiritual milk, the Word of God. To be filled we have to come to Him in hunger and thirst. When we are hungry and thirsty for the Word, the Holy Spirit prepares a table before us in the presence of our enemies to feast and celebrate the abundance of life.

> *You prepare a table before me in the presence of my enemies; you anoint my head with oil; my cup overflows. Surely goodness and mercy shall follow me all the days of my life, and I shall dwell in the house of the Lord forever (Psalm 23:5-6, ESV).*

Every day fill yourself in the Word of God until your cup overflows and your goodness affects your surroundings. You will start celebrating your victory of defeating evil with goodness in the presence of your enemies.

December 28

~ Love covers all sin ~

> *Above all, love each other deeply, because love covers over a multitude of sins (1 Peter 4:8, NIV).*

A good mother is filled with unconditional love for her children that she forgives and forgets the many times her child upsets her. It's just natural for her to forgive; the compassion she has from her love covers every wrong her child does.

> *Hatred stirs up conflict, but love covers over all wrongs (Proverbs 10:12, NIV).*

Love is a fruit of the Holy Spirit, and the Holy Spirit is the Spirit of God who is love. Out from Him flows His universal unconditional love that has the power to forgive all evil and make you feel you belong. The compassion of the Holy Spirit gives us the strength to have mercy and forgive those that offend us.

> *For I will forgive their wickedness and will remember their sins no more.' (Hebrews 8:12, NIV).*

Every day grow yourself in the love of God. When the love of God grows big in us it covers things that offend us because we can't see those offences; they have been covered and hidden by love.

December 29

~ Life is full of surprises ~

> *Thanks be to God for his inexpressible gift! (2 Corinthians 9:15, ESV).*

My daughter was about to turn five years' old and I was trying to wrap her birthday present, but I was waiting for her to go to sleep so I could do it. You can't work on someone's gift if they know about it or if they are present. This is what the Holy Spirit taught me: A good wife is a gift from the Lord; God wanted to give this gift to Adam that He put Him to a deep sleep and made his gift. God gives us each day as a gift. Every night when we fall asleep, God puts us into a deep sleep so that we are not aware of anything. All we know is that we wake up every day to a new day as a gift of life from God.

A good mother knows that her children are her gift. She is always surprised at the little things her children do that shows who they are when they develop their characters. A gift can surprise you.

> *Children are a gift from the Lord; they are a reward from him (Psalm 127:3, NLT).*

The Holy Spirit is the gift to us from the eternal life in Jesus. Every time He reveals Jesus to us we are in awe at the amazing beauty of who Jesus is. God has given us life as a gift, He wraps it up in a package called, 'today' and gives it to us. This is why we do not know what our life will be, who we will marry or how many children we will have. A gift has to be a surprise and this is what life is: A gift.

The best life to find and live in is Jesus. The Holy Spirit is the best gift of life from Jesus. His gift of life is all about joy and peace.

> *For the kingdom of God is not a matter of eating and drinking but of righteousness and peace and joy in the Holy Spirit (Romans 14:17, ESV).*
>
> *For the wages of sin is death, but the free gift of God is eternal life in Christ Jesus our Lord (Romans 6:23, ESV).*

Surprise someone with the gift of life from the fruit of life that the Holy Spirit produces inside you. Be good, kind and patient. Do it joyfully to the glory of God.

December 30

~ *The seven Spirits of God* ~

> *The Spirit of the Lord will rest upon him, the Spirit of wisdom and understanding, the Spirit of counsel and power, the Spirit of knowledge and fear of the Lord. (Isaiah 11:2, ISV).*

A good mother knows that for her body to remain healthy, strong and fresh, her spirit has to breathe in the seven Spirits of the Lord. THE SPIRIT OF THE LORD, THE SPIRIT OF WISDOM, THE SPIRIT OF UNDERSTANDING, THE SPIRIT OF COUNSEL, THE SPIRIT OF POWER, THE SPIRIT OF KNOWLEDGE and the SPIRIT OF THE FEAR OF THE LORD.

> *From the throne came flashes of lightning, rumblings and peals of thunder. In front of the throne, seven lamps were blazing. These are the seven spirits of God (Revelation 4:5, NIV).*

Every day she seeks God for wisdom in His Word and asks Him in prayer to give her wisdom. With the wisdom God gives, she gains knowledge and understanding of who God is and how He works for good in her life in all situations. She also understands why people act the way they are, and so she is not judgemental towards others. The Spirit of counsel gives her advice not only to run her house in the fear of the Lord but also to counsel her so she can be that good mother to counsel her household to always remain and walk in righteousness. The more she sits in the counsel of the Lord in His Word, the more God's power builds up the immune system of her spirit to be stronger against any evil attack. It's the fear of the Lord that makes her afraid to walk into sin or live with sin. Sometimes she may fall into sin but she quickly stands upright and asks for forgiveness and walks out of it.

While her spirit is fully connecting to God's seven Spirits, her body is in action in the nine fruit of the Holy Spirit.

> *Grace and peace to you from him who is, and who was, and who is to come, and from the seven spirits before his throne, (Revelation 1:4, NIV).*

> *But the fruit of the Spirit is love, joy, peace, patience, kindness, goodness, faithfulness, gentleness, self-control; against such things there is no law (Galatians 5:22-23, ESV).*

Her spirit is living in a body that is designed to live on earth while her spirit is designed to access and live in heaven through the Holy Spirit, so she can be living heaven on earth.

December 31

~ *God tastes so good* ~

For no matter how many promises God has made, they are 'Yes' in Christ (2 Corinthians 1:20, NIV).

Just like the Holy Spirit who is a comforter, mothers have this instinct that can make them uncomfortable when something is not right. A good mother draws out God's goodness from His Word. She has tasted and seen the goodness of God upon all that is in her concern. And so she is always comforted by God's Word when the world's trouble tries to make her uncomfortable. She has an unshakable trust.

O taste and see that the Lord is good: blessed is the man that trusteth in him (Psalm 34:8, KJV).

The Holy Spirit is the perfect goodness of God in action within us. He comforts us with the goodness of His fruit. Nourishing our spirit, soul and body. He is the one Jesus promised to give us. He is the Spirit of God, and all the promises of God in Christ are yes and amen in Him.

For you were once darkness, but now you are light in the Lord. Live as children of light (for the fruit of the light consists in all goodness, righteousness and truth) (Ephesians 5:8-9, NIV).

Every day fill yourself with the promises from God's Word for the Holy Spirit to make all these promises of God that are 'YES' in Christ to come alive.

www.ingramcontent.com/pod-product-compliance
Lightning Source LLC
Chambersburg PA
CBHW071959150426
43194CB00008B/935